Guerrilla P.R.
WIRED

Waging a Successful Publicity Campaign Online, Offline, and Everywhere In Between

Guerrilla P.R.
WIRED

MICHAEL LEVINE
Author of the bestselling *Guerrilla P.R.*

McGraw·Hill

New York   Chicago   San Francisco   Lisbon   London   Madrid   Mexico City
Milan   New Delhi   San Juan   Seoul   Singapore   Sydney   Toronto

The *McGraw·Hill* Companies

Library of Congress Cataloging-in-Publication Data

Levine, Michael, 1954– .
    Guerrilla P.R. wired : waging a successful publicity campaign online, offline, and
everywhere in between / Michael Levine.
        p.   cm.
    Includes index.
    ISBN 0-07-138231-3 (hardcover)
    ISBN 0-07-138232-1 (paperback)
        1. Industrial publicity.   2. Corporations—Public relations.   3. Internet.
I. Title: Guerilla P.R. wired.   II. Title.

    HD59 .L483 B35   2001
    659.2—dc21   2001044552

    3 4 5 6 7 8 9 0   LBM/LBM   0 9 8 7 6 5 4 3 2 ¡

ISBN 0-07-138231-3 (hardcover)
ISBN 0-07-138232-1 (paperback)

Cover design by Amy Yu Ng

McGraw-Hill books are available at special quantity discounts to use as premiums and
sales promotions, or for use in corporate training programs. For more information, please
write to the Director of Special Sales, Professional Publishing, McGraw-Hill, Two Penn
Plaza, New York, NY 10121-2298. Or contact your local bookstore.

This book is printed on acid-free paper.

This book is dedicated with genuine respect and affection to Craig Nelson, who helped create the concept of Guerrilla P.R. almost a decade ago.

His continued encouragement and passionate support inspire me.

CONTENTS

FOREWORD

Today's business leaders and managers are inundated with change, much of it coming in the area of technology. For those of us who run smaller companies, change seems to occur at a rate faster than we can process. It's not, but that's not something you can tell anyone who's trying to meet a payroll.

For many of us, the Internet is both a fantastic opportunity and a source of intimidation. It offers untold amounts of information in seconds; it reaches millions of people in the time it takes to blink your eyes. For a small-business owner, the Internet is both the Great Equalizer and the Great Mystery. Sure, your business might have a website that looks as good as GE's, IBM's, Microsoft's, or Disney's, but what good does that do you if you can't attract visitors to the site? With companies like GE, IBM, Microsoft, and Disney making huge strides online, what room is there for a sixteen-person manufacturing company in Painesville, Ohio? How can that company even hope to compete, or to attract attention to itself?

Technically, there's plenty of room left on the Internet, and websites are being created and improved every hour of every day. Small businesses are using the Internet more and more creatively to introduce and promote themselves to customers they never dreamed they could reach. But not everyone who owns a small business (or a large one, for that matter) is an expert in public relations.

Michael Levine, on the other hand, is. Founder and owner of one of the most successful entertainment public relations firms in the country, Levine has dealt with everyone from Charlton Heston to Barbra Streisand, and many more. He has written a number of books, including *Guerrilla P.R.: How You Can Wage an Effective Publicity Campaign . . . Without Going Broke.*

When that book was published in 1993, Michael revolutionized the idea of promotion for businesses that could never afford someone like, well, him. He laid out the ideas that can help entrepreneurs and small companies draw attention to themselves for free, and his words were read everywhere from Harvard University to the White House. His Tiffany Theory is the centerpiece of a dynamic marketing concept. Breaking new ground in publicity for businesses on a budget, the book managed to explain the concepts of public relations to business owners who never had considered them before, and ended up teaching companies much larger than that, as well. *Guerrilla P.R.* became the standard for introducing newcomers to the concepts of publicity campaigns.

The only problem with it was that it neglected something that was still just a word to most people in 1993: the Internet. *Guerrilla P.R.* can hardly be faulted for not concentrating on Web technology; the term barely existed in 1993. Levine himself confesses, in the pages of the book you're about to read, that he resisted all attempts to bring him into the wired world until just a few years ago. That is another way in which he is very much in tune with the audience for whom he writes. The Internet, of course, is a constantly evolving entity, and Levine understands that. He knows a little bit about being under the gun and always being asked to move to the next level. Publicists have to know about things like that; it's part of their job.

Melding ideas of *Guerrilla P.R.* and the wired world was inevitable. Michael Levine knows that publicity is a form of communication, and in this day and age, communication happens online. When communication is done right, it can persuade, and when it persuades someone to take a closer look at a company, that is publicity.

This book, after all, is not just about getting people to look at your website. In fact, that's a relatively minor lesson compared to the ones about how to use your website to get coverage in publications, on television and radio, and on other websites that concern themselves with your industry.

Levine has written a book that explains the step-by-step process of publicity online, but he's also included some basic ideas on promotion. His sections on dealing with the press (since I am a member of the press, I get to speak with authority here) are exceptional in that they take my viewpoint into account. As the editor in chief of a business magazine, I'm constantly receiving E-mail and "snail mail" from companies that want us to "publicize" their product. I can't tell you how many of them would benefit from a mere ten minutes with Levine. He'd tell them not to assume the press exists as your personal promotional tool. He'd make sure they don't call every hour on the hour to find out if their pitch has been received, read, and accepted. And he'd be sure to mention that they should never send anything to me unless they have read my magazine and understand the kind of material we publish. Let me say that again: he'd be sure to mention that they should never send anything to me unless they have read my magazine and understand the kind of material we publish.

For that alone, I consider this book a great aid. If one entrepreneur takes the time to study my publication and send me a pitch that actually meets my needs, then this book is a boon to the world of publicity. The first time we publish an article whose pitch mentions this book, I will take Michael Levine out to lunch.

But that is a very small benefit compared to the help Levine offers the owners of businesses, small and large. Here is the opportunity to find out what you can do to get your website up and running with the kind of information you want the public to see. Here are the dos and don'ts of promotional campaigns, guidelines for deciding what to put on a home page and what to omit, procedures for taking publicity from the Web to the off-line world, and much more. With his perspective on publicity campaigns and his own newfound devotion to the Internet, Levine provides the best of both worlds, blends them, and gives the reader the chance to create his or her own campaigns.

He provides examples of businesses, large and small, that have made a splash on the Internet, know how to use E-mail, and have blazed a trail for others to follow. He also tells a tale or two about companies that have faced adversity in their Web-related promotions and have prevailed. This book will empower the reader and inspire the businessperson to take a crack at this whole Internet publicity thing and see what happens.

Levine also avails the reader of his own experience in public relations and clearly distinguishes between publicity and public relations. They're both valuable, but they're not the same thing.

If you read this book with an eye toward learning from the master, you can have every expectation of creating a successful campaign on the Web. You'll also find that you'll never be able to pass by Tiffany's or see a Mr. Magoo cartoon in quite the same way again. You might very well start to question some of your ideas about everyday life, and not just your business. Because what Michael Levine does here is to apply everyday life to the business of publicity, then tie publicity to the Internet.

Read on, and you'll see what I'm talking about. And remember: NO E-MAILS WITH SUBJECT LINES ALL IN CAPITALS!

George Gendron
Editor-in-Chief, *Inc.*

ACKNOWLEDGMENTS

So much gratitude, so little space.

I find myself in endless debt to many people for their inspiration and encouragement on this book.

Jeff Cohen, a tremendous support in creating this work. Jeff helped immeasurably and assists me in continuing to create the concepts that you are reading.

Tara Griggs, an earnest and very talented young woman who assisted and worked tirelessly researching this work.

My office staff and interns: Ian Baca, Gia DelliGatti, Jeff Veal, and Mica Youngfellow, who work hard and long with me, day-to-day, hour-to-hour in running Levine Communications Office in Los Angeles.

Blessed associates and friends, who assist, support, and encourage me when it is not always easy to do so: Peter Bart, Marilyn Beck, Rich Buhler, Adam Christing, Paul Coughlin, Jim Erickson, Kit Harper, Richard Imprescia, Mark Joseph, Karen Karsian, Phil Kass, Arthur Levine, Patty Levine, John McKillop, Nancy Mager, Cable Neuhaus, Alyse Reynolds, Steve Shapiro, and David Weiss.

Interns interested in working in Mr. Levine's Los Angeles office can contact his office at levinepr2@earthlink.net.

INTRODUCTION

*"Every heart that has beat strong and cheerfully has left
a hopeful impulse behind it in the world, and bettered
the tradition of mankind."*

—ROBERT LOUIS STEVENSON

What Alan Canton did was simply to turn a horror into a miracle.
And he did it by writing a column and posting it on a website.

On June 18, 1999, B'nai Israel Temple of Sacramento and two
other synagogues in Sacramento were devastated by fires started by
two arsonists. Canton, a member of the B'nai Israel congregation,
said insurance covered much of the structure's rebuilding, estimated
at $1.2 million, but the temple's Sosnick Library contained about
5,000 rare and antique materials, which were not covered by the
insurance policy. And they had been reduced to ashes.

Canton, a publisher of technical books and software, attended
a special service the Friday night after the arson, and he and his
wife, Jane Schweitzer, were surprised to see a large percentage of the
congregation's 700 families present, only a day after the building was
burned.

"We figured there would be 50 or 100 people there," he says.
"But everybody showed up."

Also at that service was the Rev. Faith Whitmore, a Methodist
minister who had collected $6,000 from Methodists at a nearby
convention to be put toward the restoration of the temple. Canton
was impressed and moved.

He was also inspired.

The next morning, he wrote an article about the temple and the
generosity of the Methodists as part of his weekly column called "A
Saturday Rant." The column, which is distributed via a few pub-
lishing-related E-mail lists, would reach a few hundred people, most
of whom Canton knew from his business. In it, he asked those he

knew—and some of whom he felt owed him a small favor—to send $10 or so toward the restoration of the building and the library.

"I knew about 250 guys who owed me a $10 favor," Canton says. "And I figured, what a deal. I can give a check to the rabbi for $2,500, and I can be kept out of the committee work."

Canton did get the money he expected from his publishing friends—and just a little more. By the time the rant had spread via E-mail to hundreds, then thousands, more names, and publications had picked up the story, and there had been local coverage by radio and television stations, the check Canton could hand to his rabbi had increased substantially.

"I'm a professional writer, and I'm used to people reading my stuff," he says. "After a while, the thrill wears off. So I'm giving permission right and left to anybody who wants to reprint the rant. You want to send it by E-mail? Go ahead. You want to publish it in the condominium newsletter? Sure."

Money started pouring in through the mail, some of it in cash. Some of it in Swedish kronor and German marks. The temple was getting calls. By July 4, contributions totaled $40,000.

One Southern California high-tech entrepreneur sent $18,000. Over 17,000 books were donated to the library. The checks kept coming in a steady stream until sometime in September.

By then, Canton said, the check he gave to his rabbi amounted to over $201,000.

"I wasn't trying to do this. I was just trying to get out of the committee work," he says. "I'm a good writer, but nobody's that good. There was another force at work here."

At the risk of sounding blasphemous, the other force at work here is probably the Internet.

Levine's Lessons for Guerrillas: Lesson #1

The power of Internet communication is awe-inspiring. Consider that Alan Canton wasn't trying to raise $201,000; he was trying to shame 250 friends into sending $10 each. Never underestimate the potential of putting your message online—but always consider the message, since it will be available to virtually everyone.

Besides making it easier to communicate with friends and relatives and retrieve information on virtually any topic on the planet, the Internet has opened the doors to possibilities for publicity and public relations that would have been absolutely unheard of as recently as ten years ago. And the best part is this: you can do it for very little—and sometimes no—money. That means *everybody* can take advantage of the publicity capabilities of the World Wide Web and do so quickly, cheaply, and effectively.

The key, of course, is knowing how. Fortunately, the "how" doesn't involve writing technical code or troubleshooting the latest version of Windows. Technical expertise isn't the point here. It doesn't even enter into the equation. What's important is creativity, vision, imagination, and the courage to use them. What's important is believing in yourself and your abilities and understanding the capabilities of this medium, now in its toddler stage. You can draw major media attention to yourself and your product or service without leaving your office, spending tens of thousands of dollars (or more), and hiring teams of people to do it for you.

The Internet lets you react to situations on the fly, capitalize on events of the day, and elevate your business's success to a new level, perhaps one you haven't even dreamed of yet. This is not an empty promise; it has already been done, more than once:

- When a few young filmmakers took their $35,000 investment in a horror movie with no on-screen monster or mayhem and used a website they designed to create a myth on which the movie was based, did they expect to make the most profitable film in history? Probably not, but with *The Blair Witch Project*, that's exactly what they did.
- When the support group for parents of children with a little-known neurological condition couldn't get the medical community to take it seriously, was it logical that diagnoses would start taking place on computer screens and that distraught parents would start understanding their children's illness by getting clues from others, living thousands of miles away, in the blink of an eye? For ASPEN, the Asperger Syndrome Parents Education Network, it's now happening at the rate of over 1,000 times a day.
- Did the founder of a website devoted to the history of Los Angeles radio expect to receive a special day devoted to the topic—and the website—at the Museum of Television and Radio? Probably not, but for the founder of laradio.com, it happened.

There are hundreds, maybe thousands, of similar stories. Businesses, groups, and individuals are all benefiting from the spread of the Internet. And here's the best part: it hasn't even really started yet. There are millions of people for whom ownership of a computer, or access to the Internet, is just now becoming possible. It's estimated that by the year 2005, the number of Internet users will *double*. That means more than 200 million people will be logging on, in one way or another. Consider them your target audience. And you can reach them for pennies at a time.

In 1993, I wrote a book called *Guerrilla P.R.* That book has been translated into many different languages; has been part of the curriculum in colleges, universities, and graduate schools; and has made its way into boardrooms, homes, and even the White House under two presidents. It's become the most widely used introduction to public relations in the world. I'm flattered to hear from some colleagues that it is considered the undisputed guide on low-cost, down-and-dirty public relations techniques. It's a book of which I am proud.

But the world has changed since 1993, and the medium of change has been the Internet. From a time when most people had never heard the word *online* to the present, when it's impossible to imagine a world without that kind of instant communication, things have changed.

Consider: In 1993, the World Wide Web consisted of 130 sites, mostly owned by government agencies and enormous corporations. By 1997, there were approximately 650,000 websites, ranging from Disney.com to individual pages created to keep Grandma up-to-date on the family. Since then, believe me, the number has grown geometrically to well over a million.

So, while the concepts of Guerrilla P.R. remain the same, the methods of putting them into action have changed. The outlets for your ideas have multiplied beyond expectation. The speed with which you can execute your plans has increased beyond description.

In other words, Guerrilla P.R. hasn't gotten older, it's gotten *easier*. The only trick is knowing how to use it. And that's what this book is about.

If you haven't read my first book, don't worry. I'll explain the concepts, expand on some, and update others. If you carry a dog-eared copy of *Guerrilla P.R.* around at all times, don't you worry, either. This isn't some rehash of ideas you already know. This is the opportunity of a millennium.

The Guerrilla P.R. concept takes the ideas of urban warfare seriously, because it's not just a jungle out there—it's a jungle filled with deadly snakes, quicksand traps, and charging rhinos. Business is an area Charles Darwin would recognize immediately—sometimes not even the strong survive.

But the business jungle is also a place where the smart, well-equipped warrior can quietly—and sometimes not so quietly—establish a beachhead and go on to win the battle, and sometimes the war, all on his own. If you think a small, unheard-of company can't rise out of nowhere and make its owners wealthy, try to get Bill Gates on the phone and ask him how he started.

Because of Mr. Gates and a lot of other people who developed the information technology industry into what it is today, there is a road map through the jungle. There are safe havens where a guerrilla can hide out, plan strategy, and be ready to pounce. There are proven, successful techniques. And there is a medium at our disposal to aid in the quest for publicity victory: media coverage.

Just think: Alan Canton managed to raise $201,000 in three months, and he *wasn't even trying*! He wrote one E-mail message and brought in close to $17,000 a week. That illustrates the enormous potential of this new medium, and especially its enormous impact. It's all out there for you to use. And there's no time like the present to start. So let's begin, shall we?

Guerrilla P.R.
WIRED

1

GUERRILLAS IN THE MIDST: LOW-COST P.R. IN THE TWENTY-FIRST CENTURY

"The average man does not know what to do with his life,
yet wants another one which will last forever."

—ANATOLE FRANCE

The older I get, the more I realize the truth of the old saying "Life ain't no dress rehearsal." You're not going to get a "take two" on your life. There's no use in putting something off or assuming you can go back to your life the way it was before. This existence goes on no matter what we do about it, so we'd better be ready for what it has to throw in our paths.

Life in the twenty-first century is much more complicated than it was one hundred years ago. By the same token, we can assume that life in the year 2100 will be geometrically more complex than the day-to-day tasks we face now. Some of this is the result of growing, expanding, changing technology, and some of it is simply the nature of the human species: we rarely simplify things, no matter how hard we try. We tend, instead, to add layer upon layer of artifice in the name of "simplification" and congratulate ourselves for our ingenuity. If Thomas Edison were alive today, brilliant innovator that he was, do you think he would immediately understand the complexities of the Internet, CD burners, wireless phone technology, DVD players, and streaming video (all of which humans created to make our lives easier)? Sure, Edison could catch up, but it would take time, and it would take education. Gadgets are fun, and they may perform tasks we find beneficial, but they don't actually *simplify* our lives; they make our lives more complex.

I've long believed that technology is the enemy of reverence. The more we innovate, the more we expand the level of our technological expertise, the less reverent a society we become. After all, the internal combustion engine has made our lives infinitely different, but it has also contributed to the deterioration of the ozone layer. What Nature provides, we erode through technology.

Does this mean that we should throw away our technology, live in a utopian society in the woods, wear animal skins for clothing, communicate with drums, and eat only that which we find growing in our garden? Of course not. What exists is there for us to use. We have to learn to use it responsibly, and well.

Using technology well is what *Guerrilla P.R. Wired* is all about. We may balk at the first introduction of a new device—some people still argue that vinyl LPs sound better than CDs—but if we learn to use that device, and use it with creativity and ingenuity, we can certainly turn it to our advantage. Remember that the fight for publicity is a war, a guerrilla war, and those of us who fight it have been cut off from our armies, left in the jungle with nothing more than a canteen full of water and our wits. We can dress up our circumstances with computer screens, telephone headsets, and fax machines, but don't let that fool you—this is *war*.

The first, and most important, weapon you can wield in this war is speed. There are two speeds for Guerrilla P.R. wired: fast and dead. If you don't react quickly, if you can't make changes on the fly and make decisions in a heartbeat, maybe you should find a nice job working for someone else. The true guerrilla publicist is faster than a speeding bullet when there's an opportunity, and *hesitation* isn't in the Guerrilla Dictionary.

NOT IN THE DICTIONARY

Take a look at the list of words that you won't find in the Guerrilla Dictionary. These words aren't chosen at random. Let's examine each one so you can see why you should avoid them.

10 Words Left Out of the Guerrilla Dictionary

Can't	Slow
Excuse	Spam
Hesitation	Uncertainty
Me	Won't
Never	Worry

Can't

The guerrilla publicist has never heard the word *can't*—or, at the very least, has never said it. To a true guerrilla, everything is an opportunity, not an obstacle. If you can't do it, someone else can. So don't come up with reasons you can't do something; come up with ways to do it.

Excuse

Also avoid saying "excuse," as in, "I can't, and here's my excuse." Excuses are for people who are looking for reasons not to do something. You're looking for ways to accomplish goals, not for excuses. There is no excuse for failure among guerrillas; there is only the next guerrilla waiting to take up the slack. No excuses.

Hesitation

If you have millions of dollars and a 73 percent share of the market, you might have time to hesitate, because once you decide on a course of action, you'll have the resources to put it into effect immediately. But for the guerrilla, who is operating on a promise and a couple of postage stamps, there is no hesitation; there is simply the time between what just happened and what happens next. Learn to turn on a dime and act with confidence, and you'll be the last guerrilla standing.

Me

Let's get one thing clear. Publicity on the Web isn't about you. It's about the customer you're trying to attract. Show prospective customers how you can help them accomplish their goals, and you'll be a success. Show them what a cool person you are, and they'll move on to the next website and never come back.

Never

Do you remember the James Bond movie *Never Say Never Again*? The title came from Sean Connery's wife, who was tired of hearing him say he'd "never" play the superspy again. If something has "never" been done, that just means nobody's done it *yet*. If you "never" do that, it means somebody else does—and guess who'll get the business you're trying to attract?

Slow

If you're slow, you're not a guerrilla.

Spam

In the Internet world, "spam" is not canned meat. It is promotional E-mail sent to people who have not asked for it, nor expressed an interest in the topic being discussed. Publicists and Web experts agree that there's nothing more annoying than spam, and if you use it, you run the risk of alienating more potential customers than you attract. Do the math; that's bad business. Guerrillas don't spam.

Uncertainty

It's a speed thing. There's no time for uncertainty. Develop a "golden gut" and trust it. If you think something's a good idea and you can get it to market faster than everyone else, you have an obligation under Guerrilla Law to do it. Remember, faster is better.

Won't

What won't a guerrilla do? Nothing. The only reasons to dismiss an idea are that it costs too much, it won't work, or it would cause global annihilation. Actually, that last one doesn't come up very often.

Worry

A guerrilla has no time to worry. Does that mean a guerrilla doesn't care? Of course not. But if a plan of action doesn't work, worrying ahead of time won't make it work. A successful guerrilla is always *thinking*, but never *worried*. Worry is counterproductive. Eliminate it from your dictionary.

WORDS TO LIVE BY

Now let's look at the words you *should* use.

10 Words Highlighted in the Guerrilla Dictionary

Always	Fastest
Can	Innovation
Confidence	New
Fast	Will
Faster	You

Always

Do say *always*, as in "We always deliver on time," "I always concern myself with your business," and "We're always thinking."

Can

James Cagney once said that if someone asks you if you can do a particular thing, you should always say yes. If you say, "I can," you'll get an opportunity you didn't have before, and you'll learn a new skill. Someone asked Cagney if he could ride a horse. Cagney had never been on a horse in his life before that. Even so, he said yes— and was cast in a role that started his movie career.

Confidence

The word *confidence* has dual meanings. It means the positive frame of mind that makes things possible. It can also mean trust, as in "keep this information in confidence." The smart guerrilla observes both meanings of the word, and exercises them.

Fast

The most important word in the guerrilla language is *fast*. Because we are operating on a shoestring budget, our most important weapon is speed. Without it, we are simply cheap.

Faster

What's better than fast? Faster. Move faster than the rival company trying to do the same job. The Internet provides infinite opportunities to be fast, since plans can be implemented almost immediately. Be faster than the next guerrilla, and you'll be the successful one.

Fastest

What's even better than faster? The competitive spirit is essential to the hungry guerrilla. It's not enough to be fast, or even to be faster than one competitor. The goal is to be the fastest, most dynamic company in the business, and that's the best reason for turning to the Internet. Nothing is faster or as widespread.

Innovation

The lifeblood of the guerrilla is innovation. Most tried-and-true methods are either stodgy and boring or prohibitively expensive, so the guerrilla has to be continuously innovating. Another variation on this word is *creativity*. The more creative your approach, the better your message will be received.

New

Put *fastest* and *innovation* together, and you get *new*. The most effective tactics and tools are those which haven't been seen before. So come up with something that's new, that's unpredictable, that's fresh, and you will be noticed. Being noticed is the goal for every P.R. Guerrilla.

Will

Another two-sided word is *will*. First of all, there's the will of assent: "We will do that." Coupled with that is another use of the word, the will of determination: Have the will to do what you set out to do, and you will do it!

You

Instead of saying *me*, use the opposite word, *you*. Keep in mind that your customers' needs, not yours, are the most important component in your efforts. If you fill those needs—and exceed them— your own needs will be met as well.

WHAT IS "GUERRILLA P.R.," ANYWAY?

If you're going to apply the principles of Guerrilla P.R. to the age of the Internet, you have to know something about Guerrilla P.R. itself. In case you have not worn out a copy of *Guerrilla P.R.* or have forgotten some of the finer points since that book was published in 1993, let's take a fresh look at the concept. After all, the world has changed.

Public relations is the art, as one of my colleagues put it, of "offering people reasons to persuade themselves." In other words, we are not Madison Avenue; we don't tell people what we want them to think. Rather, we give them evidence, facts, and opinions that help them reach a conclusion. If we're good at what we do, they will reach the conclusion we've been hired to promote.

The differences between traditional public relations and Guerrilla P.R. are relatively simple. First of all, public relations firms like mine are available to people with a lot of money, because we charge what we consider to be reasonable fees, which are out of reach of many small or one-person businesses. So entrepreneurs and small-business owners need to learn and apply the same skills I use every day in service of their larger, more well-heeled rivals. But these skills can't be used the same way, since they require more money than most small businesses can afford. Not everyone can buy a minute of time on network TV to get the message across.

That's where Guerrilla P.R. comes in. This down-and-dirty off-spring of the traditional method is based on an idea I developed called the Tiffany Theory. The Tiffany Theory is an idea that sounds simple but, like most such theories, is so basic it contains numerous truths.

My Tiffany Theory states that a gift delivered in a box from Tiffany's will have a higher perceived value than one in no box or a plain box. That's not because the recipient is a fool; it's because in our society, we gift-wrap everything: our politicians, our corporate heads, our movie and TV stars, and even our toilet paper. Tiffany paper places a higher *perceived* value on things.

In effect, what I do each day is gift-wrapping. I take a message and wrap it in the finest paper from Tiffany's. No matter what the message may be, I try to make it sound more appealing, more interesting, and more useful. If I do my job correctly, the consumer (who gets the message through television, newspapers, radio, or the Internet) will get the message. But first, that message has to go through editors, producers, reporters, and website managers. The Tiffany paper adds perceived value and cachet.

Notice, now, I said, *perceived* value. In public relations and publicity, perception is truth. It isn't what happened that counts, it's what people *think* happened. This is the absolute day-to-day currency of politics, entertainment, and most other industries. In our case, we're looking at how the public—that is, the segment of the public you believe is your customer base—perceives your company. Not what your company actually might be.

Does that mean you should lie? Never. Lying, besides being morally wrong, is quite literally indefensible. That means, at some point, you're going to be found out. And even if you weren't, you would have to start living the lie—remembering what you told the people interested in your business, and hearing people call you what you said you are. It's too hard, and it's not worth it. Besides, it's plain bad business.

When I say that the perception of the truth—rather than the truth itself—is the stuff of great publicity campaigns, I mean that the truth will take care of itself. But you have to make sure that the image you project, the perception you offer to potential customers, is what you want it to be.

For example, a man named Dave Schwartz decided he'd start a car rental company that would lower rates to the consumer by featuring cars that weren't 100 percent new off the showroom floor. He had a choice to make in terms of the perception of his new company, and he chose to beat critics to the punch with a strong sense of humor and a catchy company name: Rent-A-Wreck. Now, Dave didn't lie (his cars weren't wrecks, they drove just fine, so maybe he exaggerated a little), and he didn't fall into the trap of emphasizing price. After all, his competitors already had names like Thrifty and Budget. He hit you in the funnybone, made his impression of a fun car rental company—with the implied promise that the cars would cost less because they weren't brand new—and launched a very successful business.

It's all in the perception. But is this a contradiction of the Tiffany Theory? Did Dave actually wrap his cars in Kmart paper to make his point?

Not really. Dave still wrapped *his message* in Tiffany paper. He made sure local news outlets, publications, and media companies knew about his company, and he emphasized exactly how reliable and economical the rental cars at Rent-A-Wreck would be. By downplaying the appearance of the cars—calling them "wrecks"— he allowed the media to expect dented, scratched, beat-up cars. When they toured his facility and saw cars that were only slightly used, Dave didn't have to say a word. The message got out that the "wrecks" in question were very reliable, attractive cars that would be available for a lower rental rate because they were used. A brilliant, subtle piece of Tiffany wrapping.

Levine's Lessons for Guerrillas: Lesson #2

The Tiffany Theory applies to the Internet in ways it never could with traditional media. Keep in mind that more information is available on the World Wide Web than you can possibly track, let alone control. So it's always important to keep your information *true*. But unlike information in newspapers or magazines, the data you provide on a website is yours, and you provide the Tiffany paper. Use photographs, charts, quizzes, and prizes, if you can, to keep surfers' interest alive on your site. And remember to wrap every fact in a nice neat piece of Tiffany wrap.

THE BLAIR WITCH GUERRILLAS

Don't be confused: this is not a book about building and maintaining your own website, although we will touch on how to do that. It's not about doing P.R. on the Internet. It's about *using* the Internet to attract media attention from *other* websites, from television, radio, and print news outlets. It's a way to take what has traditionally been an expensive, slower-paced activity and dragging it, kicking and screaming, into the twenty-first century.

In other words, this isn't about getting people to look at your website. It's about using your website to get you on *Oprah*.

A key example of this—perhaps *the* key example, and one we'll refer to many times in this book—is the Web promotion that turned *The Blair Witch Project* from a microbudget indie film with a chance at distribution into a monster (you should pardon the expression) hit and, considering the ratio of production budget to gross ticket sales, the most profitable film ever made.

The business story rivals the movie script: A group of young filmmakers got about $35,000 together and shot a horror movie, chiefly in the woods in Maryland, in eight days on a $400 video camera. The film, bucking current trends, shows no blood, no violence, no monsters, and for that matter, no Blair Witch on screen. Instead, the audience sees a lot of handheld video shots of three young "filmmakers" (actors playing film students) who relate their story as they become more and more frightened about what appears to be their impending doom. By all rights, this no-special-effects cheapie would probably have ended up on the Independent Film Channel at three in the morning after a few modest weeks in ten theaters in New York, Los Angeles, and Chicago (and maybe Seattle). Instead, it grossed over $135 million and became the most-discussed, most-parodied, most-recognizable movie of 1999.

How? It was all done on the Internet.

Long before the movie was released to theaters, Web surfers would have found a site with the address www.blairwitch.com, at which there was absolutely no mention of any movie. There was, instead, the tale of the Blair Witch, the backstory for the film. Surfers could find the history of the cursed woods, where children were supposedly abducted and murdered by a madman decades before, and the alleged ties to a witch executed on the spot hundreds of years before that. All of it was presented as fact, with no hint that it was a marketing tool.

Word spread among the Internet community, and soon the Blair Witch site was getting tens of thousands of hits—incidents of people visiting the site and looking at the information—every day. Once the film was shown at the prestigious Sundance Film Festival and bought for distribution by Artisan Entertainment, the site had received millions of hits. Let me repeat that: *millions* of people knew about this movie long before it opened, and they wanted to see it.

By the time the movie, which was told documentary-style to keep the myth viable, was announced and released, anticipation of a scary experience had built to such a fever pitch that some theaters couldn't handle the crowds waiting for the first showing, and had to add additional screenings.

This may be the most perfect example of Internet Guerrilla P.R. ever executed. Let's analyze it.

First of all, the boldest move the filmmakers and marketers made was to completely eliminate all traces of the movie from the website. Any visitor without prior knowledge of the movie would have been absolutely convinced the site was dedicated to the legend of the Blair Witch, and that it was not a promotional site for an upcoming film.

Why is this brilliant? Didn't the filmmakers want people to know about the movie? Weren't they trying to get audiences to attend the film when it opened? How did this work so well without ever once mentioning the product being sold?

The key here was the type of movie being marketed. It was imperative to the plans of the *Blair Witch* team that this film seem like it really was the lost tapes of a doomed expedition. The line between fantasy and reality was intentionally blurred to play up the film's strength—the heightened sense that you're seeing the horrible events exactly as they happened—and to obscure what could be seen as weaknesses in the competitive marketplace.

After all, a horror movie that has cheap special effects is considered cheesy and laughable. But a horror movie with *no* special effects was right next to unthinkable. And that's exactly what was being marketed. If the core audience for this film—mostly young males, in their teens and early twenties—was going to shell out hard-earned money to see the movie, the filmmakers couldn't mislead them into thinking the Blair Witch would make an on-screen appearance with blood, guts, and light-saber battles. The audiences for initial screenings would have been bitterly disappointed, and the word of mouth would have been disastrous.

The canny guerrilla publicist knows not to lie. So the *Blair Witch* marketers did not imply that the movie would contain anything other than what existed—faux video of two young men and a woman traipsing through the woods and getting scared. What was important was that the audience buy into the myth of the Blair Witch, to believe that there really *was* an evil force in those woods, and that those three filmmakers were indeed in mortal danger.

Since the budget to promote *Blair Witch* wasn't going to be huge, and since the target audience spends a lot of time on the Internet, the concept of creating the Blair Witch myth online and then letting the audience find it themselves (with a few subtle nudges from the marketers) was beyond brilliant. It got the foundation of the film's story across to its most likely audience before the movie even opened. And it did so while seeming to be a fact-based website dedicated to "victims" of the Blair Witch, setting up the audience for the suggestion that the films left behind by the three latest "victims" would soon be available in theaters.

Word spread like wildfire, and soon the Internet was abuzz with word about the myth, but not the movie. Other Web pages sprung up (a casual search of the words *Blair Witch* turned up more than sixty-five sites), and soon it was hard to escape the story. Then Artisan Entertainment, the film's distributor, announced opening dates for the movie. By then, the appetite was whetted to a fever pitch, and lines appeared at movie theaters across the country and eventually around the world. (For more detailed information on how the *Blair Witch* site was conceived and executed, see the interview with cowriter/codirector Daniel Myrick in Appendix A.) If the moviemakers and the marketers at Artisan hadn't understood the product they were selling, they might have put up what has become the traditional movie promotional website. They'd have posted the theatrical trailer in streaming video, cast and crew biographies, links to other Artisan movies, and offers to download *Blair Witch* screen savers. And probably the movie would have done relatively well. Certainly, it would have covered the $35,000 production cost and the money Artisan paid to distribute it.

But it wouldn't have been a $135 million phenomenon. And it wouldn't have spawned at least one sequel. And it wouldn't have gotten its creators deals to write, produce, direct, and develop other films and television series.

It was because the people involved understood both their product and their audience that *Blair Witch* became a catchphrase, a huge hit, and a phenomenon. While your product might not end up quite as successful, you can still apply many of the same principles to whatever you're trying to publicize.

Levine's Lessons for Guerrillas: Lesson #3

Know your product. Don't overestimate the upside or the downside of your product. Know its strengths and weaknesses well, and play to the strengths. The *Blair Witch* crew took what could have been deficits—no special effects, no gore, no on-screen monster—and turned them into assets.

IT'S NOT JUST PUBLICITY

I don't generally go around quoting myself, but in *Guerrilla P.R.*, I wrote, "The notion that P.R. is simply a matter of mailing press releases is nuttier than a squirrel's breakfast." Public relations is not a simple matter of getting as many press clippings as you can—that's *publicity*. P.R. is that and much, much more.

Remember, perception is the key. What the public thinks about you and your company (or your product) is what's important, not where they found out about you. If your company is in the news unintentionally, or if a news story breaks that might paint your company in a negative light, public relations is the art of "spin," of presenting your side of the argument to alter the public's perception of you until you can recover. It's not lying; it's giving your side of the story.

In that regard, the Internet is the ideal medium. Your Web page is the one place where you can completely control the editorial content and where the message that is being conveyed is totally yours. There is no way to overstate the value of such a forum. When you can present the facts you have in the way you choose to present them, to refute untrue or confusing claims made publicly about your company or you, to present your product or service in a way that makes the public understand its use and value, you have achieved a P.R. nirvana unlike anything that has existed on this planet before.

It's inconceivable now for a political candidate to forgo a website where position papers can be downloaded, biographical information is available, and E-mail questions can be answered. Both major-party candidates in the last presidential election had Web presences, and almost all the smaller-party candidates did, too. Don't expect to ever see an election in your town, your state, or the country again where a website isn't part of the candidate's public relations effort.

Virtually every company offering a product or service, and many individuals, now have their own websites. Business E-mail addresses are essential features on business cards. There is no escaping the Internet, and if you can't beat 'em, you should join 'em, and then beat 'em. In other words, compete from within.

Part of your effort will include designing and maintaining your own business website to disseminate information about your company. You'll also need an E-mail address, preferably one used strictly for business. And I'd recommend a faster Internet provider—one that utilizes the latest high-speed connections. Dial-up service is slow and will limit your flexibility. Remember, guerrillas hate slow.

Don't be scared of the new technology; embrace it. It is the fastest, cheapest, easiest way to spread the word about you and your company to more consumers than you could have imagined ten years ago. And once you learn the basics of Guerrilla P.R. and how to apply them to the Internet age, you'll know everything you need to get started at a gallop.

Remember, guerrillas are fast. No, faster. Better, fastest.

Levine's Ten Commandments
of Internet P.R. for Guerrillas

1. Thou shalt know thine audience.
2. Thou shalt know thy product.
3. Thou shalt not spam.
4. Thou shalt be fast.
5. Thou shalt not overspend.
6. Thou shalt not lie.
7. Thou shalt send E-mail to interested parties.
8. Thou shalt update often.
9. Thou shalt seek out and provide links.
10. Thou shalt study media websites.

2

THE WEB AND HOW TO UNWEAVE IT

"A conservative is a person who does not think anything should be done for the first time."

—FRANK VANDERLIP

To newcomers, the Internet can be a scary thing. But it doesn't have to be. It might surprise you to know that I was very resistant to the Internet not all that long ago. I *hated* to be contacted by E-mail and never used it to send messages. I didn't know a website from a whale watch. I had to be dragged, kicking and screaming, to a computer terminal and then instructed in how to turn the damned thing on.

Things have changed.

My friend Jeff in New Jersey never lets me forget that I practically took his head off every time he offered to send me something via E-mail only two or three years ago. Now, he notes, I'll send him E-mail about local Los Angeles events he can't possibly attend or radio shows he can't tune in. He's always offering to come out to the party or tune in the show if I'll pay his airfare. It's the price one pays for having friends.

I came to scoff and stayed to pray.

Once I realized that the online world was inevitably going to be part of all businesses, and my business in particular, it was a fait

_ _compli that I'd have to learn how to deal with computers, E-mail, and Internet access. So I sat myself down at the computer one weekend, with some instructional books and CD-ROMs, and I forced myself into the twenty-first century.

You know what? It wasn't all that hard. In fact, it was kind of fun. Before I knew it, I was communicating with friends across the country in no time flat for free, and I was accessing all sorts of information I had no idea was even available. For a public relations consultant, this was nirvana. Because in my business—and, I'm willing to bet, in your business, too—information is power. And power is opportunity.

So let's calm ourselves down, take a deep, cleansing breath, and plunge into the online world of Guerrilla P.R. Don't worry, I won't leave you alone here.

FIRST, WHAT *IS* "THE WEB"?

The World Wide Web (the "www" in those Internet addresses) is what most people think of when they say "the Internet." In fact, the Web is just one small part of the Net (although the terms are often used interchangeably, making the whole thing that much more confusing). It's estimated that 45 million or more people access the Web itself *every day*. And that number will easily increase, perhaps by as much as half, in a year. That's a lot of potential customers, but it's also a huge area in which to create buzz and get media attention. After all, if just *one* of those 45 million people happens to be a newspaper editor or TV news producer, and your message is compelling enough . . . well, you can do the math. If one of those people is Oprah Winfrey or David Letterman, your accountant can do the math.

The rest of the Internet—that is, the majority of it, which is not covered by the World Wide Web—is devoted to things like newsgroups, which are areas in which people with a very specific area of interest (say, Alfred Hitchcock movies) can meet, start discussions (and sometimes arguments), and gather information. There is a newsgroup devoted to pretty much every topic known to humanity, and a few that are a real stretch. A rudimentary search of newsgroups featuring the subject line "Alfred Hitchcock" turned up more than 300 such areas. With a few minor modifications to the search engine, far more could have been identified. So the breadth and scope of newsgroups on the Net certainly bears examination.

The World Wide Web—from here on identified as "the Web"—is the only place on the Internet where commerce (that's what the "com" in *dot-com* stands for) is permitted. You can't sell something in newsgroups, bulletin boards, government areas, or educational sites. You can sell things, and advertise them, on the Web. It's an important distinction, because "selling" is not the same thing as promoting.

Attracting publicity is a tricky business, but the Internet rules make it a little trickier. You *can* publicize your product or service anywhere on the Internet, even where you can't advertise or offer anything for sale. But those who try too blatantly to sell products or services in newsgroups, for example, will be subject to *flaming*—an avalanche of unwanted, vicious E-mail directed to the mailbox of the entrepreneur who tried to make a product available in the wrong place or in the wrong way. It's a fine line to walk.

Think about it: you can have a fantastic product, a crack sales staff, and a strong, important, vital message that could result in major media coverage. If you choose to advertise it, rather than *promote* it—and we'll discuss the differences—in an Internet newsgroup, you could be rewarded with angry E-mail and strong suggestions that you leave the entire online community out of your marketing plans. Not exactly the kind of reception you're trying to encourage, is it?

Levine's Lessons for Guerrillas: Lesson #4

Know the medium you're dealing with. If you hadn't known that advertising in newsgroups and bulletin boards is not permitted and can hurt your business, you might have made a critical error in your plan. Time, money, and effort spent in preparation should begin with an examination of the medium you're about to enter. Respectfully, buying this book was a very good first step.

Your best bet in a new Internet venture is to concentrate—not exclusively, but pretty seriously—on the World Wide Web. You are, after all, allowed to advertise there, and it is the part of the Net that will attract most users. In the Internet world, it's called "attracting eyeballs." You want someone to *look* at your message or your website. Get the eyeballs, to paraphrase G. Gordon Liddy, and their hearts and minds will follow.

This should be pretty easy, since the Web is the most recognizable and familiar area of the Net. It is also the easiest to access, the cheapest to use, and the part of the Internet that can most easily and most quickly turn your business into a wild success. So, what do you have to do to create a presence on the World Wide Web?

First, do your research. Don't leap into anything, ever, in Guerrilla P.R. without knowing exactly what you're doing. That doesn't mean you shouldn't be fast (remember that guerrillas are always fast to react and first on the scene), but it does mean that you should avoid being rash. You should take on a venture only after you understand its ins and outs. You should never, ever commit time and money to a business without finding out ahead of time what the pitfalls are and how to avoid them. Creativity counts for a lot in the guerrilla world, but it means very little without research.

In this case, the research you need to do is on the medium you're about to enter. The World Wide Web is a difficult thing to explain: it is more a concept that *feels* like a place. On the Web, things exist only because Web users have decided to agree they exist. You can "go" somewhere without leaving your desk. You can "chat" with people who aren't in the room, and never hear their voices. You can make close friendships with people you might very well never meet.

The Web can also be a treacherous place. Those with whom you communicate might be exactly who they say they are. They might not. It's possible people are trying to trick you, to take your money, to find your credit card numbers or personal details about you to exploit. It's also possible they're kindly and warm. You can't assume one or the other.

Keep in mind, too, that other Web users have to be just as wary as you do. So if you set up a website for your company and make claims about your product or service, you'd better be able to back them up with facts and demonstrations that will convince the more skeptical surfers on the Internet that day. It's always important to tell the truth in business, but never more so than when you're dealing with people who don't know you well; first impressions are enormously important. If someone catches you in a lie, or if you make a claim on your website that you can't back up, you could lose a customer for life.

A Few Quick Stats

- In 1998, 48 percent of adults in the United States had Internet access.

- In 2002, 88 percent of adults will have Internet access.
- Of those, almost half will be business users.
- In 1999, 40 percent of businesses without websites intended to get one.
- That could add, conservatively, a million businesses by 2002.

WHY YOU SHOULD BE ON THE WEB

If you don't have a Web presence yet, chances are you're planning one. Small businesses have been the most reluctant group to get involved in the Web, but they have been finding some of the largest benefits.

The Web is the great equalizer. Your business site is just as easy to access, and is accessed in exactly the same way, as www.sears.com. The advantage that unscrupulous chat room "lurkers" have is that nobody knows who they really are. Used more responsibly, that concept can be an advantage for you. Nobody who comes across your website need know that you have only six employees, as long as you can deliver the goods—literally.

The Web makes you an international business. Without having to set up a branch office in Hong Kong, another in London, and one in Johannesburg, you can easily sell your goods and services to people all over the world. Access to the Internet is the same in every corner of the globe. It might be worthwhile to hire someone with the ability to speak multiple languages to translate some of your most pertinent information for those in other countries.

The Web is remarkably inexpensive to use. Setting up a website, given a certain amount of computer knowledge, can be done for a couple of hundred dollars. Less, if you know how to write your own computer code. Creativity is especially well rewarded here, since your website can be just as glitzy and impressive as that of huge competitors. You don't have to spend more money to have a website, as you would if you wanted to upgrade your TV commercial from local cable access to network prime time. It costs less than $50 to register a domain name, and about the same to secure a place on the Web.

You can use the Web without having your own site. Remember, Guerrilla P.R. isn't just about getting people to look at your website. It's about attracting attention from the media. And the digital age has afforded the guerrilla a great advantage, never seen before: every major media outlet, from magazines to newspapers to radio to television, has a website, and on that website is a way to contact editors, producers, and decision makers. E-mail has made the process faster, more inexpensive, and immediate. Later on, we'll talk about how to make your E-mail stand out in an electronic mailbox. For now, just take heart in the fact that you can literally get your message to *anybody* if you know how to use the Web properly.

APPROACHING THE WEB

So, how *do* you use the Web properly? There are two ways to approach the Web: from outside and from within. In other words, you can set up your own website, or you can try to attract attention via existing websites and other Internet avenues.

Or, the way I recommend it, you can do both.

It's important to set up your own website. As we've already established, it's quite inexpensive, pretty easy to do (or you can easily hire someone with experience to help you, and that's not a huge amount of money, either), and it can be extremely effective.

Do-It-Yourself or Hire an Expert?

Should you design your site yourself or hire help? This is a question only you can answer for yourself, but there are indicators to consider. If you have absolutely no Web experience (you haven't even surfed a site to buy, say, this book), it's probably too much for you to learn about the Web and about trying to design your own site at the same time. For some small businesses (twenty or fewer employees), it might be best to see if anyone on staff already has some design experience. If not, you might want to consult the yellow pages and ask friends and associates for referrals to a Web design firm.

For those with even a limited amount of Web experience, though, it might be an option to build from the ground up yourself. There are a number of helpful software packages, including NetObjects Fusion and Dreamweaver, by Macromedia, that can help. You can set up a basic website in less than a week, easily.

Design firms are less risky in terms of technical know-how but are a mixed bag in terms of the creative possibilities you might want to exercise. Make sure, if you decide to employ outside designers, to see previous examples of their work. Get Web addresses, check out the sites, and answer a number of questions about each site:

- **How quickly does the site load?** If the site takes a long time to appear on your screen, the designer might have been too ambitious, adding in lots of graphics and flashy material that looks good—if the consumer chooses to wait for it to load. What you want is a balance of neat ideas and user-friendly load time.
- **Is the site easy to understand?** Consumers, especially those on the Web, have notoriously short attention spans. If they can't grasp the information being offered, or at least how to get the information being offered, they will move on to the next site before you can say "update résumé."
- **Is the site attractive to the eye?** It's nice to be able to share information with the public. It's even nicer if the public wants to find your information. If the *home page* for the website (the first screen that appears when the Web address is typed) is not interesting to look at, if it doesn't appear colorful and intriguing in some way, it will not hold the consumer's attention and will not get the consumer to the information you want to convey. Home pages are especially important and have to be fun to look at.
- **Is the website fun?** Let's face it: most of us are not surfing the Web because we want to discover information that will enrich our lives and make us better people. Either we're doing it as part of our jobs, or we're doing it because we want to have fun. In either case, the website that is more interesting, that has more buttons to push, pictures to look at, and games to play—in short, the site that's more fun—will be the more successful one. Amuse consumers, and they will follow you anywhere. Bore them, and they will lead you to the front door and give you a good swift kick on your way out.
- **Is the message clear?** Site content isn't necessarily the domain of the Web designer, but when you're looking at someone else's website, one of the first questions you should ask yourself is, Is it clear what information is being given and what the message means? If you have to think about it too long (like more than a few seconds), something is wrong. Even if the message is as simple as "buy my product," it should be presented in a plain, uncomplicated manner, so that it's easy to understand in a short time. Web publicity is like any other kind: you've got to grab attention immediately and hold it throughout.

- **Is it easy to contact the company through the website?** At a website, any area of your screen where you can click to go to another website or another area of the same website is called a *link*. A good site will include a link marked "contact us" or words to that effect. Clicking on that link will immediately call up an E-mail form for sending a message that should be read by someone in the company and answered (if the company is efficient) as quickly as possible. If it is difficult to contact the company that owns the site, or if it is impossible to do so through the website, that's a problem.

PLANNING YOUR WEBSITE

Once you've seen examples and selected a designer or if you've decided to create your company's website on your own, you're ready to begin.

What information should you include on your website? Keep in mind that your objective is to create a site that will attract attention. So in designing (or in supervising the design firm that will create) your website, you'll want to include a number of essential elements:

- The company's name, address, and contact information are a basic starting point.
- Describe what the company does—products you sell, services you offer—clearly and briefly.
- If you offer products, you should post pictures of the products whenever possible.
- If you offer services, you should use graphics to depict the services offered.
- There should be links to related websites. Be sure to contact those websites, and ask them to add links to yours.
- If you sell a product, determine whether you're selling the product through the website (consumers tend to expect this now). If so, the button beginning the ordering process should be easy to locate, and the order form should be short and clear.
- A search function is especially helpful for consumers who have a specific mission when visiting your site. If they're interested in one—and only one—aspect of your business, they'll be grateful to cut through all the red tape and get to their area of interest immediately.

- A press area is extremely important. Remember, you're not just trying to sell things on the Web—you want to get press coverage. Your site should offer reporters, editors, and producers easy access to company information, press kits, photographic images, and interview subjects. Ask for E-mail addresses, so you can "keep them informed" with news when it happens.

Now, what *don't* I include on my website? Creativity is nothing more than a series of choices: I will paint the Mona Lisa this way, but not that way. I'll include this scene in *Citizen Kane*, but I won't include any of an infinite number of other scenes I could use. Given that, if you choose to include certain elements on your website, which ones should you unquestionably leave off? Here are a few suggestions:

- Complicated graphics are great, but if they're going to take forever to download, you don't want them.
- Detailed testimonials to you personally, or even to your company as a whole, are going to turn away the viewer—or the media decision maker. Even if every single word is true, testimonials will sound like hype. Don't go overboard. It's OK to say, "We offer the finest products available," and it's not OK to post a six-page description of your career and how you came to buy these materials so you could make the finest products available. Keep in mind the short attention span of the viewer.
- Materials that are likely to offend some viewers, or that parents will consider objectionable for their children, should be left off. Yes, including offensive material will get you noticed, but it will get you noticed in the wrong way. Contrary to the popular expression, there is such a thing as bad publicity. The only time this rule doesn't apply is when your business is dealing in such material. I don't judge; I merely advise.
- Long, detailed descriptions of your product or service will provide an incredibly small percentage of your potential audience with more information than they will ever want to know. Don't overload them with details. If you feel it's absolutely necessary, offer a specific package of information as a download, which means the customer can ask for that packet and receive it as a file they can save or read. This way, you

won't be taking up valuable space on your website for something only a few of your (hopefully) many visitors will find interesting.

DON'T JUST POST YOUR SITE, MANAGE IT

Once your website is up and running, you'll be able to troubleshoot it, refine it, and continually upgrade it. In the words of Don Barrett, founder/publisher of laradio.com, the Internet site devoted to the history of Southern California radio, "You have to be willing to throw a grenade into your site periodically."

That means you have to keep the site vital and interesting, and you must be constantly in the process of redefining and updating it. Why? Because people aren't going to visit your site just once; they're going to come over and over again. And if they find the same information, delivered the same way, over and over again, guess what? They'll stop coming. And you'll lose a golden opportunity to keep the interest of someone who was clearly a potential customer or a media pro who could help promote your business. Keep it current.

Portrait of a Guerrilla: Don Barrett

My friend Don Barrett is an example of someone who turned his passion into a very successful website. A veteran of the Los Angeles radio scene, Don founded and developed laradio.com, the definitive Web presence devoted to, as he says, "preserving the rich history of Southern California radio." Usually, sites concentrating on something that specific will receive hits in the area of a hundred or two per day. Don's receives about 30,000 hits from unique visitors (that is, not one person going there 30,000 times) every day.

He says it's his interest in the subject that keeps the website fresh and vital. "I was passionate about the subject, so the subject was easy for me to wrap my arms around," he says. "People have to feel that if they don't go there every day, they're going to miss out on a vital component."

Toward that end, Don makes sure the news provided on laradio.com is always fresh, and he does so himself. He has the industry contacts and the drive to make sure that nothing—absolutely nothing—happens on the Southern California radio scene without being reported on his website.

"When people come to the site, they have to find something that's vital and alive," he advises. But "throwing in the grenade" and starting the website from scratch isn't something that can be done too often, to avoid removing the things that people liked about it in the first place. "If you throw the grenade in every day, it won't work," he says. "Work slowly to build their confidence and credibility."

Other advice from the sage of the radio website:

"I've never spent a dollar promoting the website. I've never taken out an ad. But I promote all the time. Thou shalt not let one day go by that you are not marketing your website.

"They [Web surfers] have to believe you're doing it for them. If you think you can be the star of the universe, you will eventually fail.

"Spam may get someone to look at you once, but if they're not interested in your subject matter, it doesn't matter what you do. Spam isn't worthwhile."

Don can be found at www.laradio.com.

USING THE WEB FROM OUTSIDE

Generating publicity with the Internet doesn't have to entail having your own website. It's possible to create buzz for yourself using other websites, and non-Web sections of the Internet. It takes a little more ingenuity, a little more sneakiness, but that's what being a guerrilla is all about, isn't it?

First of all, remember that the Internet is, above all, a medium of communication. Information is available, and users can access it at any time, for any reason. Therefore, your priority, as a guerrilla, is to make your information both available and unavoidable to users who might be searching for something related to your area of expertise.

To make information available without building your own website, you might consider *banner advertising*. You'll notice that many websites have these ads, which generally appear at the top or bottom of the Web page, and usually offer links to other sites where products can be purchased or information on the product or service can be found. You can certainly buy a banner ad on any site related to your business, and it will work pretty much the way an ad in any medium—print, radio, TV—would work. People will be informed of your existence and the product or service you offer.

The problem with banner ads, from a guerrilla's point of view, is that they cost money. Advertising, no matter which medium, is a for-profit endeavor, and the Internet is no exception. Depending on the site in question, and the length of time the ad will run, the cost of a banner ad can be quite high. It would be cheaper, and more effective, to build your own website and solicit other companies to advertise on yours, to offset the cost of running your business.

Let's remember our guerrilla training: we need to be fast, we need to be effective, and above all, we need to be *cheap*. Money is at a premium, and after all, if you just wanted to spend money to attract publicity, you could hire a P.R. firm to do it for you.

Instead, get yourself a little attention *without* spending money. On the Internet, this is simply a question of making a splash on appropriate websites.

First, compile a list of websites whose subject matter would include your business. Make this as broad a list as you want, but don't go so far from the core topic that you start getting into completely unrelated sites. When you start making your presence known, you don't want your reputation to be one of a spammer.

Internet bulletin boards and newsgroups are very good areas to post your opinions, and some facts, related to your business. You can even mention that you have a business. But don't try to solicit customers or lure people to your website through posts. Instead, establish yourself as an expert in your field, and let people start to ask you questions.

Some websites have been set up in exactly this way. For example, www.askme.com is a site devoted to having questions answered by experts in the field. Some of the experts are indeed impressive. Those who have questions about screenwriting, for example, can ask questions directly to William Goldman, perhaps the most respected screenwriter in Hollywood, whose credits include *Butch Cassidy and the Sundance Kid*, *Misery*, *The Princess Bride*, and *Hearts of Atlantis*.

It's easy to set yourself up as an expert in your field at this site. Merely fill out the questionnaire that is accessible from the home page, include some information about yourself (mentioning the name of your business is certainly within reason here), and choose your area of expertise. Before you know it, you'll be fielding questions, so you'd better really *be* an expert, because your answers will usually be posted for anyone with an interest in the topic to see.

That's one example of a website where you can establish your credentials. In newsgroups and bulletin boards, the procedure is somewhat less obvious. You sign up for a group in a topic related to your field. Before joining in the discussion, read the posts you get for a few days. Make sure you're not repeating someone else who has already posted on the subject here. Be charming, be witty, and above all, be part of the group. Don't try to lord yourself over these amateurs as the only "professional" in their midst; you'll just alienate the very people you're trying to attract. Eventually, if you demonstrate a true knowledge of the topic, you'll be asked questions. And you'll gain a reputation.

Remember Alan Canton, who wrote the column about his temple and raised over $200,000? Keep in mind that he was writing a regular weekly column for a website related to his business, which is computer publishing. You can write a column, too (or, if you are not a great wordsmith, you can hire a freelance writer to ghostwrite the column under your supervision), and establish yourself as an expert in your field.

It's also possible to pitch publications on an editorial, or opinion article, which generally will be printed in a separate section of the paper. You can even write such an article, establish yourself as an expert in your field, and try to get it published. The upside is that your message will be seen by a large number of people for free. The downside? You may write the piece and never see it in print. It's a small risk to take.

Levine's Lessons for Guerrillas: **Lesson #5**

The thing about being an expert, from a P.R. point of view, is that if you say you are an expert enough times to enough people, eventually you will be perceived as an expert. And because news programs and news channels are more plentiful now than ever before, the need for "experts" to analyze news stories on camera, on mike, and in print is deeper than it's ever been. Become an "expert," and you will definitely gain publicity.

E-MAIL: GOD'S GIFT TO GUERRILLAS

The easiest, cheapest, fastest way to communicate with potential customers, media executives, and editors on this planet is E-mail. For the cost of maintaining an Internet connection (which can be as little as $0, admittedly for a low-speed, ad-heavy connection), it is possible to E-mail virtually anyone you can think of, and the message will be delivered not in days, not in hours, not even in minutes, but in *seconds*. This is, indeed, a godsend to guerrilla publicists. I can't remember how I got by without it.

E-mail does, of course, have pitfalls, some of which we've already discussed. For one thing, keep in mind the commandment Thou shalt not spam. It's easy to get carried away with the power and speed of E-mail, and send promotional messages out to every single address you can get your hands on. Resist this impulse; it will be your undoing. Remember that if your first impression on a customer or an editor is a bad one, you won't get a second chance.

Instead, you want to send your message to people who have already expressed an interest in your area of expertise. You can purchase E-mail lists from some services, or better yet, make agreements with related websites to include links to your own. But if you have no website, you need to start compiling an E-mail list of your own, right away. Most E-mail programs have very simple features that help you compile an address book, which is really all you need. If your list gets too long, you can create a new file or edit down your list, getting rid of the names that haven't panned out or have requested that you stop E-mailing to that address.

As a matter of fact, you should *always* remove a name immediately when the recipient requests it. Continuing to send E-mail to that address is a form of spamming, so it's absolutely against the rules of Guerrilla P.R. Make sure the only people receiving your E-mail are the ones who have expressed an interest, or at least have expressed an interest in your topic. If they ask you to stop, you stop. That minute.

Compiling your address book or E-mail list should begin with contacts you've already made. If you have a client list, make sure you get E-mail addresses from as many as possible. Clients should be pleased to get your latest information the instant it's made available.

Beyond your existing list, it's possible to buy E-mail lists, as you would purchase mailing lists for conventional, or "snail," mail. These lists are not horribly expensive, and you can control the cost by specifying the lots of names you wish to buy. (You pay by the name, usually not more than a cent or two.) If you want 1,000 names at a time, you can buy 1,000 names at a time. You can also buy 10,000-name lots, and so on.

Taking E-mail addresses from your newsgroups and bulletin boards is more problematic. If you don't get some sign from the recipient ahead of time that your information is welcome, you'll be spamming. No need for me to reiterate how wrong that would be.

Once you compile or purchase your list, consider the message you wish to send. E-mail messages should be sent regularly, not just once, and each new message should contain new information. If you're running a sale on some product, E-mail is the place to promote it. Many businesses offer coupons or direct links to a website where the product can be bought at a discount offered only to E-mail recipients.

Don't flood your clientele with E-mail messages. Once a week is plenty, unless you have some breaking news story you want to discuss. In fact, once every two weeks, or even once a month, may be enough. You know your business. The golden rule: never send E-mail unless you have something to say.

If you're trying to get your face on TV, *and you have a legitimate story to tell*, you might try E-mailing some local or national media outlets. Choose carefully, try to get the E-mail address of a specific editor or producer (a list of media outlet URLs and E-mail addresses appears in Appendix C), and always, always, always make sure you're not wasting their time. The rule for first impressions is never quite as imperative as when dealing with the media.

Rules for E-Mailing Media Outlets
1. Tell a real news story.
2. Tell the story first; tell them how wonderful you are later.
3. Get a specific person's address when possible.
4. Don't blanket all media at once; start with the most desired outlets.
5. Don't E-mail now if you'll have a better story next week.
6. Know your prey: watch, listen, read the media, and know which is which.
7. Don't waste their time.
8. See Rule #1.

Remember, public relations is about creating an impression, a perception of the person, product, or service you're promoting. The *Blair Witch* filmmakers didn't blanket the media with stories of how they'd created this great website that was fooling people and producing excitement about their movie. They created a real, vital news story and then *let the media find out for themselves* how it had happened. That strategy added legitimacy to the news item itself (the media love to think they've discovered a story on their own) and made the filmmakers seem more pure and brilliant. Next thing you knew, CNN and other news organizations were reporting on this movie with great buzz and an air of mystery, and the rest was box office.

What does this have to do with E-mail, since the filmmakers didn't directly E-mail news organizations? Well, people who had seen the website *did* E-mail, and that happened naturally, without hard nudges from the people involved with the website. Yes, the film made it to prestigious festivals on its own, but it became a news story and a media phenomenon when the public took it upon itself to let news gatherers know something unusual was happening. You can't ask for a better publicity scenario than that.

Also, the film's enthusiasts—and even those who didn't know there *was* a film but had heard about the Blair Witch "myth"— started E-mailing each other, an even better result of great planning and good luck. A public groundswell built around the project, and that meant there was interest that had grown up around the product—in this case, the movie—without any media mentions and without any direct, traceable effort by the producers. People were interested because something unusual was happening, and they were given the joy of discovering it for themselves.

Levine's Lessons for Guerrillas: Lesson #6

Don't force-feed the public your information. The more people think they've found something interesting themselves, the better they'll feel about it. The key, remember, is to create a message so compelling that it will take on a life of its own.

Make sure your E-mail messages to the media are direct and to the point. Editors and producers have very little time to consider each nugget of information they're given. If you don't tell them something they want to know right away, you may not get the chance later on. If you're sending a message that provides news, get to the news right away. And tell it in the most compelling, dramatic, fascinating way you can *without lying.* Avoid adjectives like *amazing, fabulous,* or *fantastic,* since they are clearly opinions and send up red flags to media professionals. Try instead something like *groundbreaking* or *innovative*, since they indicate that you are conveying something new, and therefore newsworthy.

When you receive E-mail from a client, potential customer, or (perhaps especially) a reporter, producer, or editor, reply as quickly as possible. Always offer more information, make sure you mention more than one way to get in touch with you (E-mail, phone, fax, cell phone, snail mail), and make yourself available whenever the interested party can find the time. The last thing you want to do is lose an important contact or a lead on a client because your schedule was too full.

Once you have established a contact in the media, you must treat it very carefully. Always be honest and forthcoming with reporters, although you don't have to volunteer information that would hurt your business's public perception. You can respectfully opt not to answer a question, but don't *ever* lie to a reporter or producer; it's the kiss of death for any news coverage you may get in the future.

Also, it's important after establishing a relationship with a media professional to make it clear you're not going to waste a reporter's time. Offer information only when you have a real news story to tell, and E-mail only when you have something to say that will be of use to the reporter. A healthy relationship with the media can be a strong help for your business, but it can evaporate quickly if you don't know how to curb your E-mail impulses. Never, ever send jokes, poems, recipes, or chain letters to clients or the media: in fact, I'd advise you never to send those annoying things to anybody! Certainly never send any to me.

E-mail can be a powerful tool in any publicity campaign. But it has to be used carefully, even artfully, to be as effective as possible. The chief rule of E-mail is a derivation of a much more general, classic rule: E-mail unto others as you would have others E-mail unto you.

What Have We Learned?

- The World Wide Web is *not* the Internet. It is a *part* of the Internet, where information, products, and services are available. It is the "www" in website addresses, or URLs.
- Other areas of the Internet (or the Net) include newsgroups and bulletin boards, where people post messages and discuss topics that all relate to a common interest they share. Newsgroups and bulletin boards are open to members only, and

they sometimes charge membership fees (especially for bulletin boards).

- The Web is the only area of the Net where products and services can be offered for a fee.
- Do your research. Know the websites and terms you're using. Don't make your presence known until you have a distinct message and the means to deliver it.
- You can build your own website, a great way to draw attention to your business. If it's not going to be too elaborate, or if you have excellent Web skills, do it yourself. Otherwise, you might want to carefully select and supervise a Web development professional.
- Make your website easy and quick to download, attractive to the eye, and easy to understand. No sense dazzling people if they're going to be bored waiting for the page to appear, turned off by the design, or confused by the content.
- Make sure people can contact you through your website.
- A good website includes company information; links to other, related sites; a search function; and a "press room," among other features.
- A good website should not include confusing or slow-to-load graphics; long-winded testimonials, offensive material, or too much detail.
- "Throw in a grenade" and update your site periodically.
- Generate excitement outside your own website with banner ads if you have an advertising budget. If not, use newsgroups, bulletin boards, and websites to build a reputation as an expert.
- E-mail is as valuable a medium for P.R. as has ever been devised. Use it often, but use it wisely. Don't ever spam. Instead, compile a workable mailing list of clients, potential clients, and media outlets.
- Establish good relationships with media professionals. Do this by offering only legitimate news stories and always telling the truth.

3

WHAT IS INTERNET P.R.?

Oh, Magoo! You've done it again!

—QUINCY MAGOO

One of the questions that most obviously presents itself to me in writing a sequel to *Guerrilla P.R.* is, How does doing a publicity campaign on the Internet differ from doing a traditional publicity campaign?

Well, the obvious answer is, You're doing it on the Internet.

Marshall McLuhan coined a phrase in the 1960s that still resonates today: "The medium is the message." And even though McLuhan didn't have the Internet in mind when he wrote that, he couldn't possibly have been more correct in today's wired society.

If the medium is the message, and the medium in our case is the Internet, then what is the message? Well, by choosing to promote our business, our product, our service, ourselves on the Internet, we are making a few statements even before we present our message. For one, we're saying that we think we have something that will appeal to people who use the Internet. Also, we think that we can present it in ways that online viewing will best accommodate. And we're making the clear statement that we're up-to-date, state-of-the-art, and in the current moment, not thinking about what happened 20, 30, or 100 years ago. If we're on the Internet, we are part of what's going on *now*.

As I said before, I was not a gleeful, willing convert to online usage. It was only after I realized that the Internet revolution was here to stay, that it wasn't going to come and go like eight-track players and Quadraphonic sound, that I was able to commit myself to acquiring the knowledge and skills I needed to operate online. But once I did, it opened up a whole new universe of thought for me. Some of it is absolutely amazing. And some of it is a little scary.

When I opened my public relations business in 1983, which doesn't seem so long ago, my office had no computers. It had no fax machine. There was, of course, no E-mail, no Internet access. FedEx hadn't started delivering yet. MTV was only a couple of years old. *USA Today* was still considered a fad among the newspaper publishers I knew; it wouldn't last. We were still writing on things called typewriters (remember those?), and in my office, we were state-of-the-art, with IBM Selectric typewriters.

Things have changed, and they've changed a lot. Fast.

In the ensuing years, all of the things I just listed have been developed, have become consumer products, and are now part of the average office environment. Except the typewriters, which have gone the way of the dodo bird and are now exhibits at the Smithsonian Institution, exemplifying the "prewired world." It's hard to think of the world as it was without them, just as it's hard to remember just what it was like to dial a phone instead of pushing a memory button. When changes are complete, they have become so much a part of our lives that we don't really think about them anymore.

There have been massive changes in technology since 1983, and many since *Guerrilla P.R.* was published in 1993. Our world doesn't even look the same as it did then, except perhaps to astronauts on the International Space Station, a concept that seemed as much science fiction as possibility in those days. Cooperate with other countries, particularly Russia, on a space project? In 1983, who would have thought it was possible?

What has changed is obvious. What *hasn't* changed, not one iota, is human nature. If we had concluded a successful business deal in 1983, I might have sent you a cordial note thanking you for your participation. This year, I'd probably send the exact same words, only through E-mail. You'd appreciate the gesture, just as you would have during the Reagan Administration, but the medium through which it was delivered would have changed.

In other words, the delivery system has changed, but not the nature of the people involved.

That is a key point: people remain the same, even when they can send messages across continents in the blink of an eye and fax documents to each other that might have taken days or weeks not all that long ago. It took the average American thirty days to receive the news that Abraham Lincoln had been shot and killed in 1865. If the same event were to happen today, the country would be alerted before the reverberations from the shot had died out. But the public would still be just as shocked, just as horrified, just as mournful. Things happen faster, and messages are delivered quicker, but they are still the same things and the same messages. Because we are the same people.

Because human nature remains the same, even as technology advances seemingly as we watch, the nature of a publicity campaign remains roughly the same, but the medium changes. We learn the rules of the new medium, and we can use it more efficiently, but we are guerrillas, and our goal remains the same: be first, be fast, be creative, be cheap.

Therefore, our fundamentals will be unchanged. We have to provide a legitimate news story, make sure the media know about it, and publicize ourselves and our businesses without spending on agencies or advertising. But there will be adaptations to the chosen medium, no?

Adaptations, yes. Changes, no. Don't let the Internet intimidate you; it's the easiest and most accessible medium for publicists in history. There's no gatekeeper! There's nobody to tell you that your story isn't worthy of print or of coverage. On the Net, you can be your own editor, your own producer. But—and this is important—to break the wall and get coverage from other media, you have to remember that the story you tell must be compelling, dramatic, irresistible—and true.

HOW MR. MAGOO HAS TAKEN OVER THE WORLD

I said before that technology is the enemy of reverence. If that's the case, then information technology is the enemy of clarity.

Not long ago, as the host of a radio show I do in Los Angeles, I noted the anniversary of the first broadcast of *Entertainment Tonight*. The next day, a number of people I know through business—not stupid people, by any means—congratulated me on my appearance on *Entertainment Tonight*. That would have been nice, had I actually appeared on the show.

What has happened over the past decade is that the media have grown faster than we can sensibly track. Our minds are full of cable channels, satellite stations, Internet connections, Web pages, magazines, newspapers, television, radio, and MP3s. This is unexplored territory; it's never happened before in any civilization. And we can't be sure what kind of impact it will have on the populace.

One thing I have noted is what I call the Mr. Magoo Effect.

Remember Mr. Magoo? Quincy Magoo was the eccentric, dotty millionaire who stumbled through cartoons in the 1960s, and his (that is, Jim Backus's) voice became so well known he eventually starred in specials adapting everything from Charles Dickens's *A Christmas Carol* to Robin Hood.

The thing most people remember about Mr. Magoo, though, is that he was extremely nearsighted. He was constantly mistaking men for women, fire hoses for salesmen, and dogs for his nephew. He was a nice enough fellow, but not all too bright, and certainly as myopic as they come. Somehow, he managed to hang on to his driver's license, although we never were terribly sure how he pulled off that feat.

Mr. Magoo wasn't blind; he was nearsighted. That is, he could *kind of* make out the images that passed before his eyes, but he quite often misinterpreted them.

Think about it. Haven't we all started to take on a Mr. Magoo–like quality? Hasn't the barrage of images, sounds, and information bombarding us started to blend in our minds just a little bit? Haven't there been times when you could remember that you'd heard something, but you couldn't remember where you'd heard it?

Likewise, the people who'd have sworn I was on *Entertainment Tonight* when, in fact, I'd merely discussed the show on the radio were not jackasses. Of course not. Did they all happen to have an off day at the same time? I don't think so. Rather, they were all suffering from the Mr. Magoo Effect.

The Mr. Magoo Effect describes a diminished capacity for clarity that exists in our present society. It takes into account the amount of stimuli we are trying to process every day. Twenty years ago, we were getting about 1,000 messages—advertising stimuli, that is—per day, but we are now receiving, as a result of increases and advances in media, some 10,000 messages. And because we use only one-tenth of our brains, we're still having trouble filtering it all into clear, understandable thoughts. At the same time, the increase in activity we see in our average day means we have less time to process ten times more messages. Because of the overload and the time pressure, we remember only bits of what we've heard and don't necessarily understand more than a small percentage of it. We can't sort, interpret, classify, and store all the information we receive, so it tends to blend together. We spend less time thinking and more time reacting, and when we have to call up some piece of information, it isn't necessarily in the same corner of our brain we stored it in originally.

Welcome, Mr. Magoo.

This society has become a large group of Mr. Magoos, all rushing around in our vintage automobiles, honking at traffic cops we imagine to be water towers, and trying to recall exactly where it was we originally started out for. It's a sad commentary on our society, and it's a frightening trend in human psychology and human behavior.

It can also be a profound advantage for the media anarchist, another word for us guerrillas.

Keep in mind that the Mr. Magoo Effect provides us with a *shift* in behavior patterns. When I was growing up in the New York City area, seven television stations were available: The networks were ABC, NBC, CBS, and PBS. There was also WPIX, Channel 11, which broadcast the New York Yankees games; WOR, Channel 9, which had the Mets; and WNEW, Channel 5, which had no baseball team but did include Sandy Becker for kids in the afternoon.

That was all the television available. No matter what technology you had at the time, that was all you could get. You could walk around with the TV schedule for every station memorized at all times. And keep in mind, this was New York, the media center of the world. Most other cities had fewer stations. You were lucky if you had five.

With the advent of cable TV, satellite technology, digital technology, and the VCR, television (and therefore media in general) options became far more broad and numerous. New York is no longer all that different from any other city, town, or borough in America. You can pick up all the stations that didn't exist in 1975:

CNN, Fox News, MSNBC, Nickelodeon, Lifetime, A&E, Comedy Central, ESPN. The list goes on and on. And it has had a profound effect.

This change has shifted the way we get our information, our entertainment, and our advertising data. And *shift* is another word, in the Guerrilla Dictionary, for *opportunity*.

In the current media climate, which can only grow and expand, someone like Bill O'Reilly can be a huge TV star. He has a best-selling book and a hit TV show on a station that broadcasts only news twenty-four hours a day. That would have been absolutely unthinkable as little as twenty-five years ago. And while twenty-five years seems like an eternity, in the grand scheme of things, it is a remarkably short time.

Believe me, I have nothing against Bill O'Reilly. I watch him on TV every night after work. But he would not have been as enormous a media star in the 1970s, when Walter Cronkite read you the news in a stentorian, important voice every night before Mary Tyler Moore came on to make you laugh. It is only with the increase in media outlets that someone like O'Reilly, or Matt Drudge, or Larry King, or the *South Park* characters can find a place to be courageous, offbeat, and maybe a little crazy. I've never met a truly successful entrepreneur who wasn't all those things.

O'Reilly and all the rest merely illustrate the opportunity that exists because of the increased number of media outlets. For a guerrilla publicist, sensing an opportunity like that is like a hungry cheetah smelling blood.

Add the Internet to that mix, and you can see the Ocean of Opportunity stretched out in front of you.

What the Net has done is to level the playing field. It permits someone with virtually no budget to compete with a huge international conglomerate, with no discernible difference. It also creates a place—albeit a virtual one—where all the businesses in your industry can be seen and compared. If you have an advantage, there is no easier or better way to exploit it.

Top 10 Advantages of the Internet for Guerrillas
1. Guerrillas are fast. The Internet is faster.
2. Your website is accessible in the same way your competitor's is, even if your competitor is the largest company in the world.
3. The Internet is inexpensive.
4. The Internet values creativity over budget.

5. The Internet is accessible internationally.
6. Your message is unedited and unfiltered. You can't be taken out of context.
7. The Internet allows for networking with colleagues you might never meet otherwise.
8. You can run a website or create publicity from your living room or the boardroom of your corporate headquarters. No one will know the difference.
9. Access by consumers can only grow over the next ten years.
10. Did we mention it's fast?

BIG FOLLOWS SMALL

In a traditional P.R. campaign—that is, one that occurred before online access was as universal as today—the procedure, although it required a good deal of art and creativity, was relatively simple. You crafted a message, be it a news item or an event, and you contacted media outlets. You would follow up with them to see if they had some interest, and some would give you news coverage. Others wouldn't. That was pretty much the way it worked, although of course it called for a good deal of nuance and expertise.

Now the pace has accelerated, but the process is, in a way, inverted. The smart guerrilla these days makes the media come to him or her. You're still trying to attract attention from newspapers, television, radio, and other media, but you can do it by starting off small. In fact, the smaller you start off, the better off you are. I've spoken with quite a few editors and producers in the course of my business, and the one thing that has always impressed me is how the most influential—the *New York Times*, *People* magazine, the *Washington Post*, *USA Today*, the *Wall Street Journal*—will always admit that they get ideas for news pieces from other news pieces, almost always in smaller publications with lower circulation numbers and a more limited range of subscribers.

In other words, big follows small.

Let me repeat that, because it's an enormously important concept for a guerrilla publicist: big follows small. A piece that runs in the local weekly newspaper might be noticed by the local cable news station, which might send a reporter out to cover it. If that piece makes it to the air, an editor at a regional magazine might see it. That can lead to an article that might get spotted by a producer at the local network affiliate, who can run a news story on the 6 p.m.

broadcast. If it's good enough, the network or a cable news channel owned by the network (since most of them have a controlling interest in at least one) could follow up on it. And the next thing you know, the little story that started in the local weekly paper is a featured piece for twenty minutes on nationwide TV.

Of course, first of all, the story has to be newsworthy. Don't expect the opening of a new pizzeria to make it to *20/20*. But if the story is truly worth telling, the concept of big follows small can be tremendously important. It means you can start off with a little item on a website and end up on the *Oprah Winfrey Show*, and it's not an impossible dream. It might be a difficult one, but nobody ever said that being a guerrilla was easy.

Put the idea of Big Follows Small to use:

- Plant little items in E-newsletters. Editors are usually very grateful for ideas.
- Write a little something for your own website. If you publicize the site well enough, the story you write will be read.
- Try sending E-mail to the news editor for your local cable-TV news station. Make sure, as ever, that your news story is legitimate.
- E-mail the editors for your town or region at the local weekly newspaper. Offer to write the story yourself if they don't have a reporter available.
- Try to get other local businesses to link their websites to yours. Offer to put a link on your website to theirs.
- Offer to write a regular column for a website devoted to your business or your community. Look at how well it worked for Alan Canton and his synagogue.
- E-mail news directors at local radio stations, and direct them to your website. Radio, because it's twenty-four hours and usually local, is always hungry for local news.
- Mention your news story—as long as it's a real news story—on Internet bulletin boards and in newsgroups devoted to a related topic.
- Watch the tiny coverage snowball.

OPEN A VIRTUAL NEWSROOM

It's one thing to allow the media to find you through a story somewhere on the Net or in a local paper. But once they do, you'd better have the information the media need.

That means, particularly when you've set up a company website, that you need a "virtual press room" at the site. You do this with a link that press members can click on when they are looking for information on your company. You can set up the link so that the reporter must establish "credentials" before entering (your website can save that information for future visits). Or you can allow anyone with interest to access the press room and gain the information you've stored there. What's important, though, is that you establish and furnish your press room well. It's the first—and in some cases, only—chance you'll have to interest a media member in your story, so you have to put your best foot forward.

The virtual press room on your website is also going to be a vital part of your online publicity campaign. But it has to be carefully designed and maintained, and you have to check *often* for E-mail from reporters, editors, and producers. These are not people you want to keep waiting.

A virtual press room is the section on the website that provides information about your company or yourself to the press. It's different than the information you provide the general public not so much in content, but in presentation. Consumers may not need to know who the officers of your corporation are or the date the company was formed; the press will. Background is always important to reporters on a story, but not always to consumers, who need answers to specific questions.

What kind of background should be included in the press room? Start with the following kinds of information:

- Provide a thumbnail description of the company. This is often the one-sentence phrase that appears at the end of a public relations press release about your company: "ABC Interiors is a company that provides wallpaper and interior design concepts to designers in the tri-state region." It's very brief but describes the company's function.
- If your company has a mission statement, post it unedited.
- List the officers of the company and, if possible, their E-mail addresses. Some executives prefer to go through a publicist or public relations specialist. In that case, make sure the contact's name, phone number, and E-mail address are listed clearly. This contact information may be the most important item in the press room, since any coverage is going to require communication between the media and the company. Never let them get away without knowing who to contact, and how.

- A brief history of the company is never a bad idea, but don't go crazy. One or two pages is plenty.
- Any recent press releases you've written or distributed about the company should be available for viewing and printing. The idea of a press release, after all, is to attract press attention. Make sure all your press releases are easy to find and use.
- If the company is publicly traded, post your financial information, including the last annual report and the stock symbol for the company.

Make sure any press releases available on your website are frequently updated; there's nothing older than old news.

Keep in mind that reporters *want* you to have a good story to tell; it makes their job easier. But don't try to sell them on a story that really doesn't have any news in it. The more honest you are with the press, the better your reputation will be, and the easier your relationship with the gatekeepers—the people who allow access to the public—will be.

Remember, too, that the press is not a race of superheroes. They're just as apt to be afflicted by the Mr. Magoo Effect as anyone—maybe more, since they spend so much of their time trying to locate and identify appropriate news stories. So you have to make your message distinctive and memorable.

How? Think about what makes your business distinctive and memorable, and that will be a start. Don't exaggerate and don't lie, ever. But do emphasize the special things you and your business do to provide the kind of product or service you think is noteworthy. If you do charitable works in a special way, make sure to mention those activities. If your product is innovative or used in some new way, that should be emphasized. If someone in the company has a special story to tell, be sure it gets told. You know your company and what makes it unique. Make sure other people find those things out, too.

Portrait of a Guerrilla: Jay Conrad Levinson

I have to admit, I'm a little in awe of my friend Jay Levinson. Author of the *Guerrilla Marketing* series of books, Jay has defined and explained the concept of guerrilla business and sold more than a million books. Because of *Guerrilla P.R.*, people often mistake me for Jay and compliment me on my fine work in the *Guerrilla Mar-*

keting series. But it's Jay Levinson who created and refined that idea, and I'm grateful that we have managed to become friends and colleagues. We recently had a conversation about changes in marketing and publicity brought on by the Internet.

Jay Levinson's theories about guerrilla marketing have embraced the Internet in the past few years, and he understands especially well how online marketing differs from the traditional kind. He agrees with me that spamming potential clients or media contacts is a deadly tactic. He says E-mail should be more of a "permission marketing" activity, sending E-mail only "to people who are anticipating your message" because they've previously contacted you or have shown interest in receiving information from you. "I don't believe in spam at all," Jay continues.

He adds, too, that Internet marketing is absolutely essential today: "Unless you are willing to move at cyberspeed, you're going to be left behind." Jay notes that for most marketers new to business or to the Internet, "the biggest mistake by far is believing that marketing works faster than it really works. Remember, the statistics show you've got to penetrate [customers'] minds nine times [with advertising messages] to get through to them, but that's not the bad news. The truth is that for every three times you present your message, they're only paying attention once. So that means you have to do it twenty-seven times!"

To attract media attention, your message has to be that much more defined, and it has to include real news, Jay says. "The media need you as much as you need them—if you give them real news," he explains. "You have to realize the importance of determination and repetition. You have to follow up on your message. You have to keep your determination."

Getting media coverage is important, however. The level of believability for news coverage is miles above that of advertising or materials that come directly from a company. Jay says it's necessary to make press coverage a key element of your promotional plan.

"When it comes to marketing, people have a built-in B.S. detector," he says. "What they read in the paper, they believe much more readily."

The Internet's reach can only expand, too. As time goes on, people in lower socioeconomic groups will gain access, and they will also be available as clients for Web-present companies. "As we progress, [the Internet and computer technology] will be integrated into the educational process, and you can see they're learning it at school *now*," Jay says. "As we're talking, I just got back from being away for five days. When I got back, 75 percent of my E-mails were spam, and I didn't pay them any attention. That's what's going to happen."

Participating in discussion groups and bulletin boards should also be part of an online marketing plan, he contends. "You can promote by publishing articles on other people's websites. That's very often free. Start with E-mailing and participating in forums tied to your area of interest."

Unfortunately, many business owners don't recognize the importance of marketing and promotion, online or off. Jay notes that the average amount of funding devoted to marketing is usually 4 percent, and he finds that terribly low, an indication that marketing doesn't hold the position it should in most executives' minds.

"People should follow the rule of thirds: invest one-third of your budget in developing your website, one-third in promoting the site, and one-third in maintaining the site," Jay says. "Bill Gates said recently that if he had $1 left in his marketing budget, he'd spend it on public relations. That's correct. And keep in mind that this is not about you—it's about the customer. You can do your bragging at the end of your press release or your presentation, but you start out by talking about them."

You can find Jay Levinson online at www.guerrilla-marketing.com/authors/jlevinson.html.

DON'T LET THE DATA SMOG SLOW YOU DOWN

A number of qualities are necessary for creating and executing a successful online publicity campaign. The nuts and bolts are simple enough, but it's necessary to understand the mind-set of the people you're trying to reach—potential clients and media workers.

To understand potential clients, remember the Mr. Magoo Effect. Potential clients are getting through the same kind of busy, cluttered day you are—dealing with increased professional expectations, family obligations, personal problems, and the simple business of getting through a day, which can include transportation, household chores, shopping, cooking, laundry, and vehicle maintenance. All that's without even taking into account the business of running a business. It's a lot to remember and a lot to keep track of.

Add to that the thousands of media messages we're all confronted with in the course of a day, and what you get is a condition I call Data Smog. Data Smog is as toxic as the physical kind, but it attacks the mind, not the body. It is an overload of information, and it is compounded by regular use of the Internet. Data Smog combines television, radio, print, and online information into a large cannonball of data, and it attacks every member of our society on an almost minute-by-minute basis.

The effect of Data Smog is that despite the increased demands on our time and our minds, we tend to move a little more slowly by the end of a day, when our brain capacity feels overloaded and our bodies aren't quite as fresh as they were after eight hours of sleep. The Mr. Magoo Effect is compounded by Data Smog, and now we can't remember those things we were supposed to remember. We might pass on information we believe to be accurate, and fail. Our conversations take on the quality of a childhood game of Telephone, where one person whispers a sentence to another, who whispers what he thinks he heard to the next, and so on and so on.

By the end of the game, you'll recall, the phrase "Let's go to the beach" has often become "Four score and seven years ago." Nobody knows how it happened, but Data Smog and Mr. Magoo have a lot to do with it.

Take that game of Telephone, put it on the Internet, and what you get is what I call a *thought virus*. This takes the same shape as an intentional online virus, starting in one person's computer and ricocheting from one to another and so on until everyone has a different piece of information, none of which is accurate.

Technology, after all, is a double-edged sword; it can be used in any number of different ways. Remember, a hammer can be used to crush a skull, or it can be used to build a hospital. Online technology works the same way. To use it well for a publicity campaign, you need these important qualities:

- **An appreciation for the zeitgeist.** That's a fancy word for the spirit of our times.
- **Courage.** People think courage means the absence of fear. No. The absence of fear is mental illness. Courage is the ability to feel fear and do what you have to do, anyway.
- **The ability to experiment.** This is an outgrowth of courage, and it is indispensable to a guerrilla. If you can't experiment,

if you have to do everything by the numbers, following carefully in previously made footprints, you can't be a guerrilla.

Now, let's not confuse Data Smog or thought viruses with laziness. Laziness should not be ignored as a problem in our society. If you go to a restaurant tonight, what are the odds that the manager will come over before you leave and ask how everything went, whether there was anything he could have done to improve your experience, and whether there is anything he can change in the future? Not very high, I'll say. Is that because everyone on the planet is too busy to take thirty seconds to ask the questions? No. It's because most managers don't want to be told things they don't want to hear, and that's *laziness*.

If you want a professional role model, use Michael Jordan. When he was playing for the Chicago Bulls, Jordan was famous as the best basketball player alive. And at the end of every season, what did he do?

Jordan went home, assessed his game, figured out where the weaknesses were, and spent the entire off-season trying to improve on them. It's like Picasso getting up early to improve on his technique or Martin Scorsese studying past directors to see what they might have understood that he doesn't. If you think you can't improve on what you do, you're not trying hard enough.

There's a saying popular among some businesspeople: "It's not about working harder; it's about working smarter." Nonsense. It's about working harder. You've got to ferret out opportunity and work at it until you see how you can capitalize. Spike Lee, the filmmaker of such impressive movies as *Do the Right Thing*, *Malcolm X*, and *Bamboozled*, takes Michael Jordan as his example: "Every summer, Mike would woodshed. Dribbling, his outside shot was kind of shaky when he first came into the league. Every summer he would take his game apart and say, 'Where am I deficient?' And that's where the work got done." Even as he gets more confident and wins more awards as a filmmaker, Lee takes time out after each movie to ask, "Where am I deficient?" and he works on those things.

Work hard. Work fast. Be a guerrilla.

And Now What Have We Learned?

- Technology changes. Human nature doesn't. Capitalize on human nature.

- Overload of information has created the Mr. Magoo Effect. This is characterized by a vague understanding of input and is an enormous opportunity for a guerrilla publicist.
- Remember, Mr. Magoo was nearsighted, not blind. People can see your message, but it has to be clear. Use the diminished capacity for clarity in society to your advantage. Be clear yourself.
- Your website should include a virtual press room where information is available specifically for the press. Include background on your company, recent press releases, and especially contact information.
- Big follows small. Let a small news break in a local weekly grow into television coverage.
- A message that comes through the media will have more credibility than one you create yourself. Try to achieve media coverage.
- Even for guerrillas, patience can be a virtue. The biggest mistake is that people think marketing works faster than it possibly can. Don't give up on a marketing campaign, even an online one, if you don't get immediate results.
- Marketing should be a major priority for businesses and is often undervalued by executives.
- Know your prey. Understand your target demographic and the members of the media you're trying to attract. Give them what they want, not what you want them to have. Tell the truth, and you will be respected.
- In creating a website, devote one-third of the budget to development, one-third to maintenance, and one-third to marketing or promotion.
- Data Smog is a condition that creates the Mr. Magoo Effect. It combines all the information we encounter in the average day, blending it until comprehension becomes more difficult.
- A thought virus begins with a piece of information online and develops into a chain of misinformation
- Laziness is an enormous problem in this society, largely unrecognized. For a guerrilla, laziness is death.
- It is *so* about working harder.

4

NARROWING DOWN

"Too much of a good thing can be wonderful."

—MAE WEST

Think of the Internet as a starry sky on a clear night: each star is a website, and each constellation a group of linked sites on a particular topic. And for each of these, there are many, many more stars, planets, asteroids, and solar systems you can't see with the naked eye.

That's a lot, isn't it?

It can be intimidating to consider, even casually, the size and breadth of the Internet as it exists today. There is a website for virtually every topic, every viewpoint, every interest humans have so far developed, and there's no end in sight. Finding your way through this star chart is more difficult than simply asking Mr. Sulu to "lay in a course for Starbase Three" and hoping he knows where he's going.

It's one thing to be surfing the Net and become overwhelmed with the vast extent of it all. It's quite another to be *using* the Net to publicize your interests and find yourself up to your neck in Web addresses (URLs), downloads, links, banner ads, and home pages.

In other words, you'd better narrow your focus just a little bit, because trying to attract attention on the entire Internet at once is like trying to staple jelly to a ceiling. It takes a whole lot of time, and it can't be done anyway.

If that's what you shouldn't do, what *should* you do? Well, it's necessary to change your outlook. Either get a telescope to examine the constellations close up and a little at a time, or focus on one star and learn all you can about it, plotting your guerrilla maneuver to best capitalize on your strengths and the star's weaknesses.

Let's take a look at this huge universe called the Internet and decide how a confident, capable guerrilla can best conquer it.

HOW BIG IS THE INTERNET?

As of this writing, there are about 116.2 million Web "hosts"—meaning permanent Web addresses. That's up from 50.6 million only two years ago. Each of those addresses can contain countless Web pages. They include educational sites, corporate sites, private sites, and others. At this rate of growth, the number of hosts could easily top 200 million in two years. If that happens, there will be a Web page for almost every person in the United States. Counting hosts doesn't even begin to calculate the number of people who visit each host every day.

Nobody said there wouldn't be a lot of ground to cover. But in narrowing your sites (literally), keep in mind that you don't want to cut out areas that might be interested in your message. In other words, don't narrow too much.

How do we go about narrowing down our area of attack? It's clear—remember that McLuhan said the medium is the message. Another way of looking at that is to say that the message is the medium. What you have to say, the news story you're telling, the product you're introducing, the service you're providing, is going to appeal to a certain segment of the population *first*. To begin with, we focus on that segment. That doesn't mean we're excluding the rest of the world, just that we're starting with this group and will move on from there.

Not every business owner has access to demographic studies and carefully compiled statistics about the people who patronize his or her business. It's hard to have enough money to commission such research, and very little of it is available for free on the Internet.

However, there is something that each business owner *can* use to help identify and target the most likely patrons, and that is observation. For example, if you own a T-shirt shop in Baltimore, you know that the majority of your customers are male, they're between thirteen and thirty-five years old, and they favor designs that feature rock bands, professional wrestlers, and sports teams.

That, by itself, is demographic research. Based upon that observation, you might be able to guess which publications this group of customers is likely to read, which radio stations are most likely to be their favorites, and roughly how much money they have to spend on T-shirts. For our purposes, it's probably possible to determine which websites they might be likely to frequent.

How is this information useful to the business owner, particularly the *Guerrilla* business owner? Well, the more you can ascertain about your core customer, the more you can target publicity campaigns, Web pages, and promotions, as well as more traditional advertising.

Keep in mind, also, that your core customer, your main market, is not the only consumer to whom you're marketing. There will be ancillary markets as well, people who on first glance wouldn't appear to have a desire or need for your product or services, but who might defy the odds and actually find themselves wanting to patronize your business. We'll get to them later in this chapter.

TARGETING

As an exercise, let's see how to define and *refine* our target demographic. We can start with a huge target—let's say every person in the United States—and then gradually narrow our focus until we can best identify our core customer, to whom we'll direct most of our guerrilla tactics. Start by answering the questions in my twenty-question quiz about target markets. By the time you finish, you may end up with a much clearer picture of your best customer.

20 Questions to Ask Yourself About Your Target Market

1. Is my product/service more likely to be used by one gender or the other?
2. Is my product/service geographically based (that is, tied to one physical area)?
3. Is my product/service too expensive to appeal to every demographic in my area?
4. Is my product/service more likely to be used by people of one age range?
5. Is my most frequent customer most likely to be from an urban, suburban, or rural area?
6. What kind of car does my most likely customer drive?

7. In what publications would that car most likely be advertised?
8. On what television/radio programs is that car often advertised?
9. Which websites best attract the eye of my target demographic? Why?
10. What kind of music does my target audience listen to?
11. Does my core audience listen to Howard Stern or NPR?
12. Does my core audience watch *South Park* or *Masterpiece Theater*?
13. Is my most frequent customer more likely to have a white-collar or blue-collar job?
14. What other products or services is my target demographic likely to need?
15. Where are these things advertised?
16. Which websites might these products or services support?
17. Have I seen celebrities endorsing products or services similar to mine? Who are they, and what do they represent?
18. Is my product or service most likely to be used by one particular ethnic group? Why? Can my audience be broadened to include others?
19. Does my target audience travel much? What might be some typical destinations?
20. Does my target demographic own/operate a personal computer?

Once you have answered the quiz questions, you can begin to construct a vague picture of your most likely customer. But in answering the questions, be honest. There are no right or wrong answers, only the truth. If your product really isn't more likely to be used by one gender, don't pretend that it is. Remember that one of the commandments of the guerrilla is to "Know thy product."

If you've answered the questions and determined that your average customer is a male between the ages of eighteeen and thirty-two, more likely to have a blue-collar job, listen to Howard Stern, dine at Hooters, and root for the Dallas Cowboys, don't try to market to him as if he were a seventy-six-year-old woman from Boston whose hobbies include embroidery and who never misses *Live from Lincoln Center* before heading out to the local Ethiopian restaurant for an elegant dinner. In other words, be honest with yourself. Don't try to turn your customers into something they aren't. Instead, market to those customers, since they are the most probable consumers of the product or service your business offers.

But where's the online part of this process? After all, targeting customers would be the same if you were trying to get publicity off-line through the usual press releases, events, and advertising.

Keep in mind what I've said before: technology advances, but human nature remains the same. There is a difference in marketing to a demographic on the Internet, just as with any other aspect of the publicity game. It's faster, it's cheaper, and it's easier. But how do you make it work?

Simple. When you visit virtually any business-oriented website, you'll come across a button that asks, "How did you find out about us?" That tracking device, which is by no means new on the Internet, is a way of identifying your demographic in much the same way I just described, but in a considerably more direct fashion. You don't have to beat around the bush; you can ask, "Where did you hear about us?" It's another way of saying, "Who are you?" Once you've gotten an answer to that question, the rest will follow.

Include that question, and others, on your website. This will be natural, especially if you're setting up an E-commerce site that will actually allow the public to buy your product via the Internet. Demographic questions regarding age, gender, socioeconomic status, and others (ever wonder why the questionnaires always ask you if you own a personal computer or a VCR?) can all be answered directly. It's true, these questions shouldn't be made mandatory, like address and phone number, but most people will answer them anyway, and you will have a much clearer picture of your target audience.

Narrowing your focus is a process of eliminating the *least* likely consumer and concentrating on the *most* likely one. It begins with identifying these groups, and that can be done with a simple visualization: Each ring on an archery target represents a certain segment of the population. The wider the ring, the larger the group. And the larger the group, the more broadly it is defined, so the less likely it is to be exactly the consumer who is your perfect target audience.

Think of each ring as a group of people. Obviously, the best thing would be to appeal to the entire target, but that's not terribly likely unless your product is called Coca-Cola or Scotch tape. What's more apt to happen is that one of the inner rings will be your broadest possible target audience, and once you've hit the bull's-eye in the middle, you might want to start broadening your appeal, ring by ring, until you reach your widest possible demographic.

Archery Target Demographic

Let's use our Baltimore T-shirt shop as a model. Imagine an archery target. Each ring, from the outermost to the bull's-eye, bears lettering, as indicated below, beginning with the largest, outermost ring:

> Outermost ring: The population of the United States
> Next largest ring: The population of the East Coast of the United States
> Next largest ring: The population of the Middle Atlantic states
> Next largest ring: The population of Maryland
> Next largest ring: Residents of, or visitors to, Baltimore, Maryland
> Next largest ring: People in Baltimore between the ages of eleven and thirty-five
> Next largest ring: Males in Baltimore between the ages of eleven and thirty-five
> Next largest ring: Male sports fans in Baltimore between the ages of eleven and thirty-five
> Next largest ring: Male baseball fans in Baltimore between the ages of eleven and thirty-five
> Bull's-eye: Male Baltimore Orioles fans between the ages of eleven and thirty-five in Baltimore

While it might be best for our imaginary T-shirt store to target boys and men who root for the Baltimore Orioles, it's also possible to broaden that demographic to any baseball fan in that age and gender demographic. How? Offer T-shirts with logos from teams other than the Orioles, especially the team the Orioles are playing *today*. Later, you can widen your audience another notch, to sports fans, by offering Baltimore Ravens T-shirts, and those from other local and visiting sports teams.

Beyond that, you can widen your target to males in the area who might not be professional sports fans, with T-shirts that have the logos of rock bands or other interests of that group. If that continues to grow your business, consider bringing in shirts that will appeal especially to the women who walk in with your core audience, and see if they'll buy shirts, too. And on it goes . . .

This same principle applies when you're putting together a website or searching for one to link to your own. Once you know the kind of person who most often makes a hit on the site, you can start to determine whether or not this Web page is appropriate for your business.

Of course, your own website is the most appropriate for you, since it concerns itself strictly with your business. But getting people to view it might involve links to other sites and banner ads on sites that are related to your own.

This does *not* mean that you should immediately begin advertising on sites that compete directly with yours. That's just giving aid and comfort to the enemy in your guerrilla assault. What it does mean is that you should consider related sites, those that offer posters, let's say, of the same bands and athletes featured on your T-shirts. Or the fan sites devoted to those athletes and musicians. There are hundreds and hundreds of them, and they are quite likely to be regular Internet stops for devotees of the people, teams, and bands you feature on your product. Imagine the numbers of interested eyeballs you can attract with mutual links between the websites or, if necessary, banner ads placed on the poster or fan sites. You could be well on the way to broadening your business in a way that the Internet does best: attracting customers who are not in your geographical area but are interested in your product. Nothing can attract them faster, in greater numbers, or cheaper than a well-placed Web campaign.

GENTLEMEN, START YOUR (SEARCH) ENGINES

Of course, you can't spend thousands of hours drifting from Web page to Web page in order to determine which sites are the best match for your own. You need to become proficient in the use of a search engine, something that helps you identify websites that serve a particular area of interest.

A search engine is not usually offered as a separate piece of software, but is a tool available at popular Web portals such as Google, Yahoo!, Excite, Alta Vista, and others. To use a search engine, you type in a keyword or phrase, click on "search," and receive a list of suggestions as to websites you might want to peruse.

Applying a key phrase in computer lingo, "Garbage in, garbage out," the relevancy of your search results will increase as you choose better keywords or phrases. For example, I tried a search on the words *George Washington* with Excite, and the result was hits on

9,386,073 websites. It might take you the rest of your life to look at all of them, so they are listed in groups of ten according to relevance. The first ten in Excite's list about George Washington included a student's guide to the first president, a guide to the university and the medical center that bear his name, and a virtual tour of Mount Vernon, Washington's home.

To be more precise, you might want to add words to your request. For example, when I typed, "speeches of George Washington," Excite rewarded me with only 2,549,030 suggestions, a considerable reduction from the first group. The top ten websites listed here included the text of Washington's second inaugural address, provided by a website called The Waiter's Digest; a speech by George Douglas Washington on energy, delivered in 1999: and information about New York Governor George Pataki. Clearly, some more specification is needed.

When I refined my request again, to read "Washington inaugural," I got a choice of 1,598,245 sites. Why the reduction? Because the search engine didn't give a listing for every website that included all the words I searched for before; it listed only sites containing "Washington" or "inaugural," so we got a lower number. Still, almost 1.6 million sites is too hard to surf one by one.

What's a searcher to do? One trick is to put your request phrase in quotes. For example, by typing in the words *George Washington inaugural*, I got a list of over 2.5 million sites containing one or more of those three words. By enclosing *"George Washington inaugural"* in quotation marks, you specify that the search engine look for the combination of all three words, used *in that order*. When I did that with Excite, my results shrank to just 100 sites. Then I typed, "George Washington inaugural address" in quotes, and the total dropped to about 60. That number of sites is starting to become manageable.

Some software programs will also allow for multiple search engines, all searching at the same time. A program called Copernic, for example, can run the same search on a number of engines simultaneously, then remove the redundancies and give you a list from which to choose. It's downloadable from the site www.copernic .com and free, unless you opt to get the more advanced versions. Unfortunately, the company discontinued its version for the Macintosh, but Windows users can still find Copernic and its helpful functions.

A search engine can take you only part of the way, however. Eventually, you'll have to visit a number of the sites you're considering for your publicity campaign. Try to align yourself with sites that best define your business, then contact the owners of the site (usually through the online "contact us" link) and ask if they're interested in swapping links to your site.

It's also helpful to have your website listed on search engines in order to increase traffic to your site. It's easy enough to submit your site to Yahoo!, Alta Vista, Excite, iWon.com, and so on. However, each one charges about $199—a one-time charge—for a business site submission, and there are many search engines available. Some of them are very specifically concentrated on one topic—for example, search engines that specialize in certain trades, like public relations consultants. If you aren't familiar with the search engines that focus on your area of business or target market, it can be very difficult to maximize your search engine presence one engine at a time.

The solution to this problem is to spend less money, more often. Submission services will make sure your site is listed on every directory pertinent to your business and your goals. Something like Submit It! (www.submit-it.com), for example, will handle submission onto large search engines like Yahoo! and Alta Vista, as well as smaller, more obscure ones, which might be more useful because they are used by people in your business. The cost is only $59 per year, and that's money well spent. There are other, similar services, which cost less or more, depending on the kind of service you require.

GET LINKED UP

Of course, the easiest, cheapest way to get interested Web surfers to your site is with links. If someone is already viewing a related website and sees a possible link to yours, all it takes is one click to bring a new set of eyeballs to your home page, and possibly a new customer to your business.

That seems easy enough, but how do you go about getting a link on another website? It's a simple matter of agreement between two cyber-colleagues, you and the owner of the other site. If you see a site you think is compatible with yours and doesn't compete with yours directly, you might E-mail the owner(s), via the "contact us" button, usually found on the side of the screen in the menu of functions.

Don't simply write, "Hi, I saw your site and thought I could attract some customers if there was a link, so how about it?" Try something similar to the sample message I've provided, which establishes a certain relationship between you and the other site's owner, then offers a link from your site to theirs in exchange for the reverse on their site.

SAMPLE LINK PROPOSAL

Dear Ms. Winston:

I must compliment you and your company on your extraordinary website. Because my T-shirt business sells products like your posters, I have explored your site extensively and find your information easy to understand and interesting. Congratulations.

Since my business, T-Shirt World, put up its own website, www.t-shirtworld.com, a few months ago, I've been receiving E-mail from customers, some of whom mention your products. They're always very happy with your posters and ask if we have shirts featuring the same personalities.

Our businesses appear to be linked in our customers' minds, and I believe our websites should be linked, as well. If you would be interested in having some of my customers view your website, I'd like to add a link to your site to the "links" section on t-shirtworld.com. And I hope that you would also add a link to my site from your own.

If you're interested, please contact me via my E-mail address, bob@t-shirtworld.com, or call my business at 410-555-5555. I would like to discuss this matter with you further, and hope to hear from you soon.

Sincerely,
Bob Robertson
Owner
T-Shirt World

But before you start writing your message, examine the website you're writing to. The names of the executives should be included in the site's information about the company or organization. Choose one to whom you'll address your E-mail. Also, read about the company's goals, personality, and history. That will help you personalize your message and persuade the other executive that your company—one he or she might never have heard of before—is compatible.

Of course, it's always possible to buy advertising on some of the most popular sites, including search engines. For example, iWon.com has a sliding scale of ad rates, depending on your preference to advertise to the whole site or to a specific "channel" on the site, specifications to be linked to certain keywords, and your ad design (for example, animation costs more). It's not cheap: there's a $15,000 minimum buy for filters that target certain demographics, geographic regions, interests, and other specifications, assuming your ad runs on the site as a whole. If you want to have your ad run only in specified areas, there is a $100,000 per quarter minimum.

Not exactly guerrilla pricing, is it?

Also, remember the ancillary markets? The people who might not appear to be interested in your service or product, but who might end up patronizing your business anyway? Well, they are the reason you don't want to narrow your focus too much. Keep in mind that your links and advertising should be done on *related* sites, not sites that compete with you or operate in exactly the same area of the industry that you do. Keep in mind what that voice kept whispering to Kevin Costner: "If you build it, they will come." In this case, "build it" means to build a message about your business. If you build it well enough, and publicize it loudly enough, ancillary customers will find you.

TELL YOUR STORY WITH E-MAIL

The real example of guerrilla pricing is E-mail. Here, for absolutely no cost, you can communicate with as many people as you'd like in virtually no time flat.

I host a radio show every Sunday night in Los Angeles, and not too long ago, we began broadcasting for two hours every week. To inform my friends, colleagues, and other interested parties, I wrote an E-mail message and sent it to my entire address book, a collection of about 500 names.

In other words, I communicated a fact about my career to 500 people who live all over the world, in one second, *at no cost*. In human history, that has never been possible before. And it was so easy, it was almost embarrassing.

If you want to duplicate, or better yet, increase on, my success, the process is simple. First, you compile a mailing list. Then you decide upon a message. Once that message is complete, you draft an E-mail, and after you have it in its best possible shape, you send your E-mail to the list. If it were any easier, it wouldn't require breathing.

Compile Your List

Perhaps the toughest part of this procedure is compiling a mailing list. This should comprise E-mail addresses, and you can start with the postal mailing list you already have for your business. Surely, along with snail-mail addresses, phone numbers, fax numbers, cell phone numbers, and home phone numbers, you've managed to collect a few E-mail addresses, too.

Start with that list. Add any people who have signed the "address book" section at your website, as well as any E-mail addresses that have come in through links to other websites. You should have a good, working E-mail address book by now.

Decide on a Message

When you know who you will communicate with, you are ready to decide on a message. This should also be relatively easy, since you know what information you want to impart. If yours is a new business, you want to announce its formation. If your business has posted a website, that is your news for today. Sales, specials, new product lines, or additions of executives can also be among the messages you're sending. You can also highlight a special promotion, particularly one that might attract media attention (free T-shirts on your birthday, T-shirts made for each city council member, etc.), and these can be the subject of a special E-mail message.

Draft and Review Your E-Mail Contents

With your main idea in mind, draft your E-mail message. Writing a message or press release to send by E-mail is exactly like writing one that's going out on paper. The only difference is the medium upon which it's being sent. In other words, there is no difference.

Five Extremely Quick Rules for E-Mail
1. Have a real story to tell.
2. Remember, it's about them, not you. Emphasize why they should be interested. What's their benefit? What's in it for them? Everyone's favorite radio station is WIFM: What's in It For Me?

3. Be complimentary without being transparently solicitous; don't gush.
4. Tell your story before you talk about yourself.
5. Don't be so formal it hurts, but don't be so casual it's cutesy.

Read your E-mail to yourself, out loud, before you send it. Revise anything that sounds phony, awkward, or just plain wrong. Read it over a couple more times, and then get ready for the fun part:

Send It Out

Finally, you simply send your E-mail. Just click on that button on your E-mail program that says, "Send now." There! You're done.

Your E-mail went out, in the time it takes to say, ". . . ," to as many people as you could gather in one address book. The message you so carefully crafted has now reached each and every one of those people. And it cost you, if you prorate the amount you spend on Internet access for a month, approximately 1/100 of a cent. And that's if you have high-speed Internet access. This technology thing isn't all that bad after all, is it?

Don't Go Overboard

The whole process is so easy, you may be tempted to flood your mailing list with "friendly reminders." But remember that there is a fine line between upkeep and harassment where E-mail is concerned. You don't want to send so many messages so often that the people you're trying to impress—your potential client base—become annoyed with you. Spamming, sending unwanted E-mail, is obviously wrong. But even with people who genuinely want to hear about your company, burying them under a deluge of letters, coupons, and press releases, so they delete your messages before reading them, is wrongheaded, too. This overzealousness can doom your online publicity campaign before it gets a foothold.

That means you must be thoughtful. Send news only when you *have* news to send.

ONE LAST POINT

Most of the information you need is already in your possession. You know your business better than I do, especially since, in all likelihood, we've never met. So use your common sense, and your business sense. Think about what has worked for you in the past, and apply it to the Information Age.

For example, your E-mail address list will more than likely be based, if not entirely, to a great extent on your existing phone book and mailing lists. Those clients, associates, and media members for whom you have E-mail addresses will be included on your list, and as you meet new people, you should ask for and receive E-mail addresses. It's a common courtesy in this technological time.

Also, since you have Internet access, you've probably already located some of the most popular websites pertinent to your business. Watch them closely, on a weekly basis at least, and observe what makes them work and what, in your opinion, they could do better. Apply those observations to your website if you have one.

Join newsgroups and Usenets as you would based on your own interests, and subscribe to E-zines and other online publications, but do so with a mind toward using such publications for your campaign. In other words, keep on doin' what you're doin', but make sure your Internet ambitions are always in your mind while you're doin' it.

What Have We Learned This Time?

- There are more than 116 million websites. That's a lot.
- Letting the size of the Internet intimidate you is unproductive. You have to narrow your focus and use the areas of the Net that can work for you.
- Start by identifying the people most likely to be interested in your message.
- Observe your clientele and make calculated guesses based on their purchasing and behavior. Create a model demographic for your primary customer.
- Start by asking yourself questions about your clientele, then make a chart narrowing the profile of your customer a little bit at a time. The bull's-eye is your core audience, and the outer rings are ancillary customers who might be interested if your message is presented well.
- Your own website is a good place to gather information. Ask visitors where they heard about you, and about themselves and their buying habits.
- Make links with other websites that might have interests similar to yours. Do this with well-considered E-mail to key personnel in the companies that run the related sites.

- It's possible to advertise on websites and search engines, but not at guerrilla prices. Focus on publicity, not advertising.
- Search engines can help you find related information, and it's worth having your site listed on them for potential customers who might not know about you.
- Submission services can get you listed on search engines for a reasonable fee.
- E-mail is the most cost-effective, speedy, efficient way of communicating with large groups of people ever invented. Make sure you use it, but don't abuse it. Send out bulk E-mail only to people who have some interest in your business, and only when you have something of interest to say.
- Use your common sense. You know your business. Now use the Internet to grow your business.

5

READY, AIM, . . .

"'Cheshire Puss,' she began, rather timidly, as she did not at all know whether it would like the name; however, it only grinned a little wider. 'Come, it's pleased so far,' thought Alice, and she went on. 'Would you tell me, please, which way I ought to go from here?'

'That depends a good deal on where you want to get to,' said the Cat.

'I don't much care where—' said Alice.

'Then it doesn't matter which way you go,' said the Cat."

—LEWIS CARROLL, *ALICE'S ADVENTURE IN WONDERLAND*

That's exactly the point, isn't it? If you don't know where you're going, it really doesn't matter how you go about getting there.

Determining your goals and making them realistic, attainable, and ambitious all at the same time can be a daunting proposition. Before you begin your guerrilla campaign, you have to determine what victory will look like to you, or you won't know whether you've succeeded at any given moment.

Business owners typically want their business to continue to grow and make more money. But that's a little too broad a goal for guerrilla purposes. For your publicity campaign to succeed, you have to know ahead of time exactly what "success" means for your business.

Keep in mind that there's no such thing as "winning" a publicity campaign. You can achieve a victory, or a succession of victories, but each one will merely lead to a new battle. You have to aim at winning each battle, and by accumulating victories, win the war. For the purposes of a guerrilla publicist, a victory can be defined as achieving the level of media coverage you set out to attract. And since, as we've discussed before, there is a snowball effect to media coverage—big follows small—the best course is to start by aiming at smaller media outlets. Then you progressively up the ante until you're dealing with the producers of the network shows, editors of national magazines, and reporters from large-market newspapers.

How small is too small? There's no such thing. If your area has a weekly newspaper, chances are it's *starved* for feature story ideas. If your story is a good one, it'll be noticed by the local daily paper. Or the local radio station. E-mail a few press releases to local media, and see what happens. The key is to start small.

You're not fighting a protracted war here; you're going on a series of guerrilla raids. For each one, you will have a specific goal in mind and will plan it well. You will set out to accomplish the goal, then begin work on the next goal. But the thing to remember is that the first raid will be followed by a second, no matter what the outcome.

A TEST CASE

Let's set up a small business to use as an example, and follow it through a typical series of guerrilla raids. Let's say we run a small photo-developing studio in Milwaukee. We've been open a year, and business is OK, but we haven't really been able to establish ourselves as a distinct presence in the market just yet.

It's time to inaugurate ourselves on the Web, as well. We're about to launch our new website, which was designed by an outside consultant, under our supervision. The site contains information about our company, the services we deliver, our principles, and for consumers, an offer of a free roll of film to those who register with our site. There's also a very well designed press room, where all this information, plus press contacts, is available.

We'd like to publicize the free-film promotion, so we accumulate a list of local Milwaukee press contacts through the websites of Wisconsin television and radio stations and the local papers, including weeklies and free handouts (although not the adults-only editions). Low-tech though it may be, the phone book is another good place to find phone numbers and addresses for local media. Call to get a specific editor or reporter's name.

When you get the E-mail address for a press contact, always save it to your address book in a special file you open for press release mailings. A program like Outlook Express from Microsoft or Netscape Communicator can be downloaded for free and will have the capability you need to create and store such a file.

Once that's done, we draft a press release about the promotion. Especially if you've never seen a press release before, study the example.

SAMPLE PRESS RELEASE

Milwaukee Photo Labs, LLC
1515 Saycheese Street
Milwaukee, WI 41414
Voice: 414-555-5555
Fax: 414-555-5556
www.milpholab.com

For more information:
Michael Levine
Milwaukee Photo Labs, LLC
414-555-5557
414-555-5558 (cell phone)

FOR IMMEDIATE RELEASE

April 26, 2002

MILWAUKEE PHOTO LABS OFFERS
FREE FILM TO CONSUMERS

MILWAUKEE, WI—**Milwaukee Photo Labs, LLC**, a leader in photo processing in the Midwest, has made a special offer to consumers: register at our website, and we'll give you free film.

The offer, for one free roll of 35 mm film, was announced by Milwaukee Photo Labs President I. M. Age as the company unveiled its new website, **www.milpholab.com**. Mr. Age said that any consumer who registers at the site by providing information like name, address, and phone number will receive a free 24-exposure roll of film.

The website has been developed to provide consumers with information about Milwaukee Photo Labs, from store locations to pricing and an explanation of the high-quality process that makes Milwaukee Photo Labs the area's leader in sharp, clear color reproduction. It also includes games and puzzles for children, and contact information for consumers wishing to communicate with the company.

Customers who have sent film to the company for processing can check on their order status, and request their order be delivered, for an additional fee.

"Our website is only the beginning," said Mr. Age. "We intend to expand our presence in the Midwest to make it more convenient for photographers who want to see their photographs reproduced more accurately than they might be used to."

Consumers who register with the website are not charged to be listed and will receive the free roll of film, he added. The company expects to announce future promotions soon, according to Mr. Age.

The free-film promotion will be good until the end of this month, so consumers are urged to register with www.milpholab.com as soon as possible.

Milwaukee Photo Labs, LLC, is a high-quality photo-processing company with four locations in Wisconsin and Illinois. Its patented film-processing equipment creates images that are sharper and clearer than conventional photo processors, for comparable prices.

For further information, contact Michael Levine at 414-555-5557.

This sample press release has a few characteristics that should apply to all releases you write and try to place:

- It includes a contact name and phone number. Reporters have to know who to call and how to reach that person.
- The story—in this case, the free film promotion—comes first. What a great company you are should be last. Get readers interested before you sell to them.
- It's OK to quote an executive in the company, but you don't have to name each one in every release.
- The last paragraph contains a description of the company, some boilerplate that reporters and editors can use to better understand who you are.

Chapter 6 provides more detailed guidance in writing press releases.

AIMING YOUR MESSAGE

Once you've written your press release, you can send it the conventional, snail-mail way, or you can send it to your entire press list in the blink of an eye via E-mail. Actually, it's not a bad idea to do both.

Both? Actually spend money on the postage and the printing and the envelopes and all that, and then E-mail it to your whole list anyway? Well, if your goal is to obtain press coverage, you should make sure you're covered from all angles. For one thing, you may not have an E-mail address for everyone on your list. Even if you do, it can't hurt to send a hard copy.

If time is not pressing, the easiest and least costly plan would be to E-mail the whole list first, then wait a week or two. See if you get any calls from the E-mail press release. If some time goes by and no coverage results from the announcement, definitely send the release via regular mail. It's possible that editors or reporters didn't get the E-mail, or that they weren't the correct people for you to contact.

Even better, tailor your press list to local media first, in order to maximize your series of guerrilla raids. Trying to conquer the entire territory at one time, remember, will require too much personnel, too much material, and too much time for guerrillas. Better to take the smallest hill first, climb to the top, and see what horizons are beyond.

Keep in mind that in every business relationship, there is a buyer and a seller. Here, you are the seller, trying to interest a buyer (a reporter, editor, or producer) in your story and your message. The better a salesperson you are, the more success you'll find, assuming you have a legitimate product—your story—to sell.

The key rules in a buyer/seller relationship for the seller are: (1) Find out what buyers want; and (2) Get it to them. Understanding your quarry, here the "gatekeeper" editor or producer, is essential.

That means you have to read the magazines, watch the TV shows, listen to the radio. There is nothing an editor likes less than being pitched a story that ran last week. There is nothing that will get you a rejection quicker than trying to sell a story that is clearly outside the publication's coverage area. Know your quarry. Find out what your buyer wants. Deliver it.

So the first thing you should do is narrow your focus. Decide on the most realistic chance for press coverage, which might be the local weekly newspapers. Address your first press release to the E-mail boxes of editors at the local weeklies and the local cable access stations. After a day or two, make a follow-up call.

A follow-up phone call is a standard part of any P.R. campaign. The idea is to remind the editor that he or she has received a press release from your business, and to "follow up and make sure you received it." This is a way of asking whether the editor is planning any coverage on the news item you suggested, while making it sound like you're simply checking on the reliability of your E-mail system.

All those phone calls might sound like a lot of work. Is it necessary to call, rather than following up with E-mail? Yes, it's absolutely necessary. E-mail is fine to deliver the message, but you can't logically E-mail to ask if the E-mail you sent was received. Get on the phone and make those calls!

How to Call an Editor

I know what it feels like to have to make cold phone calls to editors, reporters, producers, and other media types. It's intimidating. But it doesn't have to be a big deal. After all, the editor (I'll say "editor" in place of the more cumbersome "media person") *wants* to hear a good news story. It makes the editor's job easier. And remember, you're calling on a professional basis; not asking this person out on a date. This is part of the job for both of you, and if you treat it that way, your stress level will drop. If that's not enough to calm you, ask yourself, "What's going to happen if they say no?" Will you lose your job? Your car? Your family? Will people turn their heads away when they see you in the street? No! If this editor says no, you simply call the *next* editor.

Once you've overcome your fears, here's how to call an editor (and remember, the first one is the hardest; after you've done it once, it becomes a piece of cake). Use these guidelines only as guidelines, not as a script.There's nothing worse than a follow-up call delivered in a stiff monotone. When you use these ideas, make the words your own.

First, refer to your master list. Make sure you know how to pronounce the person's name. Make sure you know whether you are calling a man or a woman; names like Chris and Pat can be deceptive. When in doubt, throw yourself on the mercy of the assistant.

Make absolutely sure the number you're calling and the person you ask for match up. Too many people operate off a list that's confusing, and they ask for an editor who works at the wrong newspaper. This, believe me, is a business faux pas. Check twice.

Once you have the name and phone number lined up, simply dial and ask for the editor, by both names (this helps if the first name is gender-ambiguous): "Hi, is Pat Masterson there? This is Michael Levine of Milwaukee Photo Labs."

When connected with the editor (and sometimes they do, in fact, answer their own phones, particularly at the smaller newspapers), introduce yourself and state your purpose. "How are you? (Wait for answer.) This is Michael Levine from Milwaukee Photo Labs. I sent a press release by E-mail a few days ago, and I just wanted to follow up and see if you'd received it."

The rest of the conversation will depend on the response you get, so be prepared for any of these alternatives:

- "Hi, Michael. Yes, I remember your press release. I'm glad you called; I'd like to assign a reporter to the story. Can you give me your number again, please?" This doesn't happen often, but it certainly is not unheard of. Count your lucky stars and give the editor your number; you're home free.
- "No, I don't recall getting your E-mail. What was it about?" This editor either truly didn't get your E-mail or got it and didn't keep it, or doesn't remember. In any event, you have to encapsulate the press release into one sentence: "It's about our promotion to give away free film that ties in with our new website," or, "We're giving away free film to draw attention to our new website." The conversation will either progress or end on that note, depending on the level of the editor's interest.
- "Yes, I received the E-mail, but we don't have any interest in that story." Well, there's nowhere to go from here. You can't change someone's mind at that point, particularly if you want to keep the relationship active for your next guerrilla raid, which might work better. So you say thank you and get off the phone. Dial the next editor's number and start over.
- "You know, I'm not the editor for this story. You need the city/business/Internet/whatever editor. Let me transfer you." This keeps a possibility alive. Start over with the new editor. Wait until that person comes onto the line, identify yourself, explain that you have an E-mail press release you'd like to

send, and ask for the editor's E-mail address. You'll either get
a new E-mail address or be asked to explain your story on the
phone, as before. Comply with either preference, and see how
things progress.

- "Gee, I don't know. I can't find the E-mail right now. Can you
call back in a few days?" This editor truly doesn't remember
or is hoping you'll go away. But remember, a guerrilla is tena-
cious. Politely thank the editor for his or her time, then do,
indeed, call back in a few days. Keep this up until the editor
gives you a straight answer or moves on to another job.

Once you've completed your phone call, if no coverage has been
guaranteed, move on to the next editor. The phone calls get easier
to do with repetition, and you have a voice to go with the name on
your list. From such guerrilla raids is a relationship with the media
born.

BROADENING YOUR AIM

Since you have a narrow focus for your first raid, you sent the press
release only to local weekly newspapers and local cable stations, and
they are the only media outlets to receive follow-up calls. Let's
assume a local weekly paper wants to print an article about our free-
film promotion.

Great! If the staff is large enough, a reporter will call or visit
our business headquarters and interview you for the article. The
paper will not allow you to see the article before it's printed; that's
only allowable with advertising copy or in some "advertorial" sections, like many local real estate sections. Such articles are always
labeled "advertisement" in the paper, and we're getting editorial, or
news copy. In other words, free publicity!

Some weeklies (and monthlies) are so small they can't spare a
staff reporter (or don't *have* a staff reporter), and they will ask you
to write a draft of the article yourself. This is just a rewrite of the
press release, with more detail about the promotion and no contact
information. This does not happen terribly often, except on the
smallest of newspapers.

Keep in mind, too, that not all newspapers appear in print format. *E-zines, online newspapers,* and *E-papers* are all legitimate
media outlets that may attract the notice of potential customers and
other media. For example, *Desktop Journal*, Wisconsin's computer
newspaper, might be an online source in which to place our story.

Once the article is printed, we buy copies of the paper (and ask the editor if he or she can spare some "extras") to take out the article about our business. We can now copy this article and use it as a press release, a news clipping (or, in the business vernacular, a *tearsheet*) that you can show to potential customers (who hopefully buy the newspaper and have seen it) to demonstrate the merit of your message and to other editors as an example of something they might want to consider. Remember the key rule: big follows small.

Of course, we don't expect the staff producers at *Good Morning, America* to subscribe to every local weekly newspaper in the country (although they should). Instead of trying to make the jump from the *Isthmus*, the weekly newspaper for Madison, Wisconsin, straight to network TV, maybe we should move up to a daily paper. The Milwaukee *Sentinel-Journal* and other dailies are the target of our next guerrilla raid.

The procedure is the same. First, target E-mail addresses. Then send out a press release (you might want to revamp the old one to include a new promotion, if it's taken longer than a month to reach this point—perhaps a sweepstakes to give away a camera or a month's worth of free developing). Last, follow up by phone.

This time, though, you'll want to include a copy of the weekly article with the press release. If you have a scanner, you might want to include it with the press release in your E-mail copies, and just make paper copies for the times when you're sending snail mail. If you don't have a scanner, just refer to the previous article in your press release ("Milwaukee Photo Labs was the subject of a recent feature article in the *Isthmus*, Madison's weekly newspaper").

Another huge media outlet is rarely thought of but can be an enormous help to the guerrilla publicist. Trade publications exist for virtually every market, every industry, every business in the world. Often more than one covers each business. They are not terribly well funded, for the most part, and do not have large editorial staffs. But the good ones (and there's at least one good one in each business) are well respected in the industry, read from cover to cover, and always looking for interesting stories to tell.

Trade publications ("trade books," as they're known) are not sold to the general public on newsstands or through the mail. Before you can subscribe, you have to prove you are a participant in the industry being discussed. So the coverage a publicist gets isn't as wide-reaching as that of a traditional (consumer) magazine or newspaper. But trade books are often an excellent place to start.

After all, establishing yourself as a leader in your industry, among people who work in your business, will enhance your reputation. The consumer press is more likely to see you as an "expert" on your business when it's time for interviews on related articles. And, since the big-follows-small rule applies here as well as anywhere, consumer publications and radio and television stations read trade books and often get story ideas from them. Don't discount trade publications; use them effectively.

Assuming that this guerrilla raid is also a success, it will be time to move up to local radio and television coverage, and so on. The chain of raids should be constantly moving to larger potential audiences, which can take in more area in terms of geography. Just for illustration, your battle plan should look something like the "growth" chart on the next page.

Notice that with each successful guerrilla raid, the target audience gets bigger. The goal, after all, is to grow our business by attracting attention from as many people as possible. That means each story we tell will have to be interesting to just a few more people, with just a little broader focus, than before. Start out very narrow, then open up to the point that anyone, anywhere could find your story interesting.

It may be a good strategy, then, to emphasize the local angles in our story as we start out. Make sure the editors (and therefore the public) understand that this is a local business, with the values and concerns of local residents in mind every step of the way. Maybe the first promotion should be a free roll of film to anyone who registers on the website with a Wisconsin address.

Once coverage starts happening for us, though, we need to broaden our focus to fit the media we're targeting. If we go from a local weekly to a statewide newspaper, we should emphasize the state, rather than the city or town, in which we operate. If we're trying to become a regional business, and therefore target regional media, we should discuss Midwestern concerns. And once we decide we can go national, our theme should remain the same, but our story—the part we're emphasizing to get people to notice us—should be something that anyone in the country can relate to.

It's important, after all, to distinguish between our *story* and our *message*. Our message is going to stay the same throughout the campaign: This is the best photo processing you can get anywhere, and you need to come to us in order to get it. But our story will continue to change. The free-film promotion is a story; its goal is to be told in a local context. When we want to move up to the next level in the media, there has to be another story. But the message, the

PUBLIC RELATIONS DEVELOPMENT

Weekly newspaper

Local access cable TV; national trade publication

Local daily newspaper, feature section

Local radio broadcast

Local TV broadcast

National cable TV (CNN, Nickelodeon)

National radio

National TV news segment

Network or syndicated national TV talk show (Today, Good Morning, America, Oprah Winfrey, Rosie O'Donnell) point we're trying to make overall to our listeners, readers, viewers, and Net users, will remain constant. We're telling people that we believe in our service enough to offer free items, sweepstakes, prizes, and other incentives to try it—once. The circumstances of each promotion, each incentive, will change, but the point that we have the best process and will use it for you remains the same.

The most important thing is to set clear goals. Before you go into battle, you have to know what victory looks like to *you*. In our example, the first victory is getting a small article in a local weekly newspaper. That's victory. You may not feel like breaking out the champagne, but you have done what you set out to do. Then it's time to go out and set a *new* attainable goal, a realistic one. That's the local cable access station. And then the daily paper. And so on.

Each step is a victory, but it's been carefully planned. You have to picture the victory before you can have it, and recognize it when it's been achieved.

What Have You Learned?

Here's a pop quiz. Answer each question without looking back over the chapter. Give yourself 5 points for each correct answer (answers follow the questions). Then, look back over the chapter again to learn the parts you missed.

1. Victory is: (a) conquering your enemy; (b) achieving your present goal; (c) making more money; (d) all of the above.
2. The first basic rule of media coverage is: (a) big follows small; (b) sit on Dan's left side; (c) never E-mail; (d) call only editors you know.
3. Winning a publicity campaign is: (a) possible only when you understand your product; (b) a matter of contacts; (c) impossible, since achieving one goal only sets up the next; (d) all of the above.
4. Because big follows small, you should always: (a) aim for the biggest, then work down; (b) buy clothes that are too big for you; (c) start with a small goal, and work up; (d) always sweat the details.
5. How small is too small? (a) smaller than a breadbox; (b) anything that reaches fewer than 10,000 people; (c) there's no such thing as "too small"; (d) none of the above.

6. Local news outlets can be identified: (a) in the yellow pages; (b) from their websites; (c) through addresses and phone numbers in the publications; (d) all of the above.

7. All the information in a press release: (a) should be included in your website's virtual press room; (b) should discuss only the story you're trying to place; (c) is made up; (d) none of the above.

8. Always included in a press release is: (a) your previous year's earnings; (b) the name of every executive in the company; (c) a contact name and phone number; (d) all of the above.

9. Press releases should be sent: (a) the day they are written; (b) via E-mail; (c) via snail mail; (d) both (b) and (c).

10. The first guerrilla raid should have as its goal: (a) to get news coverage from a local source; (b) to get on the *Tonight Show*; (c) to get on radio; (d) to announce a company's formation.

11. In every business relationship, there is: (a) an exchange of money; (b) a buyer and a seller; (c) publicity; (d) big follows small.

12. To follow up on the press release, always: (a) send another press release; (b) write a letter to the editor; (c) make phone calls; (d) all of the above.

13. It's always important to: (a) be familiar with the media you're trying to attract; (b) start small; (c) keep victory in view; (d) all of the above.

14. The following is *not* a rule of the buyer/seller relationship: (a) find out what the buyer wants; (b) lower your price; (c) both (b) and (d); (d) get it to them.

15. Follow-up phone calls should be: (a) short; (b) to the point; (c) relaxed; (d) all of the above.

16. If an editor says he or she can't use your story, try to: (a) convince the editor of the story's merits; (b) pitch another story; (c) maintain the relationship for the next assault; (d) none of the above.

17. Use a small article in a local weekly to: (a) wallpaper your den; (b) attract *Oprah Winfrey*; (c) impress your friends; (d) attract the attention of a local daily.

18. Trade publications are: (a) magazines dedicated to a specific industry; (b) stepping stones to consumer media; (c) avenues to be recognized as an "expert"; (d) all of the above.

19. When starting with a local paper: (a) act the same as with a national TV network; (b) visit the office yourself; (c) emphasize the local aspect of the story; (d) all of the above.

20. Goals should, more than anything else, be: (a) ambitious; (b) attainable; (c) painted yellow; (d) none of the above.

Answers: 1-b; 2-a; 3-c; 4-c; 5-c; 6-d; 7-a; 8-c; 9-d; 10-a; 11-b; 12-c; 13-d; 14-b; 15-d; 16-c; 17-d; 18-d; 19-c; 20-b.

6

. . . FIRE!

"Never mistake motion for action."

—ERNEST HEMINGWAY

"You have all eternity to be cautious in when you're dead."

—LOIS PLATFORD

Academic theory is a fine thing, but after a while, there's nothing left to discuss. It's time to take the bull by the horns. Get into the game. Jump in with both feet and see what your guerrilla skills will do for you. "Ready . . . aim . . . " is OK, but now it's time to *fire!*

You'll know when it's time to begin. You will have absorbed the information I've given you up to this point, understood the concept of the Guerrilla P.R. practitioner, and identified your goals. You'll know exactly what you're setting out to accomplish, and what your first steps should be to accomplish it.

So, what's holding you back?

Fear, pure and simple. And don't worry about that; it's natural. The first time you do anything, it feels unfamiliar and uncomfortable. But if your goals are really important to you, and if you truly believe you can achieve them by publicizing your business in the guerrilla mode, then take a deep breath, suck in your gut, and get ready to start your first guerrilla raid.

THE RAID

First, let's assume you've constructed and launched your website (a process we'll cover completely in Chapter 7). There's no point in drawing attention to the site if you still have an Under Construction sign where a website should be. That will just annoy the very people you're trying to attract—customers and media gatekeepers. So make sure the website (if you're planning on having one) is in place, with a "contact us" link and a virtual press room, *before* you begin your guerrilla campaign.

With that out of the way, you're ready to start in earnest the process of Guerrilla P.R. online. Here's how it works:

1. An attention-getting device creates a news story about your company.
2. You package that news story for the media outlet you're targeting.
3. You alert the media outlet to your news story.
4. You establish a relationship with the media gatekeeper.
5. You continue to provide fresh information via your website and other online vehicles, and move on to the next guerrilla raid.

Attention-Getting Device

Did you know you can order a Pizza Hut pizza online? You probably did know that, because when the service was initiated, Pizza Hut went out of its way to make sure the story was covered. In this case, the information was carried on traditional media sources, like television, radio, and newspapers, as well as appearing on the company's website. The coverage was extensive, and while it wasn't entirely free (television and radio advertising contributed to the attention-getting blitz), it was certainly effective.

Your first move, then, must be to create a news story that will command and hold the public's attention. To construct such a story, let's consider what qualities made the Pizza Hut story work:

- The announcement that Pizza Hut takes online orders draws attention to the fact that, in case someone didn't know, Pizza Hut is in the pizza business.

- It gives the media a reason to say, "Pizza Hut" repeatedly without advertising dollars being spent.
- It conveys the message that there is a new way to order Pizza Hut's product.
- It projects the image of Pizza Hut as a forward-thinking, progressive company moving ahead with technology.
- It gives the public something fun to do that makes them feel good about Pizza Hut.
- Not coincidentally, it can directly increase Pizza Hut sales.

Lessons from Pizza Hut This news story, although certainly not as serious as a presidential veto or a fluctuation in the stock market, got covered by a wide-ranging spread of media, in newspapers, radio, and television, in addition to online news services and other websites. The Pizza Hut model provides many lessons that you can apply to your business:

- Try to be first at something in your business. Pizza Hut was the first large pizza chain to offer online ordering. It's much less likely that the fourth got media coverage.
- Tie your story to the Internet, preferably to your website. Get people interested enough to visit your website, where there is lots more information about your company and your product or service that they may find interesting.
- Make sure the story has something to do with your product or service. Notice that Pizza Hut didn't just give away a new car; it made sure the news item mentioned pizza. Don't hold a raffle for a ham unless you're in the pork business.
- The news story—and I've said this before—has to have *news* in it. Media members aren't easily fooled, and they've heard it all before. If you're merely kicking off the launch of your website, you're going to get a big yawn. Pizza Hut managed to be first at something in its business and told you about it. They didn't mention having sold some pizzas that day, because that isn't news.
- Tie your news item to an idea that benefits the customer. Remember, it ain't all about you. If the customer doesn't see something in the story that he or she can use, your response will be an enormous shrug. Keep a voice in the back of your head that speaks for the customer, and all it says is, "What's in it for me?"

Creating a news story isn't the same thing as creating a website; you can't assume that people who read the press release you've written are doing so because they're already interested in your business. You are approaching the media gatekeeper, whereas people who come to your website are approaching you. An interest has already been established, or they wouldn't be bothering to seek you out.

The Ingredients of an Idea When you create a press release (see Chapter 5 for step-by-step instructions), remember that you're concentrating on the news story, not the overall story of you or your business. So the news story you create has to be compelling, intriguing, attention-demanding, and *real*. Where do news story ideas like that begin?

Promotions, like the free film I used as an example in Chapter 5, are one way to create a news story. But the promotion has to be very specific to be of interest to a news organization. Keep in mind that reporters, editors, and producers also are asking, "What's in it for me?" So if you're targeting a weekly newspaper that covers just your town, tailor your promotion to your town. If your business is a retail store that is new to the town, create a promotion that requires the customer to show proof he or she is a resident. Create a benefit to customers who happen to be residents or, to be more specific, likely readers of that newspaper.

Innovations are even better news stories than promotions, because they don't feel "manufactured" by the business owner and will be more palatable to gatekeepers. The announcement of Pizza Hut online ordering is an example of an innovation that worked beautifully. In beating its competition to a practice that would certainly become inevitable in the industry, Pizza Hut managed to create the image of a cutting-edge company by adding a benefit its customers could enjoy.

Charitable acts your business may perform make good press releases. It may sound a little crass to consider making publicity hay out of an act you perform with only the best intentions, but think about this: not only does a large donation or charitable event create good press, it also raises the profile of the charity in question and may actually help increase donations from outside sources. Donate from the heart, but don't hide your light under a bushel, either.

Events are terrific publicity attractions. Hold a contest or a performance in your town, and let the local media know. True, your business name might not be in the opening paragraph of the news story, but it will appear somewhere. Sponsor events for very little money by creating a contest or exhibition that ties in with your business, and hold it outdoors, near your business, on a weekend or whenever street traffic is expected to be highest. And let the press know you're hosting.

Packaging for Your News Story

The type of promotion or event you decide to publicize should be made with a keen eye on the specific media outlet you're targeting. Remember the concept of big follows small, and begin with a smaller, more accessible target.

As I said earlier, local media are attracted to publicity aimed at local residents—in short, their audience or readership. That's because the media gatekeepers are beholden to local advertisers. In other words, when a reporter or editor asks, "What's in it for me?" about your news story, the answer has to be, "Serving your readership, which in turn patronizes your advertisers." Editors and producers are always looking for ways to engage their readership, so if you're pitching a local newspaper or radio station, the key is to tell the gatekeeper exactly how your story will interest the paper's readership or the station's audience.

This concept is absolutely essential to P.R. generally, and Guerrilla P.R. specifically. So let's condense it to as few words as possible, recite it over and over, and commit it to memory: gatekeepers answer to audiences. Think about that. The person you're ultimately trying to engage is the one who buys the newspaper, turns on the radio, watches the television show. This actually makes the process easier, because that person is, or should be, your target consumer, as well.

You choose to target a media outlet for one reason, and one reason only: because the people who might patronize your business are audience members of that outlet. They read the newspaper, they listen or watch. That's it. So if your aim is always to interest your customer, and your customer is the person the editor or producer is trying to please, then your only course is to keep your customer in mind when conceiving a news story and pitching it to the media.

How do you do this? Consider: you are not a shill, and you're not a prostitute. You're not trying to get a reporter to do anything the reporter wouldn't normally do. And you're not going to change or compromise your business principles for the sake of a little press coverage.

Rather, you are an *aid* to the reporter. Learning to think like a newsperson will be extremely valuable. The reporter's job is to find and report news, usually in a particular area of interest or geography called a *beat*. A beat can be a physical area, like the city of Los Angeles, or it can be an area of interest, like technology or entertainment.

One of the hardest parts of the reporter's job is finding news. This entails talking to experts on the subject ("sources"), scanning documents or websites, reading trade journals and other publications, and in some cases, just brainstorming about the topic until a question arises that would make a good news story.

The ABCs of Journalism: Five *W*s and an *H* News stories begin with a question. And in journalism, the questions most frequently asked are known as the five *W*s and an *H*:

$W1$ = Who?
$W2$ = What?
$W3$ = Where?
$W4$ = When?
$W5$ = Why?
H = How?

A reporter tries to answer as many of these questions as possible in each news story. Who did something? What did they do? Where did they do it? When did the incident take place? Why did it happen? How was it done?

You can help the reporter by answering as many of these questions about your news story as possible, preferably in your press release. Remember that the press release stresses the novelty, the drama, the excitement of your story and is not about you. In the sample, the news release helps reporters by answering the five *W*s and an *H*.

Press Releases That Answer Reporters' Questions Consider the following sample press releases that answer reporters' questions and keep the focus on the five *W*s and an *H*.

Michael Levine [who], author of *Guerrilla P.R. Wired: Waging a Successful Publicity Campaign Online, Offline, and Everywhere in Between,* is offering an online seminar on Internet publicity campaigns [what] at his website, www.gprwired.com, [where] this Thursday at 8 P.M. [when].

Levine, a renowned Los Angeles publicist and author, will host the seminar because, he says, "Not everyone can afford the services of a publicity firm like mine, so I think we should help small businesses learn the down-and-dirty tactics of Guerrilla P.R. for the Internet Age." [why] He will conduct the seminar from his offices and will end the session with a 15-minute question-and-answer chat, so small-business owners can ask their own questions [how].

Then, after more details about the event, will come a description of the person whose business is being publicized, as follows.

Michael Levine is founder and president of Levine Communications Office, one of the country's most prominent entertainment public relations firms. He is also author of 12 books, including the most widely used introduction to P.R. in the world, *Guerrilla P.R.,* which has been studied and used by Wharton Business School, Harvard and Stanford universities, Nordstrom, the U.S. Navy, Ben & Jerry's Ice Cream, Emerson College, USC, Eastman Kodak, Chase Manhattan Bank, Microsoft, Apple Computer, Yahoo!, General Motors, American Airlines, *Success* magazine, and the White House under Presidents George H. W. Bush and Bill Clinton.

In this sample, all the information about the business credentials comes after all the details about the news story, providing background for reporters who are interested in the news item but might not be familiar with the business being discussed. In other words, you hook 'em with the story, then give 'em the message after they're interested.

Because, in this fictional case, the event being planned is not local but does contain elements of: technology, the Internet, P.R., small businesses, publishing, and publicity, the P.R. focus should be not on a local newspaper or cable access talk show, but on publications and radio and TV stations that cover those topics. For example, this press release, if it were real, would be sent to trade publications for public relations, like *PR Week,* to publications for computer and Internet enthusiasts (also known as "buff books") like *Wired* and *Inc. Technology*, to mainstream newspapers like the *New York Times* and the *Chicago Tribune*, and to cable news stations like CNBC, Fox News, CNN, and some of the larger-cities' radio and TV stations, particularly in Los Angeles, which is the home base of the business in question.

That doesn't mean we'd leave out local outlets, since they are still the stepping stones to media that are more widely read and seen. But we shouldn't target the story toward a local angle; the news item is not about the Los Angeles area, nor do people have to be from the area to participate. By definition, an Internet event can be viewed and appreciated by people anywhere in the world with computer access. So, there's no need to rewrite the sample press release to cater to local media.

Tailoring the Press Release Still, one release can't cater to technology publications, trade magazines about publicity, Los Angeles business radio shows, a cable TV program on innovative websites, and a CNN reporter with the book-publishing beat. We will have to prepare more than one draft of the release, with minor changes to emphasize the area of interest for each media gatekeeper. You can send the same letter to editors at competing publications that deal with the same topic; that is, the release can go to both *Inc.* and *Entrepreneur* magazines, but a letter with a technology bent that might be right for, say, *Wired* probably won't have the same slant as one aimed at the *Boston Globe*'s business section.

Remember, our mission is to give the reporters what they want, and that is a news story that will appeal to their readership. After all, gatekeepers answer to audiences, and each audience is going to want a different angle on the story.

Let's examine the first paragraph of the press release we simulated above, and determine how it would be changed to appeal to each separate market segment. The original copy read:

> Michael Levine, author of *Guerrilla P.R. Wired: Waging a Successful Publicity Campaign Online, Offline, and Everywhere in Between*, is offering an online seminar on Internet publicity campaigns at his website, www.gprwired .com, this Thursday at 8 P.M.

That straightforward approach can work for local newspapers, radio shows, and TV programs that deal with general-interest or business topics. But for publications or other media outlets that specialize in technology or the Internet, it might be altered this way:

> There's no better publicity tool than the Internet, but not every small-business owner knows how to utilize it to its ultimate extent. That's why Michael Levine, author of *Guerrilla P.R. Wired: Waging a Successful Publicity Campaign Online, Offline, and Everywhere in Between*, is offering an online seminar on Internet publicity campaigns at his website, www.gprwired.com, this Thursday at 8 P.M.

As you can see, it doesn't take much to cater to the gatekeeper of your choice. Let's say, then, that we want to make the story more attractive to the small-business press, magazines for start-ups and entrepreneurs like, well, *Entrepreneur*. How would the opening paragraph have to change in that case? Here's one approach:

> Let's say your business is a year old, but the growth rate isn't quite what you were projecting in your business plan. The answer, of course, is to attract publicity. But you can't afford a public relations firm. Luckily, there's an ultra-low-cost publicity tool available to virtually every small-business owner—the Internet.
>
> Your readers can make effective use of online technology to publicize their businesses, but they may not know the intricacies of the Internet P.R. game. So, Michael Levine, author of *Guerrilla P.R. Wired: Waging a Successful Publicity Campaign Online, Offline, and Everywhere in Between*, is offering an online seminar on Internet publicity campaigns at his website, www.gprwired.com, every Thursday at 8 P.M.

Notice that a few changes have been made. First of all, the opening paragraph is now two paragraphs. That doesn't matter; it just keeps things readable for the editor being wooed. A more significant change is that the online publicity seminar has grown from a one-time session set for "this Thursday" to a weekly meeting that takes place "every Thursday."

Why? Because a monthly magazine like *Entrepreneur* won't be interested in something that takes place this coming Thursday. Its editors are probably working on an issue that's at least three months ahead of today's date as you read this. So if an event isn't an ongoing enterprise that can help their readers *at the time of publication*, there's no point in even attempting to gain their attention about it.

If, instead, we're trying to get coverage from a reporter whose beat is the publishing business, we have to emphasize that the event being discussed is tied to a book. After all, the book is the element of our story that we hope will command the reporter's attention. Here's a way to revise the original press release:

> A new book from Contemporary explains the best techniques for small-business owners to attract publicity on the Internet, and the author is putting his commitment where his mouse is.
>
> Michael Levine, author of *Guerrilla P.R. Wired: Waging a Successful Publicity Campaign Online, Offline, and Everywhere in Between*, is offering an online seminar on Internet publicity campaigns at his website, www.gprwired.com, this Thursday at 8 P.M.

It's admittedly a little cute, but it gets the point across, and it emphasizes the book, which is the angle this editor wants and the other ones don't. This technique can be altered to fit any market you might happen to be aiming at, as long as you remember to emphasize what the editor or producer needs over what you want each of them to cover. Fill their needs, and they'll cover exactly what you want them to cover.

Time Out: Levine's Favorite Clichés of the Cyber-World

- Home is where you hang your @.
- The E-mail of the species is more deadly than the mail.
- A journey of a thousand sites begins with a single click.
- You can't teach a new mouse old clicks.
- Speak softly and carry a cellular phone.
- The modem is the message.
- Too many clicks spoil the browse.
- The geek shall inherit the earth.
- There's no place like http://www.home.com.
- Modulation in all things.
- Give a man a fish and you feed him for a day; teach him to use the Net and he won't bother you for weeks.

- You can lead a horse to www.water.com, but you can't make him download it.
- Spam is the root of all evil.
- To baud or not to baud; that is the question.

Alert the Media

Remember that the press release alone isn't going to guarantee you coverage in the media, unless you're promoting an event so earth-shatteringly exciting that you could whisper the information out your front window at three in the morning and be on *The Today Show* by seven. Your guerrilla raid is going to have to take place on more than one front at a time.

First, declare yourself your own press agent. Remember "press agents"? Those guys in the wide-brimmed hats in the 1940s movies who ran around smoking big cigars, talking on three phones at once, and using words like *kiddo* and *sweetie?* Well, public relations isn't like that anymore (and it probably never was), but for the sake of your guerrilla campaign, you're going to have to pretend that it is.

You have to get on the phone and start talking to reporters and producers, especially the ones at radio and television stations. Not every assignment is made via E-mail or snail mail, and it's too easy, particularly in the broadcast media, for print press releases to get lost. One-on-one contact is going to be necessary, and the phone is the best way to make it work.

But do your homework first. Find out which reporters are assigned to the beat you're pitching a story in. If it's technology or online activity, call the station (or check the website) to find out the name of the reporter and/or producer involved in that area. If it's the business desk, do the same thing.

Telephone pitching of broadcast media is no different in its preparation than print or E-mail pitching of print media. You still have to get the reporter's name right, and you still have to have a legitimate news story to offer. And you still have to be familiar with the program you're pitching. Make it a priority to watch or listen to that show more than once so you can be sure you know which segment might apply, and which on-air talent should be involved.

When you call, be sure to ask for the proper reporter or gatekeeper, then identify yourself immediately. Don't try to pretend you're a publicist; admit you're the business owner in question. And then say that you've got a strong news story you think they'll be interested in covering.

Get right to the point. Remember that you're trying to help the reporter do his or her job. And remember that the reporter has more than one thing to do today.

The Average TV Reporter's Daily Workload The average TV reporter's daily workload is a laundry list of things to do. Keep these tasks in mind as you stalk your prey.

- Arrive around 9 A.M. (for a 6 P.M. newscast), answer phone messages, E-mail, and snail mail, at a rate of about twenty phone messages, thirty E-mail messages, and fifty letters.
- Attend "budget" meetings, which determine what stories will be ready for broadcast that night.
- Finish editing yesterday's assignment, and write voice-over narration to be recorded later.
- Get sound and camera crew, and go to location to interview people for upcoming feature.
- Receive assignment on breaking news story, rush to scene, conduct interviews.
- Head back to office for writing, editing.
- Attend second budget meeting.
- Finish returning phone calls from the three hours you've been out.
- Call sources on breaking story; get quotes.
- See rough cut of breaking story footage; record narration.
- Prepare for broadcast.
- Deliver breaking story on-camera during 6 P.M. broadcast.
- Update breaking story after dinner for 11 P.M. broadcast.
- Put finishing touches on yesterday's feature assignment.
- Return phone calls from your dinner break.
- Prepare for 11 P.M. broadcast.
- Deliver breaking story and yesterday's feature on 11 P.M. broadcast.
- Set up tomorrow's assignments before leaving at 1 A.M.

Maybe you can understand how your press release might not be at the top of the reporter's To Do list.

Keep your phone call short and to the point. Make sure you tell your story without "hyping" it; don't make any claims you won't be able to back up if the reporter is interested. If your story is strong enough, it will sell itself. You have to be your own press agent, but you don't have to blow everything out of proportion.

Establish Relationships with Gatekeepers

The telephone is still the most direct and best instrument of communication with journalists. While E-mail is gaining in popularity, access to higher-profile (mostly broadcast) journalists is increasingly hard to manage. You can't always get the E-mail address of the reporter you're trying to reach.

Keep in mind, too, that you can't control the content of what appears if a journalist decides to cover your story. The reporter's job is to observe, ask questions, and present the story as the reporter sees it. Although the goal is usually to be objective (when not editorializing or appearing on a show that takes a particular point of view), there's no denying that each reporter will handle the story in that reporter's style. You can't tell the media what to say, and even if you do, they won't listen to you.

Total control over the coverage of your story is limited to your own website. There, you can oversee (or write) every single word that appears, so the message delivered will be exactly the one you choose to send. But in dealing with the media, no such guarantee is offered.

You can, however, attempt to guide the media. You present your story the way you see it, and in some cases, the reporter will see it your way. Certainly, innocuous events like store openings covered by weekly local papers tend to be presented in a positive fashion, much the way the business owner would cover the story if it were possible. But even when you're dealing with more widespread media, it's possible to guide the reporter to your point of view. The reporter might resist being led, but that's the chance you take.

The wording of your press release and/or your phone call is naturally the first step to presenting your spin on your story. Particularly with the written release, it's possible to present the story from your point of view, as in the case of the "he's putting his commitment where his mouse is" line from the fictional press release in the previous example. That sentence shows that the author is committed to his subject, has a sense of humor, and is using the Internet to make his case. All good points, none of which has to be said in so many words because the press release has been constructed to imply them.

But no one story is as important as the overall message. Therefore, even more important than the way you word a press release are your efforts at cultivating and maintaining relationships with the media (or, more specifically, relationships with various members of the media—never forget they're people). Don't jeopardize your future relationship with a reporter by lying, exaggerating, or in any way misleading the media.

Decide who will be the *spokesperson* for your company. It could be you, but it doesn't have to be. It *does* have to be someone who is comfortable and relaxed talking on the phone, particularly to the press. It has to be someone who has a good working knowledge of your business and knows what is and is not confidential. And it has to be someone who, if he or she can't answer the question on the spot, knows who in the company to ask.

List your spokesperson as the contact on your press releases, and have that person make the phone calls to the press. If it's you, get to know the reporters who will talk to you. If they don't want to cover your story or simply can't right now, keep the phone number and E-mail address, and let the reporter know you'll be contacting him or her again. Remember, the long-term relationship you cultivate may be infinitely more important than the single story you're pitching today.

Keep a good, working press list. Assuming you're the company spokesperson, make sure your address book—including phone numbers, E-mail addresses, and snail-mail addresses—is organized and backed up electronically. Don't let a single computer crash wipe out months of work and jeopardize more months of future publicity opportunities.

Be a Fountain of Fresh Information

Whether a particular story gets you coverage or not, you'd better have another ready in a few weeks. Don't inundate reporters with story after story. One a month is probably enough, depending on the media outlet you're discussing. After a few campaigns, you'll know which reporters are especially receptive, and which ones wouldn't cover you if you went bungee-jumping off the Sears Tower in Chicago.

Make each guerrilla raid part of a continuing guerrilla war. You don't have to ignore journalists just because they haven't covered you before; keep trying. Remember that a guerrilla is persistent. But you might want to give special attention to the places where you've succeeded before.

On a regular basis, continue to generate news releases. Make sure you respect the rules. Most importantly, don't send a release with no news in it. Continue to refer reporters to the website, where you should have posted previous press releases and made them available for reference at all times.

Plan your events carefully, and take your time with them. It's better to have one or two high-quality events per year than monthly events that won't generate any news coverage and will lessen your reputation. A guerrilla raid is a sprint, but a guerrilla war is a marathon. Keep that in mind.

It's possible to establish and maintain relationships with journalists, but keep in mind that they should be professional relationships, not friendships. Reporters are professionals, and they will report the news about your company, good or bad. They won't create news coverage for you, because they are not your spokesperson or your publicist. You'll know some of them for years, but remember what kind of relationship this is: a business one. And in a business relationship, there is always a buyer and always a seller. You will always be the seller of information, and the reporter will always be the buyer.

Maintaining a strong professional relationship with members of the press is a vital part of the Guerrilla P.R. experience. Be polite, be concise, be friendly—but be a professional.

Your next campaign should be ready to roll as soon as this one is complete. You can overlap campaigns, but make sure they're all legitimate and worthwhile news stories. Don't offer a press release every few weeks just because you don't want the journalists to forget your name.

The goal remains the same: press coverage and recognition for your company. But you can work against yourself by providing information that isn't newsworthy. You're not doing yourself a favor if a journalist winces when he or she sees your name on an E-mail message or an envelope, or if you start getting voice mail instead of a live human voice when you call. A broken relationship with a reporter is a difficult thing to repair; try not to damage it to begin with.

A Quick Chapter Review

- There are five steps to a successful guerrilla publicity raid: (1) An attention-getting device creates a news story about your company. (2) You package that news story toward the media outlet you're targeting. (3) You alert the media outlet to your news story. (4) You establish a relationship with the media gatekeeper. (5) You continue to provide fresh information via your website and other online vehicles, and move on to the next guerrilla raid.
- A successful campaign will include a real news story, create a reputation for your company as a leader, create media coverage for your story, and direct consumers to look for more information about your company.
- Try to be the first in your industry at something. Companies that break new ground are seen as innovative, forward-thinking—and successful.
- Always listen for a little voice in your ear—it's your customer, and the undying refrain is, "What's in it for me?"
- News stories can be built around promotions, innovations, charitable acts, events, and other business-related happenings and efforts.
- Target specific media outlets, beginning with local ones, keeping with the rule that big follows small.
- The people to whom you're trying to sell your story are media gatekeepers—the producers and editors who decide what's covered and what's not. They answer to their audience. That's the key: gatekeepers answer to audiences.
- Your job as publicist is to help the reporter find news (yours) and report it. Help by offering real news and access to the newsmakers.
- Newspeople operate with six questions, the "five *W*s and an *H*." These questions are who?, what?, where?, when?, why?, and how?
- Tailor your press release to the branch of the press you're targeting. If it's a business story, lead with the business angle. If you're sending it to a technology reporter, stress the technology part of your story.
- E-mail and snail mail aren't always enough; call journalists with your story. But make sure you've done your homework. Get to know the publication, program, or segment you're targeting by watching or reading it.

- When calling a reporter, be concise and to the point. They're busy and will appreciate your being professional.
- Designate a spokesperson for your company—you or someone else. This official press contact will offer information and control access to company officials.
- Continue to offer new information regularly. Be realistic about your ability to generate real news stories, and don't waste the journalist's time.
- Establish relationships with reporters, editors, and producers. Make sure these relationships remain professional, and make sure your behavior is always professional.
- Once a guerrilla raid is finished, another should already be planned and ready for implementation. Sometimes raids can overlap, but don't inundate reporters with useless information about your company.

7

IF YOU BUILD IT,
THEY WILL COME

*"Hide not your talents, they for use were made.
What's a sundial in the shade?"*

—BENJAMIN FRANKLIN

In this chapter, I'll show you how to build a website.

No, this book has not suddenly lost its way and become a technical manual. If you want to learn how to write Hypertext Markup Language (HTML) code, you've come to the wrong place. But there's no way to overemphasize the importance of a website in your publicity campaign. And if you're going to have a website, you're going to need a guerrilla's-eye view of one.

The goal of this book is still to help you get on *The Today Show*, not to win your website an award for website design. However, although some people believe that a website will get you publicity, they are dead wrong: a good website will help you get publicity; a lousy one will drive people away like a skunk in your living room.

Clearly, the easiest way to deliver your message and draw attention to your business is to create your own arena—that is, a means of saying what you want to say and having people find it on their own. If the public can come to you, it's a hell of a lot easier than having to go to them.

That's why I heartily recommend creating and maintaining your own website. From a publicist's point of view, a website is nirvana, a place where there are no gatekeepers, where your statement isn't cut down to a sound bite, where your quote can't possibly be taken out of context. It is the haven of control, and you are the controller. Nothing can happen here that you don't approve ahead of time.

Still, a great website is a delicate balance. You want to keep it simple, so the public can understand the information you're offering, and so it doesn't take so long to download to the average person's PC that the user who had some interest in your company becomes irritated and decides not to bother. On the other hand, even a relative novice on the Internet has seen sites that are technologically advanced, exciting in their graphics, intriguing with little animations and buttons to click. With those expectations, you don't want your site to come across as boring and a waste of time.

What's a guerrilla to do?

Strike a balance. Creativity, the guerrilla's best friend, is perhaps never more on display than at the guerrilla website. Yes, include bells and whistles, but you don't have to be so up-to-the-minute with technology that you bust your budget and alienate consumers using slow dial-up modems. Of course you want to convey your message, but you don't want your site to be a staid, text-driven visit that people may glance at once for thirty seconds before moving on to your competition.

REQUIRED QUALITIES

With this balance in mind, you need a website that has the qualities Web surfers care about. I've identified ten qualities that bring people to websites and keep them coming back. These are requirements for a Guerrilla P.R. website.

1. It's easy to use.
2. It's eye-catching.
3. It's fun.
4. It's interesting.
5. It downloads quickly.
6. It's informative.
7. It delivers on its promises.

8. It's interactive.
9. It changes frequently.
10. See requirement #1.

Easy to Use

Your website has to be easy to use. The reason is obvious—if it's too confusing or difficult, the user will simply choose not to bother. After all, there are millions of other sites to explore. Why bother with one that's going to take up a lot of time and be distressingly hard?

That's why the buttons that link to pages within the site have to be obvious. If you have a press room, label the link "press," so media members don't have to think about where to go. If you're engaging in E-commerce and want customers to order online easily, mark your button "order" or "checkout." There's no point in being cute or adding unnecessary steps to the project. If they want something, use the one word that tells them where to get it. Simple.

Remember that making something simple can sometimes be a very complicated process. Don't expect to set up your website, or even just your home page, in an afternoon. The process is going to be time-consuming and will require attention to thousands of details before it's done. But if you pay attention and make the proper choices, the result will be so organic and pure it will seem that it happened all by itself.

Eye-Catching

Second, your site must be eye-catching. Why do graphics matter? Because it's estimated that the average Web surfer takes roughly fifteen seconds to decide whether a site is worth exploring or moving on to the next. Not only do you have to make a good first impression, you have to make it fast.

An eye-catching home page has to be colorful but not overwhelming. It has to be functional but attractive to the eye. It has to have a point that attracts immediate attention, leading to other points on the screen that will link to other pages.

Keep in mind, after all, that your website is more than your home page. The home page is the starting point; it's where you greet your guests and bid them to come in and browse around. Other pages throughout the site will have other functions, but the home page is the most important, since it is the first thing visitors will see, and the place where they will decide whether to look closer or go check out your competition.

If you're not technologically inclined yourself, or you simply have no eye for design, your best bet in this case is to hire a Web designer to make your site more attractive. You're still in charge of the content, but the presentation of that content will be in better, more experienced hands.

Fun to Visit

Your site has to be *fun*. Why? Because the more enjoyable an experience the consumer or media representative has visiting your site, the more likely that person will remember the experience in a positive manner, and the more likely he or she will come back.

How do you make the site fun? Well, think of the best websites you've seen, not strictly from a business point of view. Which are your favorites because you need the information they provide, and which are stored in your file because you just like to go there? Take that second group as role models, not to steal their ideas, but to understand what you find enjoyable about them.

If they have games for the user and your business lends itself to games, you might want to include a simple one on the site. If you think that's not the way to go, determine what those sites do that keep you coming back for more, and see if you can adapt it to your own purposes.

Interesting

It should go without saying that your website has to be interesting. For all the reasons previously cited, especially the short attention span of the average site visitor, your home page and subsequent pages in the site have to grab the viewer's imagination and hold it long enough to move those eyeballs to the next page, and the next.

Although your business is of intense interest to you, it might not be the most fascinating thing on the planet to consumers, media representatives, or idle visitors. So you have to strive to keep your message clear, simple, understandable, and fun. While they may not mean the same thing, the words *interesting* and *fun* are linked. How can something be a lot of fun and bore you at the same time?

Don't get wrapped up in the minutiae of your business on your home page; it's the place for casual interest. Keep that page light. More detail can show up in press releases, specific Web pages designed for those with a much more serious interest in your work, and E-mail replying to those who express an interest. Too much detail to the new or casual visitor is going to be dull—the kiss of death for a website.

Levine's Lessons for Guerrillas: Lesson #7

Try this: when your website is almost ready to be launched, ask a friend—one who has no connection to your business and works in another field entirely—to look at your home page. See where your friend's mouse goes first. See how long he or she looks at each item, each page. See which links your friend chooses and when he or she loses interest. Now you have a good idea of how the casual visitor will approach, and react to, your site. Make adjustments accordingly.

Quick to Download

Requirement number five is that your website must download quickly. There's nothing deadlier to a Web visit than a slow, painful wait for a page to appear on your screen. If you've been on the Internet for more than a half hour, you know that. And the last thing you want is for your website to gain the reputation of being frustrating and slow. Remember, there are two speeds in Guerrilla P.R.: fast and dead.

To make sure your site downloads quickly, you have to make some tough choices. Yes, streaming video is a lot of fun and would be a fascinating addition to your site, but is it cost-effective, and can you get it to show up on the screen quickly enough? Other features that will slow download time include intricate graphics, extensive detail, and too many links. Remember that not everyone has a high-speed method of access; some people are still on dial-up modems at 56K and slower. Even if your home page comes up quickly on your DSL or cable modem, others with slower connections may have a much slower experience.

Yes, you want to offer as much as you can on the site, but if it's going to slow things down to the point that surfers will give up before your home page appears, you're defeating your own purpose. Make choices about what stays and what goes based on what's essential.

When you're writing the code and designing the site, the rule of thumb is that more than ten seconds of download time for any page is too much. If everything you have on the page—HTML text, graphics, and all—takes up more than 40K of memory, it's going to take too long for some users to download.

Informative

Your website also must be informative. It's great to have an enjoyable, interesting, easy-to-download site, but if it doesn't actually spread the word about your business, why were you involved in this to begin with? Your goal is to inform the public about your business, yourself, or your product or service. The tools you use are games, bells and whistles, jokes, graphics, and streaming video or audio, and, of course, your text.

The qualities are not mutually exclusive: you can be informative and have some fun at the same time. Hard-core facts should be available on your site, but they don't have to be dry, boring position papers, mission statements that read like obituaries, and annual reports that could put a chronic insomniac to sleep.

Yes, have that area where the traditional papers can be located—by those who want them. In the press room, *all* recent press releases, dating back a good few months, should be available. If the business is publicly traded, the latest annual report should be online. If you actually have a mission statement, surely it belongs here, too.

But for the general public, the consumer, the casual visitor to your site, the information you offer should be delivered in a light, breezy tone. Make it sound like conversation. How do you tell your friends about your business? Tape yourself doing just that, and then have the tape transcribed. Edit your words until they say exactly what you want to say, but in the easy, conversational tone you're looking for.

When you can, show, rather than tell. If you have pictures of your product, by all means post them, with descriptions of the product nearby. If you can demonstrate a characteristic of your business with video, see about adding a streaming video feature to your site. If graphics are better than photographs, make sure you have colorful, interesting, appropriate graphics. Keep the tone friendly and casual, and present the pictures in whatever form you feel is most appropriate. Remember that stodginess is going to be the death of your website.

Faithful to Its Promises

Like any other aspect of your business, your website must keep its promises. Don't ever offer something as a tease to get visitors to your site, then fail to deliver on that offer. Not only is that an unsuccessful way to bring visitors in, it's going to alienate the ones who show up.

The idea of *visitors* to your site should be taken close to literally. These people are dropping by your home base, and they expect to be treated the way you would treat a guest in your own home. You should be courteous and friendly, keep in mind that you are the host, and provide for your guests' needs. Don't expect anything from them, and you'll be pleasantly surprised if they decide to purchase a product, request information, or inquire about a press placement that could give you publicity.

It's important, too, to understand that your words aren't the only ones that can form promises you have to keep. When your potential visitor types keywords into a search engine and your website comes back with the results, you have unwittingly made a promise to deliver whatever those keywords might have requested. And that can't be a cursory mention. If someone types the words *Guerrilla P.R.* into a search engine, and they get a site about guerrilla warrior Che Guevera traveling to Puerto Rico simply because that word and those initials are mentioned in text on that site, I am missing out on a possible visitor. Also, the searchers are going to be irritated, not with the search engine, but with the two websites, *including mine*, when I had no intention of misleading them. It may not be fair or logical, but that's the way it will happen.

Keeping your promises also means that each link must lead to what it claims will be there. A press room should not have the same information as the home page, because the reporter visiting will not find that helpful. The "contact us" link should have your company's name, phone number, E-mail and street addresses, fax number, and any other information available for someone who needs to contact you. It should have an E-mail link, too, but clicking on "contact us" should not immediately connect with the E-mail link alone. Someone may need to call you or may want your mailing address or directions to your headquarters. They don't want to wait for you to provide that information via E-mail. You will have succeeded only in alienating the very people you've been trying to attract.

Interactive

Your website must be interactive. People who use computers do so because they are not interested in being passive viewers. If they were, they'd be watching television. They want to feel that they are involved in the process, and interactivity provides that feeling in spades.

Links are not enough. One major component of most successful websites is a search engine. While your site's search engine won't be as powerful a tool as the online search engines like Yahoo! or Excite have, it will let visitors search for a particular topic contained within your website.

Besides a search engine and links to other websites or pages within your site, the ability to access streaming video has become much more popular on websites in the past couple of years. This takes up considerable memory, can slow down download time, and can be expensive to add to a website. However, it looks really good and can sometimes illustrate your point in a way that is infinitely more interesting than anything print or a still graphic can do. I can't tell you if it's the way for you to go, but I can say it adds a good deal of fun and interactivity to a site.

Games are not just for kids, and they're not just for kids' websites. Any kind of interactive game, preferably one that isn't so complicated or so difficult that it will frustrate the player, can certainly increase the interest level in your site. Tie the game to something involving your business, and you can teach and amuse at the same time.

Up-to-Date

To keep visitors coming back, remember that your site has to change frequently. That *doesn't* mean you have to reinvent yourself, or as Don Barrett of laradio.com says, "throw a grenade into the site" often. It means the information and links you offer have to be updated as often as is practical, to keep visitors as up-to-date as they can be. It also means that some facet of the site needs to be updated, changed, or eliminated relatively often, to give the returning visitor something new to look at and a reason to drop in more than once a decade.

In the press room, obviously the update must come through posting new press releases as soon as new information becomes available. Whenever you issue a new press release, it's a good idea to put a headline or alert on the home page (perhaps next to the press room link), alerting media members to a possible hot story idea as soon as possible. Of course, that doesn't replace your own legwork in pitching your story, but it adds another weapon to the guerrilla's ammo belt.

It is also extremely important to keep your contact information as up-to-date as possible. If you experience changes in staff members listed in your contact area, be sure to update the list as soon as the personnel change occurs. There's nothing worse than listing a contact who does not work for your company or not listing one who can help if a customer or media member has a question.

Beyond that, changing features on the site helps feed other vital requirements, like keeping the site interesting and fun. Add new games, announce promotions, answer messages from visitors, highlight new products. If you haven't been doing E-commerce but are about to begin, don't hide your light under a bushel; announce the launch to the world! Have you participated in a community project or a fun promotion lately? Are there pictures you can post on the site? Showing yourself or your staff having a good time is a good way to humanize your business and make the visitor feel more like one of the family.

Every once in a while (no more often than once a year, and possibly not as often as that), you *will* need to "throw a *big* grenade in" and overhaul your entire site. If for no other reason, technology will continue to advance, and you don't want your site to be left in the dust. If you've hired a Web master or a Web designer to launch the site, you might want to look into the possibility of reinventing it periodically, or take some courses to learn the proper computer wizardry yourself. Either way, this overhaul is very important. Your regular guests, the ones who drop by the website often, will certainly get tired of looking at the same home page day after day. You will need some new scenery once in a while just to maintain interest. Keep your customer in mind at all times, and think about how you feel about the websites you visit regularly. After the fortieth or fiftieth visit, aren't they just a little bit tired? You don't want that to happen to your site. Get that grenade and pull the pin!

Easy to Use (Again)

Remember our tenth requirement? "See requirement #1." I've repeated this principle because although fun is a much higher priority than you might think, even at a business website, it's not more important than being easy to use. For a website, there is nothing more important than being easy to use. It's a cold, hard truth that if people have the slightest bit of trouble downloading or using your website, they will be gone, and they won't come back. There are so many websites happy and able to take your place, the erstwhile visitor to yours won't have to wait ten seconds—literally—before linking up with a competitor, and getting what he or she wants. What *you* could have provided if you'd built on a foundation of simplicity.

DESIGN DECISIONS

What's better: designing your site yourself or hiring a Web designer to write the code and get everything you want up and running? There are as many answers to that question as there are businesses launching websites, because each set of circumstances requires a different set of decisions. What's your budget for developing the site? If you spend money on a designer, will you have enough left to maintain the site properly when it's ready? If not, you either need to design the site yourself or raise more money, because the game certainly doesn't end the day your site launches.

A program like Macromedia's Dreamweaver 4 can help you set up a website. The program itself sells for $299, but you can get a thirty-day free trial from the website www.macromedia.com and download it directly, so you can be playing with the software in minutes. Fusion, from NetObjects, is only $99 but is not available for the Macintosh anymore, while Microsoft's FrontPage 2000 (or FrontPage 1.0 for the Macintosh) costs $149 from the manufacturer.

These programs are meant to be used by beginners as well as those with Web design experience, so they include tutorials and guided tours to help you through the rough spots. Still, those without some background in writing HTML code will probably find some aspects a little daunting. There are plenty of books that can give you the rudimentary instruction you need, and you can have a website up and running in a very short time.

Still, it might be a worthwhile idea to have professional help, particularly if you're well funded and lack all code-writing skills. Get recommendations for Web designers from colleagues, on newsgroups and bulletin boards that might offer some assistance, and through your own personal selection process.

Either way, there are some other choices to consider. One is whether you will store the website on your own premises or at an Internet service provider (ISP). Keeping it on the premises can mean a larger outlay of money for hardware and space, but it provides more control over the site. (You can store the site in your system and make changes when the spirit moves you.) An ISP might leave you less control, but the dedicated access line you need will be there at all times (except when maintenance is being done or the system crashes, which happens occasionally). This is a choice you have to make yourself, but either system can be workable.

You also have to decide whether you're going to solicit advertising on your site. This complicates matters, but it does pay a great number of bills. Offering banner advertising is probably over the head of most new-to-the-Net businesses, so you might want to consult an advertising agency with experience in Web ads.

THE GOOD AND THE BAD

When the Supreme Court had to rule on the question of obscenity in 1964, Justice Potter Stewart uttered a phrase that has become the rule for many subjective judgments. He said he couldn't define obscenity, "but I know it when I see it." Well, I think I've made it clear that I am not an expert on the technical intricacies of the Internet, but I know a good website when I see it.

What a Good Website Looks Like

A good website should include—but is not limited to—the following tips:

- A good website has links, but not so many that the visitor is confused. A good limit is ten.
- A good website is colorful but not garish. Don't distract the eye with so much color that visitors ignore the content.
- A good website has a permanent banner. That is, each page should have a common banner that identifies the site, so the visitor remembers where he or she is. Include the page title on the banner, too.
- A good website is clear and to the point. Remember Henry Thoreau's advice at all times: "Simplify, simplify."
- A good website keeps clicks to a minimum. No page on your site should be more than three clicks away from any other page on your site. Web surfers don't want to hit their "back" button time after time.
- A good website has links to other pages that are easy to reach. Make sure they're easy to find and use.

- A good website has clear, easy-to-read typefaces. Fancy may be fun, but if it's hard to read, get rid of it.
- A good website has a "back to top" button on the bottom of a long page. Boy, is that a relief from scrolling.

What a Bad Website Looks Like

I know what a bad website looks like, too. Check out the features I've listed. Have you ever run into a site like this? If you did, you probably abandoned it—that's what most Web users would do.

- A bad website is overwhelming. Its color, its design, and its motion upon downloading assault the eye and startle the viewer.
- A bad website is too wide for the average computer screen. It requires side-to-side scrolling to read text or see vital pieces of information.
- A bad website has far too many links, or not enough. Too many make viewers question why they're looking at this site and not one of the others. Too few indicate this is a thin, information-poor site.
- A bad website uses too much computer jargon. By the time I'm finished figuring out whether I have "Flash," whether my computer can handle "HTML," and whether I think that "emoticons" will make me "LOL," I no longer care about the message the site is trying to convey.
- A bad website doesn't include contact information. It refers only to an E-mail address or to the press room section for informational referrals.
- A bad website is difficult to navigate. Visitors don't want to scroll immediately upon entering. They should have a click to enter, and a click once they get to the home page.
- A bad website is more concerned with its own technical wizardry than its content. If streaming video and splashing colors are more important and prominent than what you're trying to communicate, you may very well have missed the point of your own website.
- A bad website doesn't make the point of its links clear. The press room should be labeled "Press," not "Media Moguls." Company information should be "contact us," not "send an E-mail to the execs."

GETTING THE WORDS RIGHT

When you include text on the site—and that will be often, since your message will frequently be conveyed with words—keep in mind that you are not writing a book. You're not writing a magazine article. You're writing a message about your business, and you are writing it for the medium we know as the Internet.

What does that mean? It means you should tailor your message to the medium you've chosen. Since the average Web user has the attention span of a ten-year-old in geography class, you have to get your point across quickly and clearly.

Each page of your website is a different chapter in the message you're conveying. So while each page has a separate theme and new information that the other pages don't include, the overall style and intent remain the same. Make sure you don't write one page very informally, then switch gears and turn on the formality with the next page.

Yes, the Internet is an international forum, but for the most part, the text presented is in English, and the odds are yours will be as well. But it might be best to keep Americanized slogans, references, and figures of speech to a minimum. You don't have to cut them out altogether, but they shouldn't be in every paragraph, either. Reading on a computer screen has been known to cause eyestrain and headaches. This is the last thing a business needs to do when trying to attract publicity or goodwill among customers. To make the read easier, vary the size, font, and color of your text occasionally. Keep your text as brief as it can be, and keep it to the point. Edit out unnecessary words. Backgrounds should be light, with colors and text dark, except on rare occasions when you're trying to create a special mood. When you absolutely must use dark backgrounds, keep your text to a minimum.

Check your spelling and grammar. That doesn't mean everything has to sound like a professor of English has approved it, since informal, relaxed speech is the rule of the Internet and of public relations writing. But it does mean that you have to fix blatant errors ("they have to take care of theirselves") before they make it to your site, or your image will be tarnished.

A well-conceived, well-executed website is an art form like any other. It is, to use an expression from Thomas Alva Edison, "one-tenth inspiration and nine-tenths perspiration." Hard work will be involved. But if you put in the time, the work, and the care required, your website will indeed be the front-line brigade in your guerrilla assault.

What We Have Learned and What We Can Learn

- A website has to be easy to use.
- A website has to be easy to use.
- Did you see those first two?
- A website has to be fun—for the *user*, not the site owner.
- Graphics are important, but they have to download quickly to be effective.
- Your home page is the opening, the introduction, to your website. It must display all the qualities you want the site to have.
- Do what you want with your website, but don't ever bore the visitor.
- Show a novice your website, and see how he or she reacts. Make the proper adjustments based on how someone with no knowledge of your industry views the site.
- Fast downloads are absolutely essential. Don't clutter your site with graphics and video if you can't deliver them fast.
- A simple rule of thumb is that a Web page that uses more than 40K of memory will download too slow. Streamline.
- Make sure your site includes the information you're trying to convey, and that the information is incredibly easy to find.
- When you can, show, rather than tell.
- Make sure your website keeps its promises. That means you have to make promises carefully, then exceed them in delivery.
- Those who click on your site are visitors. Treat them as honored guests should be treated.
- Include interactive features on your site. Games and surveys are fine, as long as they pertain to your message.
- Your site should include a search engine to guide visitors to exactly the information they require.
- Every once in a while, change the makeup and content of your site. Seeing the same thing every day is going to be terribly boring to regular visitors.
- Web sites have to be fun. Or did we mention that already?
- You can design a website yourself with help from some software programs, or you can hire a designer. The choice is yours.

- It's possible to store your website in on-site computers or to keep it with an Internet service provider. The ISP is probably less expensive, but the on-site option guarantees more control.
- Include links, but don't load the page up with them. Keep ten or fewer on a page.
- Use a permanent banner to remind visitors which site this is.
- There should be no more than three clicks between any two pages on your site.
- Make reading your message comfortable by using clear typefaces, easy-to-read fonts, and light backgrounds with dark type whenever possible.
- Don't overwhelm the eye with size, color, or motion. This is the realm of "less is more."
- Keep computer jargon to an absolute minimum.
- Make sure your spelling and grammar are correct.
- Check out my website, www.levinepr.com.
- See Appendix C for more great websites.

8

KNOW YOUR PREY, OR BE THE MEDIA

"It's not the world that's got so much worse,
but the news coverage that's got so much better."

—G. K. CHESTERTON

In Chapter 6, we took a look into the average day of a typical TV reporter. Remember what a jumble of meetings, assignments, interviews, and preparation it was, just for that two-and-a-half minutes on the air at night? Well, that's just the tip of the iceberg.

For the guerrilla publicist, it's especially helpful to be able to think like a media gatekeeper. After all, we publicity hunters are after an elusive prey—media attention—and plenty of other guerrillas and well-funded professionals are out there competing with us for the same column space or airtime. It can be as hard as pushing a wet mattress up a spiral staircase. Even in this cable-ready, Internet-accessed, information-drenched age, news coverage is a finite commodity. There's only so much to go around, and if we want our fair share, someone else isn't going to get theirs. Rules of the jungle.

And in the jungle, the rules are simple. Kill or be killed. Be on constant lookout. And above all, know your prey.

In our case, of course, the prey is that media attention we've been aiming for and hopefully getting. We have tailored our attacks to specific media; we've identified our prey, assembled the weapons we need to attack it and planned our campaigns to the last detail. But we still don't know enough about our quarry to launch the attack and have a reasonable amount of confidence that we can succeed. Remember, in the jungle, success is defined as "coming home alive."

So let's examine our quarry to see its natural habitat, its habits, and its likes and dislikes. We'll learn to think like our target, to *be* our target, and therefore, we'll learn how to conquer our target. Make sure your weapon is loaded for this trip—it's a jungle out there.

THE NATURAL HABITAT OF
THE MEDIA GATEKEEPER

The media gatekeeper, that most cunning of prey, can be spotted more easily these days than it could ten years ago. Why? Remember the *Wired* in this book's title? The Internet hasn't just added a lot of information about where to find cheap airfares, the rules of cribbage, or instructions for basting a turkey. It has increased access to all major (and almost all minor) news outlets on this planet. In short, it is easier to reach the media now than it has ever been before, and that's because every single newsperson is likely to have some spot on a website somewhere. If you look hard enough, you'll find E-mail access or at the very least a clear listing of address and phone number. (And if you miss any, see Appendix C, which lists as many Web addresses as I could find for media outlets.)

Now, some media outlets will tell you specifically not to pitch ideas to them via E-mail. Granted, they are the exception, rather than the rule, but they exist. For example, Jack Kelly, Los Angeles bureau chief for *People* magazine, says his reporters simply do not take blind story ideas over the Internet, and that's the policy his company has established. Trying to get your story into *People*, then, no matter how perfect it might be for the publication, is going to be that much more difficult, and right next to impossible if you pitch it via E-mail.

How can you know that ahead of time? Know your quarry. Check out *People*'s website, and you'll find out. Check out a publication known as the *Writer's Market*, which is published annually.

There you'll find listings for virtually every consumer, and some trade, publication in America, and tips on how to pitch them. If you see a notation that the publication does not accept electronic queries, you know to avoid that editor with your E-mail campaign. Send a fax, snail-mail a letter, or call, as indicated by the *Writer's Market* listing. By the way, *Writer's Market* is available in most library reference sections or at any bookstore. You can also subscribe to the listing service online, where it is updated much more frequently.

Know Your Quarry: Jack Kelly, *People* Magazine

Los Angeles Bureau Chief Jack Kelly knows his beat, which covers the entertainment industry and anything else that might interest *People* in the Los Angeles area. Why won't he accept E-mail pitches?

"I insist that all story pitches come to us by fax or mail," Jack says. "Our E-mail is for internal use, and it's so busy that it would add unnecessarily to the burden of processing huge amounts of data. We have a very efficient system for handling pitches when they come in, and if they start coming in by E-mail, it just gets harder to control where they go. Suppose it comes to a correspondent who's on vacation for two weeks; it just sits there."

That doesn't mean Jack and his *People* colleagues don't use the Internet. Of course they do. But they're more interested in gathering information on stories they've already decided they want to pursue, not to see ideas coming from guerrillas in the field.

"If there were a website that provided information on something we're considering, of course we would reference it," Jack says. "But 85 percent of what appears in the magazine is generated internally, and we don't want to see the pitches coming in on E-mail."

Jack stresses it's technology, and not the Internet in particular, which has increased the metabolism of his business. The pace has quickened, and in the ultra-competitive world of journalism, particularly entertainment journalism, to take a six-second breather is to fall behind the competition.

"We now deliver national-quality copy at daily-newspaper pace," he says. "There was an old sci-fi movie once about people dropping in the streets, bleeding from the ears because they were suffering from sensory overload. In a typical day, I may see 100 to 300 E-mails.

> The E-mails are totally apart from our story-tracking system, where I may see another 80 to 100 incoming pieces of story-related correspondence, and 60 outgoing every day. All that has been layered on top of the phone calls and the face-to-face interaction."
>
> Does that make it more difficult for a guerrilla to contact Jack Kelly today? "I don't know that it's more difficult," he muses. "The technology that they would use, the fax, gets a quick response for them. It might have been harder in the past for them to get through on the phone when that was their only avenue."
>
> So how does the dedicated guerrilla get through to *People* in L.A.? Kelly prefers fax before anything else. Snail-mail letters are second. Can you guess what third is?
>
> It was a trick question: there is no third!

Gatekeepers like Jack Kelly aren't all that typical. Most will accept E-mail queries these days, but guerrillas should keep one comment Jack made in mind whenever sending E-mail to a media representative: he gets 100 to 300 E-mail messages *a day*. And that's for a gatekeeper who goes out of his way to discourage E-mail pitching, so virtually all of those messages are from colleagues within his company. Imagine how much E-mail Jack would have to read if he encouraged queries via the Internet!

That lesson is central to understanding your prey. Gatekeepers are busy. That doesn't mean you're not busy, or that they're busier than you are. It *does* mean that you have to expect a short attention span when you're pitching a news story, because the odds are your gatekeeper will not spend very much time considering the idea. Remember when I said the query letter has to present the story fast and as dramatically as possible in the opening paragraph? I wasn't kidding.

Another point that Jack Kelly's numbers will raise is that of competition. Think about how many E-mailed pitches a gatekeeper will receive in the course of the average day. If Jack began to accept Internet pitches and made it public that he would accept them, would his E-mail load increase by 100 messages? 200? If that were you, would you be able to carefully read, consider, and answer all those messages, take care of the other 200 to 300 from inside your company, and do your typical daily workload? If so, please contact me and apply for a job immediately.

The point here, to reiterate, is that a guerrilla must be fast. Speed isn't an admirable trait or a beneficial asset; it's a necessity. If you're not fast—in your reactions, in your E-mail, in getting to the point—you're dead. That's it. End of ball game. F. Scott Fitzgerald said there are no second acts in American lives, but the guerrilla knows another plain truth: there are no second chances.

Websites aren't the only places to find access to gatekeepers. The traditional routes—phone numbers, fax numbers, snail-mail addresses—appear in any number of resources. *Writer's Market* is just one reference book that covers print journalism, and only periodicals. Daily newspapers are accessible through that old reliable standby, the yellow pages, in every city. You can get copies of out-of-town phone books by contacting your local phone service provider. There's a charge for some; others are free. Or use an online version of the yellow pages.

For broadcast gatekeepers, there are any number of sources. *TV Guide* prints the address of every station available in your area in the front of its listing section every week. There are many reference books for publicists and public relations professionals, available at the reference desk in your public library. Use the library's copy, since they are very expensive and require updating regularly. Many of them are also available in an online form, which requires a (sometimes pricey) subscription fee.

You can also contact media gatekeepers with a terrific technological device that you already have in your office: that's right, the thing with the buttons on it—your phone! It's one thing to have the main number of CNN's corporate headquarters and quite another to have Wolf Blitzer's E-mail address. So how do you go from having one to get the other? It's the simplest thing in the world if you call CNN's main number. The operator can either connect you with the news department, where someone will be able to tell you how to contact Wolf, or you can ask the operator for the information you need. The operator probably won't connect you with Mr. Blitzer himself, and keep in mind that I'm using Wolf Blitzer merely as an example. It's just as hard to get in touch with Dan Rather, Tom Brokaw, or for that matter, the consumer reporter at your local network affiliate station. Settle for the E-mail address or the snail-mail address, the fax line or the voice mail. That's certainly the best you're going to do on a blind phone call.

In fact, that's better than getting the reporter on the line immediately. Why? In a phone call, it's easy and fast to turn down someone with a nervous, hurried pitch. And it's even easier to turn someone down quickly if they appear to be reading a pitch from a piece of paper in front of them. It's far too easy, in fact, and that's what's going to happen virtually any time the untested guerrilla tries to pitch a story on the phone. But getting the access information—fax number, snail-mail address, whatever—gives you the ability to plan your assault as we've discussed, to word your sales tool as well as you possibly can and to present it in the best possible light. Although fast is best and the phone is the fastest communication device ever, in some cases, it's better to be prepared than to be quickest.

Once you've managed to obtain a usable address, phone number, fax number, or E-mail address for a gatekeeper, make sure you store it safely. Save it in an address book on your computer and back it up. You might want to write it down on something as low-tech as a Rolodex card or a piece of paper. These facts are gold; they are often difficult, if not impossible, to replace, and they are your ticket to the people you need the most. Never, ever treat them lightly.

THE PREFERENCES OF A MEDIA GATEKEEPER

When examining any prey, it is essential to understand the likes and dislikes of the quarry. This helps the successful hunter—and guerrillas are hunting for that elusive media placement—to think like the prey being stalked. If you know what your gatekeeper likes, you can anticipate the signals that will trigger a positive response. If you know what the gatekeeper detests, you can avoid sending out signals that will immediately cause the quarry to turn tail and run away.

Enough with the hunting metaphor. Let's examine exactly what kinds of signals a media gatekeeper is interested in seeing and what will turn the gatekeeper's stomach, causing you to lose out on a placement faster than you can say, "But wait! I was just getting to the good part!"

What Gatekeepers Like

Here is the short list of what a gatekeeper is looking for—the details will follow.

- Gatekeepers like a clear, concise statement.
- Gatekeepers like exclusives.
- Gatekeepers like their readers and viewers.

- Gatekeepers like professional behavior.
- Gatekeepers like celebrities.
- Gatekeepers like honesty.
- Gatekeepers like hooks.
- Gatekeepers like local angles.
- Gatekeepers like strong visuals.
- Gatekeepers like real news.

To attract the attention of the public, you need press coverage. To obtain press coverage, you need to gain the attention and the good graces of media gatekeepers. Let's examine each of the ten things that gatekeepers like, to determine *why* they like these things and how you can provide them.

A Clear, Concise Statement   Gatekeepers don't want to be snowed. Just tell them the story in clear, concise language, and they'll determine whether or not it's appropriate for their publication or their radio or television program. Of course, you can bolster your story and emphasize its strengths. But bolster it with facts ("Your audience responded overwhelmingly to a similar story six months ago") and emphasize only those strengths you can legitimately substantiate ("No other magazine has covered this issue in depth; you can be the first").

Exclusives   If you want to get on the good side of a journalist, offer him or her something no other journalist has. Gatekeepers are often sensitive to their competition, and offering your story—at least first—only to this news organization may give you an edge. This assumes, of course, that your story is a strong news item, not something the journalist wouldn't care about no matter who had it first.

Readers and Viewers   The audience is the faction that gives the news organization a reason to exist. Journalists have to love their audience in order to keep their jobs—and they have to give their audience what it wants. By addressing this interest in the audience, you gain two advantages as a guerrilla publicist: First, you must always be careful to remember exactly who might be in the audience for this media outlet (remember the demographic test we did in Chapter 4). Determine what that audience is going to want to watch, hear, or read. Then deliver it.

Thinking in terms of the audience can also give you a second advantage: you become part of the audience. Watch the TV news;

listen to the radio show; read the newspaper or magazine; visit the website. Take careful note of what stories the news reporters use and the stories they *don't* report. Get a feel for the content of the show or the publication. Don't offer gatekeepers something they'd never use.

Professional Behavior Does behaving professionally mean you have to wear a jacket and tie when you send E-mail? Of course not. It *does* mean that your dealings with the gatekeeper have to be mature and businesslike. Stunts like picketing outside the news headquarters to get attention might get you some negative coverage on competing programs, but they don't work with the quarry you're targeting. Act like a professional.

Remember, you want to establish a long-term relationship, not a one-night stand. If you use up all your goodwill on the first story, even if you're successful, there will never be a second story.

Celebrities There's nothing better than a famous name to attract attention, except a famous face. If you can persuade a celebrity to endorse your product or service, or if you sponsor a charitable function that just happens to be the pet cause of a major star, you will automatically attract more attention than you would have if you'd asked your mother to perform the same function. Unless your mother happens to be a celebrity.

News programs and publications are like any other business. They thrive on ratings or sales. And if you can attract a celebrity to help tell your story, the gatekeeper will sense higher ratings and increased publication sales. Think like the prey: they want to do well. Help them do well.

Honesty Gatekeepers' desire for honesty falls under the general umbrella of "Don't waste my time." When you pitch a story, the journalist will naturally have some questions about the validity of the story, or about certain points that might or might not bear on the gatekeeper's decision to use your story or not. Answer the questions honestly; don't try to overhype a story. If you do overhype and the journalist has been on the job more than a week, he or she will certainly discover that you haven't been one hundred percent honest, and your story will bite the dust. Do you think the gatekeeper will pick up the phone the next time your number shows up on caller ID?

Hooks No, the hooks that gatekeepers like aren't fishing lures. In journalism, a *hook* is a story point that will make your pitch irresistible, or at least less resistible than it would be without the hook. A celebrity endorsement is an example; another might be the fact that the event taking place will be open to area residents only, and admission is free. Better, if you, as a local businessperson, have an interesting personal story to tell, that will be a hook.

A hook need not be part of the story itself. For example, there's a hook in a sentence like this: "Since a recent survey of your readership showed that 86 percent of your readers are interested in bikinis, this weekend's *Baywatch: The Opera* presentation will certainly be of interest to them."

Local Angles Unless you're pitching at a national or international level, you're going to be dealing, in one way or another, with local news reporting. That means the coverage area of the newspaper, magazine, or radio or TV program will be limited geographically to your area, be it your town, city, county, or state. That means local media have an obligation to devote coverage to your area.

Can you imagine how difficult it is to find news that's specific to any limited geographic area, outside of a huge city or a whole state? There's nothing an editor or producer likes better than a news story tied to the the publication or station's own coverage area. It makes the gatekeeper's job easier. Tie your story to the local angle; make sure local residents have some stake in the news item. You'll be a number of steps closer to the coverage you're trying to attract.

Strong Visuals If your story has some natural picture attached to it (events taking place outdoors are great—celebrities smiling at a ribbon-cutting, for example), that gives you a very serious leg up on your guerrilla competition. It is preferable to the gatekeeper, and it's better for you. Why? In publications, the gatekeeper is always searching for "art" to go with the words, and if you can provide it along with the story, you're way ahead. (In most cases, that does not mean you have to take the picture yourself; you only need to suggest it. Smaller publications, especially, might be the exception and ask you to provide the physical art yourself.) It's better for you, too, for a fundamental, obvious reason: stories with pictures take up more space and attract more attention.

For television producers, the addition of a strong visual is imperative; television editors don't like to have a "talking head" reading the news into the camera. Producers prefer to have some-thing to videotape and show while the reporter reads the story. In radio, of course, a strong visual is, well, just silly.

Real News It can't be said often enough: if your story is bogus, gatekeepers won't just throw the story away; they'll throw *you* away, at least in terms of your ever pitching a story successfully again at that news organization. Don't ever try to sell a story that isn't true. If the gatekeeper expresses doubts about its merits for this news out-let, don't try to change his or her mind. It won't work, and it will sour your relationship for the future.

What Gatekeepers *Don't* Like

Now that you've read about what gatekeepers like, I'll bet you can guess where we're going next.

- Gatekeepers don't like people who won't take no for an answer.
- Gatekeepers don't like hype in place of news.
- Gatekeepers don't like gimmicks.
- Gatekeepers don't like interruptions at deadline.
- Gatekeepers don't like explaining the business to neophytes.
- Gatekeepers don't like being second. They *hate* being third.
- Gatekeepers don't like story ideas that have no audience hook.
- Gatekeepers don't like being bypassed.
- Gatekeepers don't like interruptions at the start of the day.
- Gatekeepers don't like "think pieces."

It may be more important to know what news gatekeepers *don't* like than what they do. If you don't know what the gatekeeper likes, you might not be able to sell your story today. If you try to give the gatekeeper something journalists don't like, ever, you can end up losing your contact and poisoning any stories you might have to pitch tomorrow. And the next day.

So, let's examine, item by item, what gatekeepers don't like. If you make one of these mistakes and discover that a producer or edi-tor is avoiding your calls, you have only yourself to blame.

People Who Won't Take No for an Answer If a guerrilla must be persistent, how can you avoid becoming the hated source who won't accept no for an answer? The answer is to know when the ship has sailed and it's time to fold your tents and go home. If the gatekeeper flat out denies your request, there's no sense in trying to change his or her mind. Remember that there will be other opportunities. Don't be such a pest that you miss out on those before you have a chance.

Hype in Place of News　Even though you think your new product is "revolutionary" and "innovative," if you try to convince the editor or producer by using those words, not facts you can prove, you're going to sound like an empty shill. Repeat this mantra: *It has to be a real story. It has to be a real story. It has to be a real . . .* You get the idea.

Gimmicks　Not only do gatekeepers despise gimmicks, they can spot one a mile away. If you're trying to get news coverage with a "doughnut" (that is, a sweet-looking story with a hole in the middle) by calling and claiming to be the president of the United States, or by hanging a fifty-foot press release out the window of the office building across the street, you're using a gimmick. The only time a guerrilla has to wait is when there's no story to tell. Wait until you have one, then give it all you've got.

Interruptions at Deadline　There's perhaps nothing more grumpy than an editor or producer reached on the phone at the exact moment the crunch is on: reporters running around frantically, staffers asking questions, clock ticking, superiors expecting action. Find out what the gatekeeper's daily schedule is like. That's relatively easy to determine by the time the program airs or the publication prints. A morning newspaper's worst time is midafternoon to evening, while an evening newscaster should only be approached in the morning, a little before lunch. Figure out the schedule, and if the editor or producer sounds hurried when you call, ask if it's a bad time, and when there's a better one.

Explaining the Business to Neophytes　Do your homework, or the gatekeeper will know you didn't. If you call during the deadline crunch, if you push a story that doesn't belong on this show, you're clearly making a rookie mistake, and gatekeepers don't have a lot of patience for that sort of thing. Be a professional, and make sure you can cover all the bases when you call or write to that media outlet. Hard work pays off; a lack of it is going to show very quickly.

Being Second For a gatekeeper, being second is bad, and being third is dreadful. Remember the rule about exclusives? This plays into the same idea. Gatekeepers, being professional journalists, are always worried about the competition. If you have a chance to place the story at one outlet, do not under *any* circumstances pursue it with another.

When you send out blanket E-mail or snail-mail releases to all the media outlets in your area, you risk having more than one outlet respond to your idea (everyone should have such problems!). Here's how to handle it: The first gatekeeper to respond positively has the inside track. Stay with that journalist until either the gatekeeper loses interest and spikes the story, or the story is "placed" (run in the publication or on radio or TV). If a second gatekeeper calls before the story is killed or placed but after the first has shown interest, you have to politely inform the second that someone else has shown interest. If the second journalist is not a competitor of the first (for example, if one is a trade journalist and the other a TV reporter), it may be possible to place the story in both outlets, although certainly with a different spin. If they are competitors, you simply have to stay with the first, thank the second, and say, "Better luck next time."

Story Ideas That Have No Audience Hook An audience hook is different from a hook for the gatekeeper, but not much. Remember that the gatekeeper serves the audience; in other words, the news outlet is trying to give its readership or viewership what it wants. So a story hook for the gatekeeper, like a local angle or a celebrity, is going to be much the same as one for the audience. What the audience wants to see is what the gatekeeper wants to show. Make sure there's an audience hook: why should the audience for this outlet be interested in your story? Answer that, and you're well on your way to finding that hook. When you find the hook, play it up to the gatekeeper.

Being Bypassed There's a saying about the jungle: there's nothing more dangerous than a wounded animal. Well, a gatekeeper who finds out he or she has been bypassed, that a guerrilla publicist has gone straight to the reporter or the editor over the gatekeeper's head, is wounded. And if you don't think they're animals, you've never been in a newsroom with five minutes until deadline. Make sure you understand the chain of command.

Sometimes it's OK to go straight to the reporter. If you're trying to pitch a local story to a newspaper, the municipal reporter who covers your town is probably the right person to call. But if the reporter refers you to an editor, *don't* continue to negotiate with the reporter; talk to the editor. If you call one editor and find out that another one handles this area, talk to the person who's being recommended. Follow the news organization's chain of command, not your own instincts.

Interruptions at the Start of the Day Not only should you avoid calling at deadline, you should avoid calling at the beginning of the workday. Again, you should be in tune with the news organization's schedule. Find out when the editor or producer gets to work in the morning. Then, wait a half hour before calling that editor or producer. Let the gatekeeper get a cup of coffee, read the headlines, fume about something that happened yesterday, and get it out of his or her system. Let the gatekeeper get used to being in the office before dealing with you.

Think Pieces A *think piece* is a long, analytical article or report about an esoteric side of a topic. These stories don't really have a strong news hook. A think piece is *not* "T-Shirt Store Offers Free Shirt to Local Customers on Birthday"; it's more like "Why Birthday Gifts Are Really Reminders of Age." It's not the kind of thing you want to pitch; it's too nebulous. Stick with strong news hooks, and leave the ethereal stuff to columnists and staff writers.

If there's one message to be taken from this chapter, it is that you must know your gatekeeper as well as you can *before* you offer a story. The more information you can gather ahead of time, the better your chances of success will be. Think like the quarry; be the quarry. The best hunters know how to do it. The best guerrillas should, too.

How Can You Recap if You Haven't Capped?

- One of the most important tactics in Guerrilla P.R. is to know your prey, and your prey is the media gatekeeper.
- Gatekeepers are editors, producers, or journalists who have the power to accept or reject your story idea.

- Gatekeepers' addresses and phone numbers can be found on the media outlets' websites, as well as in many publications, including the good ol' phone book.
- Some gatekeepers don't accept E-mail pitches. Don't try to force them; go with their rules. Faxes, mail, and telephone calls are still perfectly legitimate ways to contact journalists.
- Gatekeepers are *busy*. If you want to get their attention, don't waste their time.
- Gatekeepers have likes and dislikes. Don't waste their time with nonnews. Don't call them when they're on deadline. Do give them a local angle, or a celebrity, or a picture.
- Gimmicks can't take the place of a strong news story with an audience hook. Don't think your idea is so clever they'll love it. They won't.
- Treat media professionals as just that—professionals—and they will treat you in the same way. Remember, this is a marathon, not a sprint. You'll want the journalists' goodwill the next time you have a story to pitch.

9

THE YELLOW PAGES
ON MICROCHIP

"Don't listen to those who say, 'It's not done that way.'
Don't listen to those who say, 'You're taking too big a chance.'
Michelangelo would have painted the Sistine floor,
and it would surely be rubbed out by today."

—NEIL SIMON

"Is it progress if a cannibal uses a knife and fork?"

—STANISLAW LEM

The Internet provides the kind of contradiction usually reserved for presidential elections. On the one hand, it is the most technologically perfect, fastest, easiest, least expensive method of communication ever devised. On the other hand, it's so easy to be misunderstood on the Net that whole books have been devoted to how we should communicate with each other electronically.

We have to be careful about how we present ourselves on the Internet, and that doesn't just mean the construction of the website, as discussed in Chapter 7. It's also important to be sure we know how our Web visitors are finding us, with whom we're associating, and what the consequences might be.

This chapter is about getting your website noticed. But keep in mind while you read it that getting noticed is only as useful as the people who are noticing you. If you're attracting ten thousand people per day to your website, and only fifty of them are potential customers, you're doing something wrong. Maybe the way you publicize the site is faulty and needs to be repaired.

I THOUGHT THE WEBSITE *WAS* PUBLICITY— NOW I HAVE TO PUBLICIZE THE WEBSITE?

Your website may have a great message, but the fact is, if nobody knows it's there, no one is going to visit it and get all that juicy information you're offering.

So it's important to make your website visible and well-known. All the great bells and whistles you've thrown in and the careful construction you've done on the site are going to go down the drain if nobody comes to take a look at it. Worse, if you're attracting people who have no intention of using your product or service, you're spending money on a website that's going to be useless.

Before I explain how to attract eyeballs to your website, let's review a couple of the concepts of Guerrilla P.R. that will apply here. Remember the Tiffany Theory?

The Tiffany Theory states that a gift delivered in a box from Tiffany's will have a higher perceived value than one in no box or a box of less value. In bringing people to visit your website, you'll rely a lot on the Tiffany Theory. You can enhance your site's perceived value through the right associations. If you can link your website to Yahoo! or www.microsoft.com, that will be much more impressive than a link to www.joesautobody.net. No disrespect to Joe, whomever he may be, but he doesn't have Bill Gates's cachet. People are impressed with associations to recognizable, high-quality companies and personalities. So the Tiffany Theory, wrapping your site in Tiffany paper from a recognizable associate, is going to pay off grandly here. And by the way, don't bother to check; as far as I know, there is no www.joesautobody.net.

Another concept from Chapter 3 that applies here is the Mr. Magoo Effect, the diminished capacity for clarity that exists in our present society as we try to cope with, some ten thousand messages per day. Because of the overload and the increase in activity we see in our average day, we remember only bits of what we've heard and don't necessarily understand more than a small percentage of it. Because we can't sort, interpret, classify, and store all the information we receive, it tends to blend together. We spend less time thinking and more time reacting, and when we have to actually call up some piece of information, it isn't necessarily in the same corner of our brain where we stored it originally.

How does our friend Mr. Magoo stumble his way into this equation? Well, the thing most people remember about old Quincy was that he was extremely nearsighted. This manifested itself through his usually misidentifying people, animals, and objects, misreading traffic signs and important messages, and generally getting himself into all sorts of trouble because he thought things were what they weren't.

In attracting people to your website, Mr. Magoo's affliction will show up in incorrect assumptions and misplaced expectations. Unless you explain your site properly, make sure you're attracting the people you're trying to attract, and keep all your advertising, promotion, and linkage clear, a lot of Mr. Magoos are going to show up at your home page, expecting something other than what you're offering. And you know how people react when they don't get what they're expecting: they tend to become a little testy. First impressions can be made only once.

Of course, it's also possible to use the Mr. Magoo Effect to your advantage. Remember the example I used, of my radio mention of *Entertainment Tonight* turning into an appearance on *Entertainment Tonight* in the minds of people I know? That is an example of the Mr. Magoo Effect actually enhancing the event into something more than it actually was. You can do that, too, by creating a website that delivers more than you promise. You can take the people who stumble in unexpectedly (to you and to them) and wow them to the point that they're glad they made the mistake. Remember what Viola Spolin, the actress, teacher, and originator of improvisational theater, said: "First teach a person to develop to the point of his limitations and then—pfft!—break the limitations."

GOLDEN LINKS

We've already touched a little on the idea of adding links to your website. As you'll recall, I recommend creating links to related Web pages that do not compete directly with your own. These links help to bring more visitors to your site, establish a kind of alliance with another company (which may be beneficial to your image), and enhance your presence both on the Net and in business. The only downside is aligning yourself with a website that turns out to be poorly run or dishonest; you must be very careful about the alliances you forge through links or any other online method.

If you want to get technical about it (and this is the last time we'll do such a thing), links are actually known as *hyperlinks* in the cyberworld, because they show up on your site in what is called *hypertext*, the underlined text, usually of a different color than the rest of the words on the site. Hypertext indicates that clicking here will take you to a different page or a new site. It's possible to use hypertext even to jump to another area on the same page, as you often see in long pages that have a lot of text. Quite often, the bottom of such pages will have a "back to top" hyperlink, but that's not the only way to use links within a page.

For example, many text-heavy pages are organized in a question-and-answer format, and each question is presented in hypertext. Click on the question, and you will immediately be taken to the area of the page that answers it, with no scrolling down. That's a very simple use of links, and one that you might want to consider if you have to present a lot of text in one area.

Most often, though, links on a website will take the visitor to another page or another site. Let's examine the art of creating links to other websites—which ones to choose, how to go about getting permission to link up with another site, whether a link on their site means you have to provide one back to theirs. And, because we are guerrillas, let's look at how to do all this without paying anything for it.

Guerrillas are very thrifty. We have to be.

A pitfall of our general frugality, though, can be found in our willingness to do *anything* that's free, and that can be a problem. For example, there is such a thing as a "Free For All" (FFA) link site, where anyone can add a link to their website. On first blush, that has to sound like the deal of the century for a smart guerrilla.

And that's the problem. Think about it: *anyone* can add a link to his or her website at an FFA. That means you'll find yourself associated with anyone and everyone who's ever decided to have a website, including pornographers, hate groups, fanatical devotees to every celebrity in the world, competing businesses, and every computer geek on the planet. It also means that you will be attracting visitors from pornographers, hate groups, fanatical devotees to every celebrity in the world, competing businesses, and every computer geek on the planet.

Can this ruin your image? In a New York minute (actually, in a New York nanosecond). Can it bring in people who are guaranteed not to need your services? See previous answer. How much will it help? Not much, if at all.

Yes, your traffic will increase, but it will be useless traffic, the kind that clutters up the highways without anyone getting home for dinner on time.

Levine's Lessons for Guerrillas: Lesson #8

It's not important how many hits per day your website receives. It *is* important how much your business increases as a result of your website hits. If you're getting visited by a lot of people who aren't the slightest bit interested in your business, your website is a waste of time, money, and effort. You can get ten thousand hits per day, but if your sales don't increase significantly, why do you have that website?

Does avoiding FFA sites mean that you'll have to pay for the privilege of linking with more desirable websites? Not necessarily. Quite often, website owners make deals based on mutual admiration and mutual self-interest. In other words, if you can be helpful to the other business, it would be illogical for the site's owner to turn down your request for a reciprocal link.

But you have to be careful about approaching another site owner about a link. First of all, make sure your request is based on a true admiration for both the other website and the business it promotes. If you can't be sincere in your praise for the site you're trying to link, you need to think more than twice about whether you really want your customers associating that business with yours.

Next, narrow your choices. Remember, you don't want to have more than ten or so links on your website, so you can't ask for a link-for-link arrangement with fifty businesses and hope only the best ten ask for you to reciprocate. Decide which are the best five or six (and "best" means the best match with you, not necessarily which ones are the biggest companies or have the highest profile). Approach only those with the idea that they might add a link to your website. You may or may not be adding a link on your home page that will take visitors to their website, and it's not necessary to mention that possibility at this stage.

A Step-by-Step Guide to Linkage

This section offers you a step-by-step guide to finding the sites to link to, getting permission, and monitoring their effectiveness.

1. Determine which sites are compatible with yours. Use a search engine to search for keywords relevant to your business. You'll be surprised how many websites will come up in the results.
2. Narrow down the choices. The first priority should be compatibility not only with your website, but with your business and its image. Also, the general makeup of the site you're considering is important. One thing to look for immediately is links to other websites. If there aren't any, your chances of achieving one might be slim. That doesn't mean you shouldn't try anyway, but have a backup plan ready.
3. Once you've identified the sites you want to target, draft an E-mail message to the executives of those companies. You may need to draft a separate message for each, since the circumstances of each target website will be different.
4. The E-mail message should praise the other company's website. Mutual admiration definitely helps. Invite the executives to visit your website, and hope they'll be similarly "wowed" by your site.
5. Point out specifically why your site is compatible with theirs. Since you're not sending this E-mail to companies that directly compete with yours, you should explain the mutual benefit to links on their site.
6. Ask directly for a link on their site. Again, the key is to emphasize how the other company can benefit from this arrangement, although you will be reaping rewards, as well.
7. If you have enough admiration for their site and don't think it would diminish your site in any way, offer to add a link on your home page that will connect with their site. This is clearly an advantage for the other company and should make the arrangement more attractive.
8. Send two or three such E-mail messages at a time. When you have forged agreements with five or six other sites, stop sending.

9. See how well the links work. Chart how often visitors to your website are using the link to the other company's, and ask visitors to your site where they heard about you, including the linked site as one option. If the link seems effective, good for you. If you're not seeing any benefit, don't drop the link from your home page, but you might want to start the process again and see if links to another site might be more beneficial.

10. Check your links often. If one of the websites you're linked to goes out of business and you're still sending people there, your image will be tarnished. You can't be so trusting of your partners that you fail to keep serving your customers. A guerrilla, after all, is vigilant.

OTHER WAYS TO GET THE SITE NOTICED

Links are an excellent way to draw attention to your site. But they are far from the only tool available. While a strong link to a respected website can certainly increase your perceived standing among the Internet community, in particular among Web surfers who are interested in businesses like yours, it isn't terribly efficient. A link may bring in more people. It may not. It's hard to know, even if you ask your visitors how they first found out about your site. For one thing, a large percentage of visitors won't answer the question, and besides that, they may lie.

So while you must have the links, and make sure that you find and maintain them meticulously, you also have to publicize your site in other ways. Obviously, you should distribute to your media list the typical press releases explaining that you now have a website and what can be found there. You may not get any press coverage out of the release, but at least the media will know where to look for information on your website. Ideally, they will bookmark the site so they can refer to it easily in the future.

In fact, adding a "bookmark this page" hyperlink to your site is generally a good idea. You can make it much easier for visitors to find the site again, without their having to recall the Web address or the path they used to get to your site the first time. Bookmark links can work with the most popular Internet software packages, Microsoft's Outlook Express and Netscape Communicator. Contact Microsoft or Netscape (check the Web addresses in Appendix C) for instructions on how to add the link to your site.

Once the media know about your site, you should also let the Internet-surfing public (particularly your target audience) know, too. Links with other websites start this process, but they certainly don't finish it. Think about what your target consumer might be doing on the Web especially, and aim for that.

Naturally, it's possible to advertise on other sites in banner ads. But as we've discussed, that's somewhat expensive, and not necessarily the kind of communication most site visitors are going to find appealing. Some surfers find banner ads annoying and will take the paper you intended to come from Tiffany & Co. as a brown paper bag.

So how do you make a name for your website?

Keep the guerrilla mojo in mind: you need fast, cheap, and effective ways to announce your site and entice people to visit that site. Let's go back through our basics by taking a quick trip through the first eight chapters of this book:

- Introduction: Alan Canton wrote an article on a website and collected over $201,000 for his temple. You can write for websites dedicated to a topic close to your business.
- Chapter 1: The information you offer on the Internet is controlled by *you*. This makes the Internet the best source of free publicity ever created.
- Chapter 2: Newsgroups are great places to meet people with similar interests, find out what the hot topics are in your area, and especially to gain a reputation as an expert.
- Chapter 3: Start with a tiny newsletter run by someone in your business, and follow the principle that big follows small.
- Chapter 4: You saw that you can get your site listed on portals like Yahoo! and Excite by using submission services, which can cost as little as $59 a year.
- Chapter 5: Promotions (like the free film idea for our imaginary photo lab) draw consumer attention and use the Tiffany Theory to its best extent: they create a positive image for your business.
- Chapter 6: Remember the Pizza Hut announcement? Try to tie a promotion to your website. This not only creates goodwill, it also draws attention to your website.
- Chapter 7: One of the requirements of a good website is that it change frequently. When you make a significant change, make sure people know about it. Some who may have visited in the past and dropped by the wayside might come back.

- Chapter 8: The public drives the media. The media want to give audiences what they want to see. Give the public a reason to check out your website, and the media will follow.

Each of the principles listed is a hint to getting the public to notice you, and each has come up in a different context in this book. Information doesn't have to be used in one way only. You can absorb something and use it your own way. Creativity, remember, is the guerrilla's chief tool.

Links are one way to attract people to your site. Newsgroups, E-zines, and E-mail lists are others. Internet bulletin boards and "expert" sites like askme.com can build your reputation and drive people toward your site. Use the Internet solutions you have handy.

Remember that you have a built-in fan base: people who have the same interest that your website serves. Don Barrett could have put up the most interesting, interactive, creative, fascinating website ever devised, but if nobody cared about radio in Southern California, it wouldn't have mattered a bit. Nobody would have visited the site, and nobody would have advertised on the site. And www.laradio.com would have shut its doors and left the Web long ago.

Instead, it is a rousing success. Why? Because Barrett followed the two steps in serving the business relationship:

1. Find out what buyers want.
2. Get it to them.

Don Barrett knew there was interest in his topic, and he knew that nobody else had the passion or the knowledge he had to provide that interest group with the information it wanted. As a result, he built his site carefully and gave the buyers what they wanted. And waddaya know, people came to the site and liked it. And they've kept coming back.

The *Blair Witch* creative team didn't have a built-in fan base when they started, but they did have a group of people likely to be interested in their product if they knew it existed. So Dan Myrick, Ed Sanchez, and the people working with them brilliantly catered to that interest group, provided something the interest group didn't even know it wanted, and created a demand that became, by any logical measure, astounding.

How can you apply those principles to your site? Consider your resources, and by that I don't mean the depth of your pockets. I mean, think about what you have available to you: your product, the people likely to be interested in that product, any marketing research you've done. Think about what makes your product unique, your service indispensable, to the target audience. And exploit that. Go to the areas on the Internet (and to the publications, cable channels, and other advertising outlets, if you have the funds) that cater to that target audience. Tease the audience first, with a hint that something really interesting and new is on the horizon. Let them chew on that for a while.

Portrait of a Guerrilla: Howie Levine of www.aspennj.org

My friend Jeff Cohen in New Jersey has a son who suffers from Asperger's syndrome, a form of high-functioning autism that affects as many as two million people in the United States alone, although many of them don't know it. Jeff and his wife Jessica discovered this when their son was five, and they found that the medical community knew very little about the condition.

Luckily, there was Lori Shery.

Lori runs an organization called ASPEN (Asperger's Syndrome Parents Education Network) from her New Jersey home, and outside the medical community, she is the focal point for information about Asperger's syndrome. She introduced Jeff and Jessica to the ASPEN website, www.aspennj.org.

That site is run by Howie Levine (no relation), who owns a hardware store and is the ASPEN Web master by default, being the only one in the organization who can write HTML code. Howie says the site began three years ago from scratch and has since had over 200,000 visitors. That's with absolutely no promotion budget whatsoever, catering to an audience that is small and doesn't know where to look for help.

"It's still a pretty poor website, just text," Howie says. "I'm an electrical engineer by training, but I own a hardware store in Denville, New Jersey. I have a technical frame of mind, so I went out and bought *HTML 4.0 for Beginners*, and built a website. I had no training. I just bought a book."

ASPEN found a Web host for about $250 a year, a low price because the text-only site takes up very little server space. But when Howie put the site up initially, there was no way anyone needing its help could find it. So he went to each of the big search engines and individually listed the site on each.

"There are companies that will disseminate your name among all the big search engines, but that costs $500 or $1,000, and I could list the site on Lycos or Yahoo! or Infoseek myself."

Listing on Web search engines was the first step. Linking to other sites helped, and Lori's request that anytime any media outlet mentions Asperger's syndrome they must also include the Web address really put the site on the map.

"There are huge jumps every time something's on TV or in the newspaper," Howie says. Jeff says that when he wrote an article for *USA Weekend* and listed the website, hits soared from 50 to 2,000 per week. Television's power is even more amazing.

"I run my own business and I work weekends, and I have never put a lot of time into [the site] except to keep it up," Howie says. "You can use one of these very good programs to translate whatever you want into HTML and do all sorts of things."

ASPEN's site also gets a considerable amount of mileage out of its Web address. Lori makes sure www.aspennj.org appears on every brochure, every letterhead, and every business card associated with the nonprofit organization.

"People see it in the doctor's office or wherever," says Howie. "My name hasn't been on the brochure in two years, and I got a call yesterday from somebody who saw my name on the brochure."

ASPEN and Howie Levine can be found on the Internet at www.aspennj.org.

When a movie studio is planning to open a film, it releases what is known as a coming-attractions trailer. This short commercial, run before a movie in theaters and as an advertising spot on television, gives just a quick hint of what the movie might be about and emphasizes what's intriguing about the upcoming film. The ten-second (or so) trailer, which is produced before the longer, more explicit one, is called a *teaser*.

The same concept can be used in Guerrilla P.R. for your site. In newsgroups and small ads, for the least money possible, indicate that something really interesting is going on at a website. Later, give more detail in the same outlets. Finally, just keep plastering your

Web address over and over in the most likely places to find your target audience, and couple that with the links you've forged to other websites.

Maybe it sounds obvious, but make sure that Web address of yours is on every letterhead, every business card, every yellow pages ad, every piece of paper that has your business' name on it. Repetition is the guerrilla's friend, and reiterating your Web address as often as possible really can't be a bad thing.

Eventually, you'll draw a crowd. After that, the key will be holding the crowd's attention. But that's a subject for another chapter.

Pay Attention: There May Be a Quiz Later

- If you're attracting ten thousand people to your site a day, and thirty-five of them are in your key demographic—um, what's wrong with this picture?
- Publicity for your website is as central to the success of your campaign as building the website itself. There's no sense hiding your light under a bushel.
- Use the Tiffany Theory to your advantage. Align yourself with excellent, well-thought-of websites through links to put Tiffany paper on your own site.
- Links are forged through alliances with other sites. Choose carefully and well.
- Send E-mail to the owners of your target websites and suggest setting up mutual links. Keep the guerrilla's credo in mind: the other site's owner is wondering, "What's in it for me?" and you have to provide the answer.
- The Mr. Magoo Effect can be used to help you develop goodwill among site visitors, but you have to work diligently at it. Create a site that delivers *more* than it promises, and even those who stumble in nearsightedly, Mr. Magoos all, will appreciate the visit. Even if they can't use your service or product themselves, maybe they'll know someone who can.
- Free-for-all (FFA) link sites sound like a good idea, but they might link you with sites that won't enhance your Tiffany image at all, and they can easily be overlooked by the target demographic you're aiming for. It's better to spend a little effort or a tiny bit of money linking with sites that are clearly compatible with yours, and reputable at the same time.
- It bears repeating: It's not important how many hits per day your website receives. It *is* important how much your busi-

ness increases as a result of your website hits. If you're getting visited by a lot of people who aren't the slightest bit interested in your business, your website is a waste of time, money, and effort.

- Use E-mail lists, newsgroups, bulletin boards, and other E-avenues to create buzz for your site.
- Tease the public with a hint of your site's potential, then add a little more information about the site at regular intervals.
- Make sure to use your Web address, visibly, in every possible promotional tool your business uses. Invoices, business cards, letterheads, and more should include your Web address; it should be part of your company logo.

10

GUERRILLA MY DREAMS

*"Without heroes, we're all plain people
and don't know how far we can go."*

—BERNARD MALAMUD, *THE NATURAL*

There is no better way to learn how to do something than to study examples. A child who wants to play baseball would do well to examine Derek Jeter's methods. Someone wanting to learn to play the cello should watch Yo-Yo Ma.

Sometimes, even the way someone handles failure can provide a valuable lesson. Bill Gates and Steve Jobs stumbled and fell a number of times before founding Microsoft and Apple Computer, respectively. What matters is not the fact that they did fail at one point—it's that they persevered.

I can explain to you the many facets of Guerrilla P.R. wired, since I created and developed the concepts. I can tell you about my own experiences in publicity and promotion. Theory is necessary to understand the examples. But the examples point out exactly how the theory works and how you can apply it to your goals to achieve precisely what you want to achieve.

This chapter will be devoted entirely to examples: of business owners who embraced the Internet and of those who, like me, had to be dragged to it. Of businesses that tried to promote themselves on the Web and failed, but got up off the mat and tried again. It should give you a little more background into the way Guerrilla P.R. wired works, but it should also make your mind kick into overdrive. Take time after each example to ask yourself, What was the lesson I learned here? How can I apply that lesson to my own business? Are there similarities between this story and my own that I might be able to use?

These are my personal heroes of Guerrilla P.R. Wired. Read and learn.

HERO #1: ELIZABETH GRAY-CARR

Let's face it, there are few things most people want to deal with less than real estate. Just the words sound boring and tired. So a website devoted to a Realtor in Anderson, South Carolina, should be the dullest thing since Noah felt a raindrop.

Not so at www.callelizabeth.com, the website for Elizabeth Gray-Carr, an independent Prudential Real Estate broker in that town. Bucking the trend of making her website an extended commercial for herself—"another business card," as Elizabeth puts it—she and her husband Tom Carr set out to provide information to people who might want to buy or sell a home in Anderson. In the process, they proved that Elizabeth is the Realtor to know.

Tom, who handles the technical end of the site and built it from scratch, developed a site with Elizabeth's ideas and his own expertise. Of course, there is some promotional material about Elizabeth, but it takes a relative back seat to the information about real estate that's available in Anderson. Visitors to the site can learn when open houses are being held (not just for Elizabeth's properties), which homes are available, and what the community is like. Besides looking up general information about Anderson, visitors to the site can take virtual tours of homes on the market. Elizabeth and Tom's creative website attracted the notice of *Inc.* magazine, which awarded it first place in its 2000 Small Business Web Awards. The magazine says the site "builds relationships with customers by offering interactive tools and unusually detailed information, including personal Web pages."

The unspoken message: If you hire Elizabeth Gray-Carr as your Realtor, you're going to get all these resources, as well as the vital energy that created them. You'll get someone who will go the extra mile to get the job done and will have creative ideas about how to do it.

"A lot of Realtors have the mind-set that [the website] is just another flyer, another business card," Elizabeth says. "I had that view too, but in the past year, I realized we want the consumer to go to the website for information, and for however many seconds, see my name and the company's name in front of them. They go there for the information, we keep them there with it, and we keep them coming back."

The site offers information beyond the available homes, nearby golf courses, subdivision restrictions, and local weather. Message boards offer Anderson residents a chance to talk about their town, which can help newcomers understand the area better. Elizabeth had even offered virtual tours of the area schools but has discontinued that practice over concern for security in the schools.

Of course, because it is a real estate site, there is information about mortgage rates, local banks, recent sales, and other home-buying concerns. There is text about Elizabeth and her colleagues, but the bulk of the information is about Anderson and its real estate market.

Elizabeth finds it amazing that her competition hasn't yet copied her success on the Web, but she considers it inevitable.

"If you need to know something about real estate here in Anderson, this is the only place you need to go, and of course we're going to get some business from [visitors] if we keep them coming back enough," she says. "In our area, we are definitely way ahead of our competition on the Internet. I'm sure they will [try to duplicate her success], because when the consumer goes to the website, they want information. They don't just want to hear you say that you're a great Realtor."

Even now, though, Elizabeth doesn't write HTML code and can't do much more than answer her E-mail. Tom handles the technical end and takes suggestions from Elizabeth on what kind of content the site should have. He gave up his job at a local bank in 1999 to maintain the website and work in Elizabeth's business full-time.

"I know how to get people [to the site], and if I have something I want on there, [Tom] does it," Elizabeth says. She says it took him about six months to develop www.callelizabeth.com, and launching the site cost about $5,000.

She has learned that it's essential to update the information on the site as frequently as possible, to keep visitors coming back for the latest fast-moving real estate data in Anderson.

And even though Elizabeth now knows the Internet is more than "an electronic business card," she does combine the two. She makes sure that her Web address is on every piece of paper that bears her business's name.

"It goes on our brochures, on our flyers, on our business cards; we list it everywhere," she says. "You can promote on the Internet, but you have to make sure [customers] still go to the Internet."

Elizabeth Gray-Carr's website is www.callelizabeth.com.

HERO #2: ARIANNA HUFFINGTON

Anyone who has taken note of, or has *any* opinion on, politics in the past few years needs no introduction to Arianna Huffington. Her compassionate, humorous, and clear voice speaks to both sides of many issues and is never boring. Arianna is perhaps best known for her appearances on *Politically Incorrect* and for her byplay with Al Franken in books and on Comedy Central.

But she also has a very strong Web presence. Arianna has two websites, www.ariannaonline.com and www.overthrowthegov.com, where visitors can read about her political views, see past columns, check Arianna's schedule, voice their opinions on a number of issues, and incidentally, obtain information about Arianna's new book or other ventures she may have undertaken.

Arianna is very clear that her websites do not exist with a mandate to sell product. They are intended to be tools to build a community around the issues Arianna cares about most deeply, especially poverty in America and how to eliminate as much of it as possible. But if people want to buy a few books when they visit her site, she is not averse to making that easy to do.

"The websites are not about commerce, they're about networking with people who care about the same issue," she says. "We deliberately do not promote heavily or try to really push a book, because it would diminish the sense of community."

Arianna believes that people who surf the Web are wary about sites that pretend to be about building a community but are really meant to push products of some kind. She agrees that people *should* be wary of such things, and that people who run websites need to be very specific about their goals, so visitors understand them immediately upon downloading the first home page.

"There has to be a clear distinction about what is a profit-making enterprise and what is not," Arianna told me. "People on the Web are very sensitive about being used. You must not try to trick them."

Like other successful Web entrepreneurs, Arianna is careful about communication with her visitors. It's very easy to send her E-mail at her web sites, and she reports getting "hundreds, sometimes thousands" of messages per day connected to her column, her online newsletter, and other appearances and publications Arianna undertakes. And while she might not answer each one personally, she certainly does read everything that comes in.

"My E-mail address is on the websites, and it appears on the bottom of my column," she explains. "I read everything. We divide them up into column ideas, issues, and other categories, but I see everything that comes in myself."

No technophobe, Arianna says the quality of response from her writings is noticeably different, depending on which medium the respondent happens to choose.

"The [snail] mail we get is very different from the average piece of E-mail," she notes. "The E-mail is much more thoughtful, be it for or against [her position on the issue]. We respond, although I don't always do it personally. We often ask if [the writer] wants to sign up for my newsletter."

My Internet heroes tend to be of one voice on the issue of promoting the website, and of course Arianna is no exception.

"The Web address is on everything we do," she says. "When we had the Shadow Conventions (in the 2000 presidential campaign), the Web address was in front of the podium all the time."

Arianna Huffington's two websites are www.ariannaonline.com and www.overthrowthegov.com.

HERO #3: BRAD HALL

If you're dying to get into the entertainment industry, you have a number of options: You can be born beautiful and talented and get incredibly lucky. You can be born related to someone who is beautiful, talented, and incredibly lucky (or involved behind the scenes). Or you can work like a dog, begin at the very bottom, and claw your way up, inch by inch, to the middle.

Or, you can go to www.entertainmentcareers.net, where entertainment jobs are listed, résumés are listed, employers are listed, and they all come together to help job seekers and entertainment companies find each other.

Brad Hall, founder and creator of the website, stresses that you're not going to find listings for "female lead in multi-million-dollar movie" or any other creative job like writing, directing, or acting. What you *will* find at www.entertainmentcareers.net are jobs in the technical ends, administrative positions, and jobs you've probably never even heard of that support all those people on the screen, stage, TV, and CD player. There are listings for entry-level jobs and internships. Industry professionals who are interested in changing jobs will find listings that might help them, too.

According to Brad, www.entertainmentcareers.net is visited by about 80,000 to 90,000 people per month, with as many as 120,000 page views per month when things are rolling. "That could be 10 guys coming on each day and then coming on again the next day; they'll still be counted as a daily unique," he warns. "Ballpark per month is probably about 90,000." Not bad for a site with a very small promotional budget.

Brad issues a warning to new Internet players, however. Things are not the same as they were a few years ago, when E-commerce was just beginning and the Net was run by people who had a strong passion for the technology and a minor interest in making some money at it.

"The beauty of the earlier days on the Internet was the feeling of community. It was unrestricted. Back then, there were no rules," Brad says. "The huge break hadn't really happened. If you built a website, everyone was very interested in helping each other. It's not like that anymore. Getting a link to another site can be done, but it's not like they won't want something for what you're getting. People who have survived, and rightfully so, want to be compensated for promoting somebody."

For example, he adds, if you owned that Baltimore T-shirt company we were discussing, and you found that your customers were interested in surfing, you could go to surfing websites to request links. But expect the sites you contact to at least float the idea of affiliate programs. "The tighter your niche, the easier it is to find somebody, because they're enthusiastic about what you're doing," says Brad.

This process can be beneficial to you and to the other site. "You put somebody's link on your site, and if you refer someone to that site and it results in a sale for them, you get a percentage of 3 to 15 percent on that sale." Of course, if you get a referral from the other site and you sell that customer your product, you can expect to pay the same commission to the linked site in return.

Brad put enormous effort into his start-up, contacting no fewer than 1,000 to 2,000 websites that might be interested in his www.entertainmentcareers.net idea. He made it easy for colleges and universities to find him, supplying the site with job seekers who might have the qualifications his customers would be looking for. When www.entertainmentcareers.net was started in 1998, "The search engines were so polluted with so much stuff, it really was hard to find good-quality, best-in-class content," Brad says.

Since the website has been live, chat rooms and sites with similar concerns have found it, and www.entertainmentcareers.net has become the talk of entertainment job seekers on the Internet. "Word-of-mouth has spread, so I have that to my advantage," according to Brad. "The bread and butter of the site is to have freshly updated jobs and internships. I've got a one-on-one ability to chat with someone who wants to fill out the forms and wants to chat. They can click if they're having a hard time and have a one-on-one chat with me instantaneously." Customer service, after all, is the name of the game.

He points out that people are "just becoming comfortable with using the Web," even though the Internet is not news to most people anymore.

One tool Brad has used brilliantly is an E-mail "bomb," E-mail that goes out to ten thousand people at a time, giving them the opportunity to subscribe to a newsletter relevant to www.entertainmentcareers.net. The list includes only people who are considered likely to be interested; Brad has no interest in spreading spam. The list comes from hits to the website, and subscribers can have their names deleted by simply asking to be taken off the list.

"If people are sick and tired of getting it, they've found their job or decided not to pursue a career in the entertainment industry, they just unsubscribe to the newsletter," Brad says. "It's all automated, so it's great."

Brad makes his income from advertising he sells on www.entertainmentcareers.net and in the newsletter that accompanies the site. Neither companies listing jobs on the site nor the job seekers are charged. He spends about $200 a month on promotion, mostly on buying keywords on the better search engines, so his site will appear when job seekers even come close to asking about the entertainment industry.

I asked Brad, who is considered one of the premier guerrilla marketers on the Web, to list characteristics necessary for success in Internet marketing. Without missing a beat, he said, "strategic-minded."

"You are getting inside of the head," he explains. "Who are going to be my potential customers? Not only will they be in their college websites looking for jobs, they'll be at any career site. You definitely have to be willing to put in the time. While [online guerrilla marketing] is free or very low cost, where you pay for it is in man-hours."

Brad Hall's website is www.entertainmentcareers.net. And he'd like it cleared up that, no, he's not the Brad Hall who was a writer and performer on *Saturday Night Live* and married Julia Louis-Dreyfus. Thanks for asking, though.

HERO #4: IWON.COM

Search engines are a way to draw attention to your site; if you get your site listed on the search site, you can specify keywords that the search engine will use to find your site when someone searches for those words. There are even ways to manipulate the system, like programs that will increase requests for your site on a search engine, artificially raising your profile and having your address show up more often in casual searches. Such software requests your site automatically and repeatedly to create an inflated number of requests and raise your rating.

But search engine home sites, including yahoo.com, excite.com, and lycos.com, are also businesses. They offer news, weather, sports, and entertainment information, along with (in some cases) horoscopes, auctions, shopping, and all sorts of related services. And because they are businesses, they need to generate revenue, which (among other ways) they do by charging for advertisements on the home site.

iWon.com has found a particularly novel way to generate buzz for its site. It offers a $10,000 daily prize to a randomly selected user who has come across the site. If you make iWon your home page (the page that opens whenever you launch your browser), you increase your chances of winning, since repeated visits result in increased entries in the sweepstakes, until you reach your daily limit.

The site also awards monthly prizes and one huge annual prize of $25 million or more—hence the (trademarked) slogan, "Why wouldn't you?"

Public relations director Erica Bates says the site went live in October 1999 and immediately began to let people know what it was. Television and radio ads appeared, explaining the site and asking, "Why wouldn't you?" Every time a winner was announced (every day, including weekends), iWon's P.R. people would make sure the local media in the winner's town knew about the prize.

"If somebody wins $10,000 in a small local market, that person is kind of a hero," says Bates. "It's not a guarantee, but close to every day, we have a local market or radio or television story saying, 'Local person won $10,000.' You get human-interest stories just because of the mass of people. We generate our own content that's always different."

And iWon has continued to devote a public relations staffer to calling the local winner's home media every day. In larger markets, it sometimes doesn't translate into a news story, but Bates says her company can always at least pitch a new story every day.

"In New York City, if someone wins $10,000, nobody cares," she says. "But in smaller towns, we always have a shot at some coverage."

iWon has advertised on TV and radio and in print, because the Internet alone wouldn't generate the kind of participation the company expects and needs to survive, Bates says. "You do some on the Web, you can do some radio, some TV. My mother is rarely on the Internet. If I wanted to attract her, advertising only on the Internet wouldn't be very wise. You also go to a radio or somewhere that people go to for their information. It makes sense to advertise in all the media."

That doesn't mean iWon does no online promotion; to the contrary, Bates says. "We do some barter stuff with a variety of sites, which is fairly common practice, and programs that intertwine offline and online. We did a promotion with Don King, who was promoting a boxing match in Las Vegas, and we were the online element. We deal with *Survivor*. You'll have TV spots and on-site signage."

The annual Tax Day prize of millions is the site's biggest promotional event of the year, and there's increased activity in pitching the media around the country and on-site promotion to remind iWon users and (especially) nonusers that someone is going to win millions of dollars simply for using a search engine much like the ones that, um, don't pay millions of dollars.

"We send out E-mails to users promoting it, we send out media alerts, Don Imus is doing a huge promotion, Montel Williams is promoting it," she says. "It's sort of the same thing we always do, just that $10 million is ten times more than a million and one hundred times as much as $10,000, so it warrants that much more attention. In New York City, again, if someone wins $10,000, no one cares. If someone wins $10 million, now we're getting into the ballpark. They pay attention to that."

The search engine web site is www.iwon.com.

HERO #5: TOYSRUS.COM

The headline in the San Jose *Mercury News* on a Sunday in December 2000 read, "Toys on Time." It must have felt awfully good for Jeanne Meyer.

Jeanne is the vice president of corporate communication for ToysRUs.com, an affiliate-based private corporation aligned with the New Jersey–based toy giant. For her, the 2000 holiday season was a breath of fresh air. In 1999, ToysRUs.com may very well have been, as Jeanne says, "the poster child for things that can go wrong" on the Internet.

When Toys "R" Us, the largest U.S. toy retailer, unveiled its E-commerce site in 1999, expectations were high, largely because of the company's reputation and a considerable amount of favorable press received in anticipation of the Web launch. (Although Toys "R" Us did have a Web presence before 1999, and had done a little E-commerce by then, in 1999 the full-blown site was spun off from the rest of the company and opened to the public in a big way.) In the toy business, up to 70 percent of sales volume occurs in the last eight weeks of the year, so the lack of a Web presence for the 1999 holidays was unthinkable. "This was the year that people really saw E-commerce validating itself. There was a real sense of get out there or you will never get a second chance,'" Jeanne says.

But the Toys "R" Us site experienced glitches right away. In early November 1999, when the retailer released its "Big Book," a huge flyer sent out to tens of millions of homes and advertising toys for the holiday season, the site experienced such an increase in traffic that it crashed temporarily, and sales were lost. Worse, the site's reputation in its first big test was damaged.

Immediately, the company quadrupled the site's server capacity, but more hard times were coming. "I think we didn't anticipate how well the Toys "R" Us brand would play online," Jeanne says.

The second week in December is, more or less, the cutoff point for an E-commerce site to deliver products for the holidays, and ToysRUs.com made sure that warnings were issued to consumers: order by a certain date, or on-time delivery couldn't be guaranteed. "We experienced a technical error which led us to the point that we realized we weren't going to be able to fulfill about a half-day's worth of orders in time for holiday delivery, which we had originally promised," Jeanne explains. "It became clear that it was a fulfillment issue, not just upgrading the shipping to overnight. It's a very complex chain of events that gets you your stuffed animal for the holidays."

This was a publicity nightmare, but Toys "R" Us did not duck the issue. The company contacted the consumers involved, sending via FedEx a $100 gift certificate to be used at a Toys "R" Us store in order to have gifts on hand for the holidays.

"This is something that other E-commerce companies were experiencing as well," Jeanne points out. "A lot of companies were having trouble with delivery. But I think because this was a real established bricks-and-mortar name, we became at this point the lightning rod for all the shortcomings that every E-commerce company had."

Angry parents notified the press, an article ran in the *New York Times*, and press coverage snowballed from there. "It generated a lot of headlines that we didn't feel good about," Jeanne says. ToysR Us.com CEO John Barber and the executive team personally phoned thousands of consumers to apologize.

Imagine! The largest toy retailer in the world making headlines for not delivering toys in time for Christmas! This is about as bad as it gets for a corporate image. At ToysRUs.com, the top priority became survival, just a few months after it had come into existence.

"Year 2000 became the year we needed to win consumers back, and to win even more consumers over," Jeanne says. "If you're offering a great product or service at a great price, consumers have short memories. But we knew we wouldn't even have a chance at a second season if we didn't significantly enhance our operations."

Throughout the difficult period, ToysRUs.com made sure it kept in touch with market analysts, opinion leaders, and some media on its efforts to improve. Lesson: don't hide under the bed, even in hard times.

Clearly, if the website were going to survive, a serious change of image was necessary. However, that was secondary to the changes needed in the way the company was handling fulfillment. Those changes came in the spring of 2000, with negotiations to create a co-branded website with an Internet giant famous for its customer satisfaction.

When John Barber came to ToysRUs.com as CEO, his family was on the West Coast, and he was working in New Jersey. He spent a lot of time in hotel rooms and spent it wisely, surfing the Net and shopping at E-commerce sites. And he concluded more than once, Jeanne says, that "Amazon was the gold standard for everything that mattered in shopping online."

Shortly after the difficulties and ensuing bad publicity, Barber approached Amazon to form an alliance, and by spring 2000, the two companies were talking seriously. In New York the following August, Toys "R" Us and Amazon.com announced a ten-year alliance. The joint site would now include the best of both worlds. "We saved what we estimate as forty cents on the dollar in operations," Jeanne says, "and it gave us the gold standard in online shopping experience. Amazon got our merchandising and marketing expertise."

Bringing the Amazon name to the site was immediately a public relations coup, but Jeanne stresses that the best P.R. in the world wouldn't have saved ToysRUs.com if the problems that had plagued the 1999 holiday season had been repeated. "We wouldn't have been able to come back if this was just a P.R. stunt," she says. So the corporate communications staff went into overdrive to make sure that the press knew what was being done to ensure fulfillment for the 2000 holiday season. Open communication had been maintained throughout the process.

"We put on a real round-the-clock effort to make sure everybody was fully briefed on the deal. In addition to the press conference, we had a phone marathon to make executives available to talk to the media. We made sure the first people we talked to were some of the more influential research analysts and financial analysts that everyone turns to for their opinion," Jeanne recalls.

On the day that the "Big Book" was picked up by 60 million consumers in November 2000, the anniversary of the first glitch in the website's slide, ToysRUs.com held its breath. The surge was bigger than the year before, but the website suffered no problems.

The biggest test, of course, was fulfillment for the holiday season, and on the retailer's "Black Friday"—the day after Thanksgiving, when a huge percentage of toy retailing is done—"we emerged as the number one E-commerce site when you combined us with

Amazon, and we were number two overall by ourselves," says Jeanne. "We emerged through the end of the holiday season with 123 million shopping visits, and ToysRUs.com tripled its sales over the year before, to $180 million. Amazon reported delivering 31 million items, with more than 99 percent on-time holiday delivery, which is the number that made us the happiest."

Communication was the key to the perception of success. "One of the reasons we went from being a lightning rod for what was wrong to being a fairly high-profile success story is that we did continually keep people informed," according to Jeanne. "We didn't crank out a lot of press releases, but we did keep in touch with our opinion leaders. We made ourselves available, which was really important."

Jeanne's point is worth repeating: no matter how good your P.R. might be, if you don't deliver (as ToysRUs.com found out can be quite literal), it doesn't matter what kind of spin you put on it. Taking the right steps for the company saved the ToysRUs/Amazon site, and strong public relations, from an outside agency and then Jeanne Meyer, the in-house communications specialist, helped with public perception.

"You can't live or die on public relations or positive press alone," she says. "No matter how masterful you are in putting on a good front and managing to get great media coverage, if your organization has shortcomings or if your business is not going to live up to its expectations, P.R. can't get you there on its own. But it can be a big factor in the success or failure of you actually making a comeback."

If there's a better example of an Internet P.R. hero, I don't know it.

The world's largest toy retailer can be found online at www.toys rus.com and www.amazon.com/toys.

What Can We Learn by Example?

- Your website isn't just "another business card." You can use it to deliver information and lead by example. The first rule of being perceived as a leader is leading.
- Don't mix commerce with community building on your website. If you're doing one, don't do the other. You can create a separate website for the other, if you want.
- One way to raise funding is to take on affiliate programs, which compensate you for a small percentage of any trans-

action done on another website if your site sent them that customer. By the same token, you have to pay the other site a percentage when they send you a customer who makes a purchase, too.

- Creating news can be a local enterprise. iWon.com manages to make a news story every day by giving someone $10,000 and then alerting the local media.
- P.R. can't handle the load alone if disaster strikes. But it certainly can help with damage control, and communication will aid in speeding the healing process. Don't hide if something goes wrong. Discuss it openly and honestly, and then emphasize what's being done to correct it.

11

MEET THE PRESS

"The making of a journalist:
no ideas and the ability to express them."

—KARL KRAUS

"The media. It sounds like a convention of spiritualists."

—TOM STOPPARD

Contrary to everything you might have heard in the past ten years, not every problem on earth is the fault of the news media. Yes, the system has been set up so that competition causes errors in judgment. Yes, there are unscrupulous people in journalism. Amazingly, there appear to be some unscrupulous people in every profession. But the press has taken the heat for all sorts of terrible problems in the past couple of decades, and that's not fair.

Most of the journalists I've met, both print and broadcast, are honorable, dedicated men and women trying very hard to do an impossible job in a world whose technology changes roughly every ten minutes. They don't get into reporting for the money, I can assure you, since the average reporter is making less than the average manager of a Burger King when she or he starts in the business. A few go on to fame and fortune, and the rest keep working at it because they believe the job to be necessary, and they love it.

In this chapter, we'll meet the press, the people whose heads we must turn if we're to be successful in our guerrilla raids. We've

already outlined what their jobs are like, as well as some of the techniques you can use to contact journalists and obtain coverage, cultivate relationships, and further your publicity agenda. Here, we'll
hear from actual editors and reporters, who'll tell us what works and
what doesn't when we're trying to get their attention. Some of their
comments will echo what I've told you before or underline a point
we may already have examined. But much of it will be new to you,
and all of it will be from the mouths of the people you most need
to meet. Listen to what they say, and take note: some day, you may
be pitching a story to these very hardworking journalists.

MEET ROBERT LAFRANCO

A former associate editor covering entertainment for *Forbes*, Robert
LaFranco is now media editor for *Red Herring*, a magazine devoted
to news about innovation and technology.

Robert finds the concept of *viral promotion* especially interesting, since he believes it will eventually be the most important component of any marketing campaign. And he notes that the publicity
for *The Blair Witch Project* was one of the first campaigns that recognized the power of viral promotion and exploited it to its fullest.

"*Blair Witch* drove home the concept of the community," he
says, explaining that the Web campaign by Dan Myrick, Ed Sanchez,
and their colleagues created a community of people who found the
Blair Witch legend and increased the site's reach by alerting other
like-minded consumers to its existence. In other words, the "virus"
they created was interest in this mythical "Blair Witch," and they
passed it along, mostly computer to computer, via E-mail, to
increase the number of their own group. Before anyone knew what
had hit them, the movie behind the legend on the Internet had
grown to epidemic proportions—the way a virus is passed from
person to person until everybody has it.

"The market that film went after, which is older teenagers and
college-age students, is naturally resistant to marketing messages,"
Robert explains. "That kind of movie caters directly to them, but
the marketing for [*Blair Witch*] was smart, because it was virally
promoted by the kids who went to the site, not on television or
radio. The website was a product unto itself. It showed the viral
component of marketing is extremely important to that group of
people, but you have to create something interesting, or it won't
work."

The importance of creating interest is not lost on *Red Herring*'s media editor. You can create the most innovative marketing campaign in history, he says, but if at its center is nothing that arrests the editor's attention (or the public's), you are doomed to failure. And just relying on viral communication won't work if you have no message, or if you convey your message incorrectly.

"There are things that come to my E-mail on a daily basis that I routinely delete, unless they come from a friend," he says. "I get twenty to fifty unsolicited E-mail [messages] a day, and if I see one whose subject heading is ALL IN CAPS, I delete it immediately. I'd also say, 'Thou shalt not send anonymous group E-mails that are supposed to be personalized,' where they stick in your name randomly."

To catch Robert's attention, a website must have a central theme, an idea it's trying to convey. "It's got to have a story to it, but one that's not heavily reliant on video or audio, because that takes forever to download," he says. "It's got to have a theme, too; it's got to be simple, it's got to tell a story, and it should be text-based."

Robert says that even with the high-speed Internet connection he has at his office, some websites take too long to download, "so imagine what it's like for somebody with a dial-up modem." He doesn't have time to spend on waiting for sites to present their video effects, especially if they're there only to enhance an idea that's not terribly interesting to begin with.

The viral component of a site may begin with a few devotees, he says, then grow into *Blair Witch*–sized mania. And that's far from the limits of the concept. Robert believes that advertisers, public relations consultants, and business owners are just beginning to understand the viral concept and will continue to become more sophisticated as they refine their technique.

"Ten or twenty years from now, viral will be the most important component of the marketing business," he says. "People don't understand just how huge it's going to be."

Asked to suggest a *Guerrilla P.R. Wired* commandment, Robert offers: "Thou shalt not send an E-mail whose subject heading is in ALL CAPS." He can be found online at www.redherring.com.

MEET DONNIE COLEMAN

Donnie Coleman's work as senior vice president with Macy-Lippman Marketing takes him into the music industry, where he has worked with such stars as Tina Turner, Lionel Richie, and Peter Gabriel. He knows music, and he knows marketing. And because he can't afford not to, he knows Web marketing.

"The Internet has drastically changed the music space, not only in marketing and promotion, but also in terms of delivery of the product," he says. "It's still an ongoing evolution. At first, people thought they could survive with just a website, but [music retailers] need a bricks-and-mortar presence, too."

Donnie works with music retailers, the people who sell you CDs, and he knows how much the Net has influenced the way people buy music. Promotionally, he says, the Internet is still very much a work in progress.

He warns against spending more money than you can afford to lose on Web marketing, since in Donnie's view, overspending on banner ads on websites and America Online (AOL) fueled a shake-out among some E-tailers in the past several months.

"The spending was going unchecked for a long time," he says. "The prices that people were willing to pay were way out of line. They were spending $1 million on a banner on a deal with AOL. That really was out of whack."

In other words, companies were acting as if they had had too much to drink before they spent their Web marketing money. Now, they've sobered up, and are finding that the Web is extremely useful but can't be a money pit.

"You direct your energies to specific things, using the Internet for things that it seems to be most tailored to, like direct marketing," Donnie says. "You keep tabs on your customers' needs and wants. It's really a great tool to hone your database."

Donnie expects that in retailing, the Internet will serve as a tool to change the way products are sold and, in some cases, the way they are made.

"As we move forward, I think, people's services and products will become more individually tailored toward customers' wants," he explains. "The Internet makes that possible."

Donnie, who edits *Lip Service* magazine and *Top 40 Restaurant Guide*, is a gatekeeper himself, so he knows what the press wants to see. He has thousands of names on his E-mail list and makes sure each one receives a message at least monthly. That goes for consumers, too.

"We sent out a thing called See-Mail, which includes a still photo file that goes out with an audio file," he says. "We used it, for example, to reach the database we have for the band Hanson. We sent each name in the database a digital postcard from the group that has pictures of the band, and an audio file saying, 'Check out our new record on March 25,' or the date it was coming out. That started viral marketing, since the fans would E-mail to other fans, and say, 'Look what I got!' It was phenomenal."

What happens when viral marketing takes hold, Donnie explains, is that the campaign "takes on a life of its own. It's self-perpetuating. The people you send the message to pass it along via E-mail, and the next thing you know, you can multiply the number of people who have seen your promotion over and over again."

Donnie's suggested commandment: "Don't overspend." His website is www.lipservicemag.com.

MEET BEN HAMMER

If you want to know about the Internet, you talk to a Web specialist. If you want to know about reaching gatekeepers, you talk to a journalist.

If you want to know about both, you talk to Ben Hammer.

Ben writes about advertising and marketing for the *Industry Standard*, a weekly magazine and website that covers "how the Internet affects all industries," he says. As a journalist, he knows about receiving publicity pitches and what interests him (plus, more importantly, what *doesn't* interest him). Because he covers the Internet beat, he knows about doing publicity on the Web. And because he writes about advertising and marketing on the Internet, he can tie all of that together.

And—pay attention, now—the thing that annoys Ben Hammer, journalist, gatekeeper, Internet expert, more than anything else is a publicist trying to waste his time.

"They're not getting to the point quickly," he says of most press releases. "They're making statements that are clearly false, about being the leading this or the number one that. If you say you're the leading maker of orange juice and you're not Tropicana or Minute Maid, I know you're lying."

Journalists are well trained, and if they have any experience at all covering your field, they will know if you're trying to overhype your product or service, Ben explains. The last thing you want to do is lie to a reporter, especially when it's so easy for reporters to know you're lying.

Another of Ben's pet peeves is using jargon that is supposed to make the press release (and the company that issues it) sound "up-to-date" or "hip." It's not going to work and will more than likely backfire in your face.

"Thou shalt not use the term *the leading* ————," is his suggestion for a Guerrilla Commandment. "And that's punishable by immediate deletion. Do not use jargon or vague terms, and use the inverted pyramid." The *inverted pyramid* is a term used in journalism that refers to the way you write a news story. A newspaper reporter knows that the average reader is likely to start reading the story and continue until interest flags. Even though there may be important information in the rest of the piece, the reader stops, and the story is done. So to write in an inverted pyramid, you put all your best information—the five *W*s and the *H* we discussed before (who, what, where, when, why, and how)—as close to the beginning of your story as possible. The story is like a pyramid standing on its point, with the wealth of information at the top, narrowing down until you get to the bottom of the article.

How does the inverted pyramid work for a publicist? In the same way it does for a reporter: make sure you put all of your best information at the top of the press release. Assume that the gatekeeper will read only the first paragraph or two closely, then stop if he or she loses interest. Do *not* use a strategy that says, "Well, I'll hold this juicy bit out until page two, so she'll get a real jolt here." You can't be sure she's still reading when you get to page two!

Ben receives about twenty-five to fifty E-mail messages a day from publicists, and about fifteen to twenty-five of those are pitches. Every day. And of that fifty per day, he responds to—maybe—one.

Why? "Most of them are not appropriate for me," he says. "We read twenty-five to fifty E-mails a day from publicists, and they should try to write from that point of view. Get to the point quickly. Journalists have come to expect immediate responses, and their desire to write about a company if they don't get those responses will fall accordingly."

And from Ben Hammer's point of view, the biggest problem with most companies' websites is one that is basic, and simple to repair: "It takes too long to get to the [link] where you can contact the press person," he says. "There are too many steps between me and the person I need to talk to. Make it easy for me to find that phone number. Now I realize that not all websites are designed with people like me in mind, but that's what I need."

Ben's commandment: "Thou shalt get to the point quickly." Find him online at www.thestandard.com.

MEET ELAINE APPLETON

Since she used to be editor of *Inc. Technology* magazine and has since moved to the senior editor's post at its parent publication, *Inc.*, Elaine Appleton knows about the Internet. She understands the importance of a good website and receives the vast bulk of the publicity pitches she gets per day via E-mail. Those facts alone don't make her unique among today's magazine editors, but she pays attention to the way people are sending her pitches, and that does.

"It can be forty times per day I'm getting a pitch via E-mail," Elaine reports. "On my voice mail, it says that if you're a P.R. person, please send me your pitch by E-mail, because I simply couldn't possibly answer the phone every time a pitch call comes in; there are too many."

She says the majority of the editors she knows, and certainly those at *Inc.*, take most pitches via E-mail these days. It's faster and easier, and unfortunately, it's much simpler for the editor to delete an E-mail than to ignore a phone call. But most of the pitches Elaine receives—like those of virtually every editor—get deleted. The biggest reason? Publicists aren't doing their jobs thoroughly enough.

"The stuff that gets my attention is the stuff that shouts at me, 'I've read your magazine, and I know what you're after,'" Elaine says. "I understand how very difficult it is for the people who are writing the pitches and managing the accounts to do that with every single publication they're going to target. It's brutal."

It is hard to know every publication, every TV and radio show, intimately when you're doing your pitches. Elaine believes that publicists in large firms should specialize, delegating the responsibility not by client, but by publication. Guerrillas can do the same thing, focusing their attention on a handful of their most desirable targets for a time and not trying for as wide a dispersion of press materials.

"You don't need to send out 100 releases a day," Elaine says. "You need to get to know three or four publications, and know them really well. Craft your pitches with an eye toward who those readers are, and what they're looking for."

See? Elaine answers to her readers, and if we want to please her (and we do), we have to think like her readers. It's part of the chain we discussed before, in which the publicist must think like a gatekeeper, the gatekeeper must think like the audience, and the publicist must think like the audience.

Too many guerrillas (and even publicists with large budgets) don't understand that, and they think that more is better, no matter what. These are the kind who used to pummel Elaine with pitches about new products when she was editor of *Inc. Technology*.

"Most of the pitches I get are generic: 'Here's my new product,'" she says. "We don't do new products. I just delete those immediately. If there was one message I could get out [to publicists], it would be, 'Make sure you read the magazine.'"

Notice that the publicists—guerrilla or otherwise—who *do* read the magazine, and *do* have an understanding of its audience's needs, will find a sympathetic eye in front of Elaine's computer monitor.

"Every now and then, I get someone who really understands that *Inc. Technology* is a magazine for CEOs of small businesses, and they want to know how to use technology in a strategic way," she says. "They have a much better chance of my at least reading their pitch."

Here's Elaine's suggestion for a Guerrilla Commandment: "Thou shalt take no for an answer, after a reasonable period of time." *Inc.*'s website is www.inc.com.

MEET MARC GERMAINE

Marc Germaine is a radio talk show host known as "Mr. KABC" on the local Los Angeles A.M. talk station. He describes himself as an "entrepreneur" who uses his sense of humor and gift for gab to entertain and provoke audiences to think. He also has a very strong sense of how to use the Internet, even though Marc himself feels that so far, radio has not utilized the Net to the extent that it could.

"In radio, a website is going to reinforce listenership," he explains. "You're not going to get new listeners by having a website, but listeners who might be intrigued by you might go to your website and become more interested in you because of the things you have on your website: pictures, sound files, and whatever."

So far, though, Marc says that radio has been lagging behind other media in its use of the Web.

"I don't think anyone has done anything all that innovative for radio," he says. "On my show, I have a moment I call "Taking the

Oath," where you pledge your allegiance to my program. We have that on the website, and I get some information about the visitor, so I get a little bit of a demographic."

This comes in useful to both the station and Marc himself. "When I left one radio station for another radio station, I sent sixteen thousand people an E-mail saying, 'Here's where you can find me now.' So sixteen thousand listeners knew I had a job at another radio station. Whether that translates into higher ratings, I don't know."

It's bad enough that Marc thinks radio hasn't done enough on the Web. But when some talk show hosts get involved in their Internet activities, he says it can become worse than just not doing enough.

"I've seen hosts get into terrible, terrible situations on the Internet," he says. "I've seen hosts get into pissing contests with listeners, and I think that's just bad for business. I think you look small when you respond to allegations made on the Web. A smear is worse when you touch it. Anyone who's interested can see. You should either hire legal counsel or ignore it. Besides, people who read gossip on the Internet take it for what it is."

Does that mean Marc Germaine would shy away from the Internet? Anything but! Marc recognizes the enormous publicity possibilities that exist on the Web when it's used properly, and he takes advantage of them, promoting his program and himself where and when he can. He says it saves him a considerable amount of money, too, since he uses guerrilla methods.

"You need to have a presence [on the Web]," he explains. "It's a lot easier and cheaper to create a website than to put out a mass mailing. It's the cheapest form of advertising. Anyone who wants to take the time to learn can put together a website. What I look for is a creative way to market my show for little or no cost. Every entrepreneur wants to get a message out that hopefully will translate into sales or recognition."

Marc believes, however, that the Internet will not always be the free and easy place it is now. At least, not free. "The Internet has been based on a fundamental that everything is free, and I think eventually that's got to change," he says. "I think there will be micropayments for everything you do on the Internet. Any entrepreneur is wise to take that into account."

Marc's suggested commandment is succinct: "To have no [Web] presence is deadly." He can be found at www.kabc.com.

MEET MICHAEL SPEIER

Mike Speier edits *EV*, a publication about online entertainment, and is assistant managing editor of *Daily Variety*, Hollywood's oldest and largest trade publication.

Surprisingly, he does not consider the Web to be an entertainment medium. Mike says he thinks those who predict that the Net will compete with movies, TV, or video games are missing the mark. The Internet, he says, will always *support* those media, but will never replace them.

"The Internet is a data tool," he says. "It's not an entertainment tool. People go there to collect information, and they go there quickly for short periods of time. As studios or companies make themselves bigger on the Internet, public relations has a huge place there, because that's where people are going to go for information."

Mike has been covering the Net and online activity for some time now, and he has noticed P.R. firms and guerrillas doing their best to get noticed on entertainment sites. He says most are unsuccessful, but he doesn't think that points to a failure on the part of the medium; he thinks the publicists aren't using the Net correctly.

"Public relations on the Web will mirror the idea of marketing on the Web, which is a growing aspect of online activity," he says. "It doesn't work when P.R. firms or individuals who are in P.R. strictly use the Internet just for press releases. I don't think journalists care about online press releases. I like faxes."

He agrees, though, with the idea of two speeds for P.R. on the Net—fast and dead. "It's cut-and-dried on the Internet. If you're not instantaneous, you can forget about it," he says.

According to Mike, guerrillas can do well on the Web, but they have to understand their opportunity and not try to do more than they can logically expect to do. "If companies want to succeed by doing public relations on the Internet, they have to realize they are competing with giants," he says. "That is to say, there's no way on earth people are going to give up their televisions, their digital cable, their satellite dishes, their Nintendos, or their feature films. The Internet is a wonderful tool that has come on in the past five years like gangbusters, but it's going to take decades to tackle all the other fun things we have. You can't assume people are going to flock to it."

Mike Speier's commandment: "Be patient. Don't make P.R. on the Internet your core business—yet. It's an ancillary." He is online at www.variety.com.

MEET RIPLEY HOTCH

I actually met Ripley Hotch, editor in chief of *Success* magazine, via the Internet. We correspond via E-mail, as I'm based in Los Angeles and Ripley is in Florida. So we are a perfect example of people whose entire relationship is based on technology, since we've never met face-to-face.

Ripley knows about small businesses, serving as vice president and editor of *Success*, a magazine devoted to small businesses. And he knows the Internet and promotion. He receives fifteen to twenty E-mail pitches per day and has advice on how to get yours noticed. (Hint: It's something I've already tried to impress upon you.)

"If somebody sends you an E-mail and they make you feel good about your own publication, you tend to read it," Ripley says. "If somebody writes and says, 'I really like your magazine, and I read it,' and there's something that indicates that they do, I tend to pay more attention."

In other words, read the magazine.

Ripley says the Internet has "come to the top in a lot of ways as a source of contact, because the contact can be quick. You can usually get right to the people you want to get to via E-mail. If you've got a good informational website, people can check you out very quickly. It saves everybody a ton of time, so people are more inclined to do electronic legwork than they would have done in the old days."

Having a company website is something that this member of the press sees as a near essential. Not only does he preach, but he practices: *Success*'s website is accessible to promoters, writers, and readers and provides easy and quick access to information all would benefit from having.

"It wouldn't necessarily be a drawback if a company didn't have a website," he says, "but it would just make the job harder. I find myself surprised if a company doesn't have one, even a very small company. I can't imagine why somebody would not have one; it's very inexpensive."

As for www.successmagazine.com, Ripley says it delivers information that any guerrilla can use to his or her advantage.

"We make it very easy for people to contact us," he says. "On our website, we list everyone's E-mail address, and we also publish them in the magazine. We publish complete guidelines for writers and people who want to get publicity on the website. And still, I can't tell you how many [pitches] come with the wrong name of the magazine on them. They sent it to me care of *Inc.* magazine. I say, 'That's really good; maybe you should go talk to them.' They get your title wrong, they get your name wrong."

It's not enough to have a website, though. You have to have a *good* website, and that includes having one that will download quickly and without problems. The technology, Ripley says, is not as dependent on the method of access (telephone dial-up modem, DSL, cable, etc.) as it is on the design of the site and the server the company selects.

"It's not just a matter of using HTML or Java or whatever," he says. "It's also a function of the server. You can get hooked up with a host that has a very slow server, and it's the same thing as having a slow connection. You should test your website before it goes live and make sure it comes down reasonably quickly for a 56K dial-up connection."

The biggest mistake Ripley can recall *Success* making when it launched its website is "trying to do too much. It's very easy on home pages to make something that's awfully crowded. You have to help people find what they want to find as quickly as possible. Most people are looking for information. That's what they use the Web for. They're not looking to be entertained."

In the future, the Internet is "bound to get more and more important; I don't think it takes a rocket scientist to figure that one out," Ripley notes. "I remember the first time I ever got on a network; the transformation is astonishing. The connection to other people is enhanced, so you can do more. Once you do that, you realize the value of that communication and connection, and anything that speeds up that process will be important."

Ripley's guerrilla commandment is, "Don't fire off something in a fit of either joy or pique via E-mail, and make sure it's grammatical!"

Ripley can be found at www.successmagazine.com.

Now That You've Met the Press, Here's What You Know

- Viral promotion is easily spread on the Web, if you have a fascinating story to tell. Target your audience, identify your message, and sell it to the people who are most likely to spread the word.

- Spending large sums for banner ads is counterproductive. Use the other methods of getting a Web presence, like links and your own website. Save your money.
- Write press releases that don't waste an editor's time. Use the inverted pyramid to tell your story with all the best information at the top.
- Some editors like E-mail pitches, and others prefer faxes. In an E-mail pitch, a strong subject line—one *not* in all capital letters—will be a very useful tool.
- Sending out a mass E-mailing to people on your list is much more cost-effective than a snail-mail brochure or press release.
- The Internet is not an entertainment medium; it's there to provide information. Present your message in an interesting fashion, but don't expect to overtake traditional entertainment media.
- Thou shalt not send an E-mail message whose subject heading is in ALL CAPS.
- Don't overspend.
- Thou shalt get to the point quickly.
- Thou shalt take no for an answer, after a reasonable period of time.
- To have no Web presence is deadly.
- Be patient (a particular challenge for my personality type).
- Check spelling, grammar, and punctuation, even in your E-mail.

12

DAMAGE CONTROL

"Success is going from failure to failure without loss of enthusiasm."
—WINSTON CHURCHILL

"When you come to the end of your rope, tie a knot and hang on."
—FRANKLIN D. ROOSEVELT

You've come a long way since you started reading this book. You've learned the principles of Guerrilla P.R. and how to apply them to a direct-wired, Internet-friendly environment. You've discovered how to design and build your own website, and how to use it to promote your product or service. You've seen how to gain attention from outside media that can help grow your business, and how the Web can enhance that attention. And you've learned from the examples of Internet heroes and gatekeepers, who have told you their stories, concerns, and requirements. You've absorbed all this and are ready to put your guerrilla skills to work. After all, sitting around discussing theory isn't in the true guerrilla's nature.

Armed with all that information, nothing can go wrong, right?

Well, no. Murphy, the inventor of Murphy's law, must surely have been a guerrilla publicist with a computer connection. Because there are lots of things that can go wrong, and if they can, you can bet your last dollar (and some people do just that) that at some point, they *will*.

You know what the bumper stickers say: "Murphy was an optimist."

Computer technology is grand, believe me, and it can accomplish things that were science-fiction dreams a scant few years ago. We can communicate with hundreds, even thousands of people in a split second, and do it for free. We can entertain and inform customers we wouldn't have had a prayer of even reaching ten years ago. We can control our message, present it pure and unedited, and reap the benefits of our honesty and hard work in increased sales and expanded businesses.

But computer technology is also fragile. Servers fail. Connections are lost. Overloads are entirely possible. Anyone who thinks websites are foolproof need only go back a couple of chapters and read what happened to the world's largest toy retailer when it first opened its E-commerce site and disaster struck.

And technology isn't the only thing that can go wrong. Your website design might not attract the consumer base you're looking for. Your message may be misinterpreted or, worse, simply contradicted by some computer wiseguy on a message board whose only goal is to cause trouble and controversy. Your competition might resort to dirty tricks online. Or you might simply link up with other sites whose reputations are sullied or whose businesses close, leaving you with a damaged image, the exact opposite of what you were hoping to accomplish online.

LESSONS FROM PUBLICITY MISTAKES

Does that mean we should stay away from computers, that we can't possibly have a chance of success in a random environment where we can't even guarantee that our connection will remain intact? Of course not. You can't be afraid of attempting something because it might fail. *Anything* can fail, but it's just as possible that it can succeed. The only thing you can know for sure is that your business certainly won't benefit at all if you don't begin guerrilla raids.

Besides, the one thing that is common to all successful guerrillas is the ability to move on from a supposed failure, learn from it, and never repeat the same mistake again. Let me help you out by recounting some common mistakes guerrilla publicists make so you won't have to make them yourself.

1. Not being familiar with the publication or program you're pitching

2. Creating a dull, unimaginative, hard-to-use website
3. Choosing a hosting service badly
4. Sending too much E-mail to an editor
5. Taking no for an answer
6. Not taking no for an answer
7. Lying to the press
8. Making your site too slow to download
9. Thinking the Internet is the only necessary medium
10. Publicizing a nonstory

Not Being Familiar with the Publication or Program You're Pitching

Every reporter, editor, producer, and gatekeeper I've ever spoken to has emphasized that the biggest stumbling block between the publicist and the press placement (that is, "placing" your story with the media) is a lack of familiarity with the publication or program being pitched. That means, in simple terms, that if you don't read the publication or watch the program you're pitching, you have almost no chance of placing your story.

The reasons are also simple. Gatekeepers need the material their audience wants to see or hear. They know their audience better than you do. If you see the kind of story they've done in the past, you can have a very good idea of what they'll be doing in the future. If you can adapt your story to fit that, your chances go up.

Too many guerrillas assume all media are alike: if one show does this kind of story, they all will. Well, that's so far from the truth you need a canteen and a road map to get back. If it's obvious from your pitch that you're not a regular audience member or reader, you just plain won't get your story placed. A mistake? You bet, and a huge one.

Creating a Dull, Unimaginative, Hard-to-Use Website

Your website is your first line of defense and your best chance to acquaint yourself with new customers and media members. If you make one so complicated that people can't understand it, so boring they don't *want* to understand it, or so unimaginative that it won't stand out, your website will soon be a complete failure. It won't do much for your reputation, and it certainly won't increase your profits.

I've said it before, but it can't be emphasized enough: your website *must* be easy to use. There is no alternative. If you have every piece of information about your company available, and you include it on a site that's so complex only seventeen computer geniuses on this planet can find it, you have spent a lot of money and a lot of effort on a complete waste of time.

Choosing a Hosting Service Badly

Most of the technological problems that happen once a website is launched are the fault of the host service (the company you've contracted with to house and provide the site on the Web). Sorry, but that's the truth.

If your website is down too frequently, if the links don't work, if the video doesn't stream when it's supposed to, the probability is that your host service is not doing its job or isn't equipped to do the job you need it to do.

This is not a horribly difficult problem to solve, but it's much better to avoid it altogether. Once the site has developed a reputation for being technologically flawed or simply too hard to download or use, it's hard to undo that reputation, no matter how many improvements you make. The best solution is to make sure your host service is up to the task before you sign the first contract.

Talk to other clients (get a list from the host service) before you sign on. Go to their websites. See how they work and how easy it is to access them.

It's possible to ask your Internet service provider (ISP) to host your site, but some companies prefer an independent Web-hosting service. When interviewing host services or asking your ISP about hosting for you, ask a few questions:

- How much disk space do you use, and how much do they provide?
- Is there at least one backup server in place, in case the one they usually use crashes suddenly? Can they keep your site online?
- Do they provide technical support 24/7?
- Can they guarantee security on your site?
- What services require additional fees? Can they provide the software to include video and audio, for example, and how much will that cost?

To get the answers you need, you'll have to provide certain information to the hosting service. For example, you'll have to estimate the amount of traffic you expect to get on your site, if the host has any kind of concerns about volume. You'll also have to explain what you expect the site to look like and how often you intend to revise it. Any outsourcing (actually housing the site not on your premises) will require that site changes be made at the host service's headquarters, not your own.

A text-based site will not require much Web space, but one with tons of bells and whistles will. That's another good reason not to go overboard. You'll have to make your own determinations about your host service, and keep in mind that you'll be signing a contract. Before you make any commitment, you should discuss the length and terms of that contract with an attorney.

Sending Too Much E-Mail to an Editor

Remember the story of the boy who cried wolf? Well, imagine it as the boy who *E-mailed* wolf. If you E-mail too many messages or press releases with overblown claims or stories the press can't really use, your future messages will be deleted before they are read. And keep in mind, "too many" messages with such content equals "one" with such content. Journalists don't like anyone who wastes their time.

Save your effort and their time for occasions when you really have a compelling story to tell. If you do, you will not only garner goodwill with the gatekeepers, you'll also increase your chances of getting the press coverage that publicity campaigns are all about.

Taking No for an Answer

Fledgling guerrillas are especially timid about their dealings with the press. If a reporter or editor gives a vague excuse about "not having the space" or this being "a bad time," these newcomers tend to nod their heads and vanish into the wallpaper without putting up a fight.

Guerrillas have to have more backbone than that. We can't make up for a lack of nerve by throwing money at a problem. We have to attack when others would retreat!

If an editor or producer tries to beg off without giving your story the consideration you think it deserves, stay on the phone. Try another angle on the story that counteracts the argument the gatekeeper makes. If his or her objection is to the lack of a local angle, have one ready. If you get a standard reply about "not enough space" or "a bad time," explain why this story is vital *now* and how the gatekeeper should consider its most newsworthy points, which you reiterate in new, compelling language.

Don't simply repeat yourself. If you do, they will, too. Remember the next classic mistake:

Not Taking No for an Answer

Don't push your argument to the point that you annoy and alienate the journalist. This isn't the only story you're ever going to pitch, and you don't want to be known as the guy who doesn't know when to quit. Give your pitch a legitimate try, but if it's clear the gatekeeper is keeping the gate closed, thank him or her for the time, make it clear you'll call again when you have another story to discuss, and get off the phone.

There's no point in getting the press angry at you. It has no upside whatsoever and doesn't even feel good when you're doing it. Not every gatekeeper you meet will be a cordial, friendly type, but you can't let your personal feelings about the person distract you from the job that person holds. Even if you don't like someone personally, you can certainly pitch that person on a story. Sometimes, they'll even take the story.

Lying to the Press

Probably the most egregious sin the publicist can commit is to lie. Think of it: in one swift stroke, you can destroy your own credibility, eliminate any chance the journalist will ever trust you again, damage the reputation of your company, and still not get your story placed in the press. Now, that's an impressive negative accomplishment. And it all stems from telling one lie to a reporter.

It doesn't matter whether your story is about an international crisis or the introduction of a new brand of soda pop—lying to the press has absolutely nothing to recommend it. It's tempting sometimes, when your story is this close to being placed, to exaggerate just one point. Exaggeration isn't all that bad when you're merely stating an opinion: "This is the best toothpaste for whitening teeth," or, "This innovative approach will redefine cosmetic surgery from this date forward." Journalists don't particularly care for this kind of hyperbole, but they will put up with it.

But when you outright lie to get a story placed—and the lie can be in the story or in your presentation of the story—you are cutting off your nose to spite your face. For one thing, the reporter will always find out. Always. Reporters are good at this sort of thing; it's their job. Don't say something like "this patented process" when the process does not actually have an official government patent, or "you're the only one I'm telling this part to" when you're saying the same thing to every gatekeeper you pitch. Such lies will always be discovered—and the repercussions will be swift:

- Your story will be immediately killed.
- The reporter you lied to will never talk to you again.
- Other reporters will hear about it, and even if they do talk to you again, they'll always have this incident in the back of their minds.

All in all, it's not a very pretty picture. So don't cringe when I emphasize this point one more time: never, ever lie to a reporter.

Making Your Site Too Slow to Download

You think guerrillas are fast? Web surfers are even faster, or want to think they are. More and more, even home-based visitors are going to graduate from relatively slow dial-up Internet connections to geometrically faster DSL and cable modems. Why? Because we are an impatient people.

Even with a quicker connection, surfers are going to be upset with a long wait to download your site. I've said it before, and I'll say it again: you've got to make sure your website downloads quickly. Part of this will involve your Web designer, and part of it will be up to your host service, if you don't host the site yourself. But no matter what technical adjustments you have to make, just be sure that your home page, especially, comes up fast and clean. Don't make your customers wait, or they won't be your customers.

Thinking the Internet Is the Only Necessary Medium

Even though the title of this book is *Guerrilla P.R. Wired*, the Internet is not my only concern. The number of people who will receive your message on the Web is minuscule compared to the number who watch even a poorly rated network television show or read *USA Today* regularly.

The reasons to do your P.R. on the Net remain the same, and they remain important—it's fast, it's viable, and it is incredibly inexpensive—but your goal should remain clear.

Your goal is not to create publicity on the Internet alone, but to use the Internet to create publicity online and in more traditional channels.

Why? Because *Oprah Winfrey* reaches more people in one day than your website will in a year. Because not every home in America is hooked to the Internet, but television, newspapers, and radio can boast almost 100 percent saturation. Because the inexpensive nature of the Internet is meant to get you to the other media, which would normally cost far more than you could ever afford to spend.

So, don't concentrate entirely on the Web in your efforts. Yes, use your online connections to attract new customers and visitors. Certainly, include press releases and information about your company on your website. And absolutely, create online events that will bring attention to your site and get more eyeballs aimed at the message you're sending out.

But don't lose sight of the fact that this is the means to an end, not the end itself. You won't be happy until Montel Williams is asking you about your business on the air. You can't be satisfied until the *New York Times* is featuring you in its Sunday business section (the Sunday paper is the most widely read of the week). Your guerrilla raids will keep up until nationally syndicated radio programs are sending your message from coast to coast, and beyond.

You can't be finished until you can afford to no longer be an active guerrilla, and then you can hire a high-priced firm to publicize your business. But remember, you'll still be a guerrilla. Watch over their shoulders, and make sure they use the Net as well as other avenues.

Publicizing a Nonstory

Pitching a nonstory as news ranks right up there with lying to the press. It's not quite as egregious, but it will achieve the same results for you. Trying to hype a story that clearly has no news in it or doesn't belong in the news outlet you're pitching, is going to get you nowhere fast. Reporters don't like it, editors hate it, and producers never even listen to it.

Creativity, creativity, creativity. If you don't have a compelling story to tell, search your soul and those of your colleagues until you find one. Create an event that will be a viable story. Conjure up a promotion that will attract the attention of local news. Dig down deep until you determine exactly what it is about your business that you think is unique and exciting, and don't rest until you have communicated exactly that to the people you're trying to reach—your target audience. Reach them through the media, but always remember that the media are not your targets—their audiences are.

DAMAGE CONTROL

Once you've become aware of the top ten mistakes and taken steps to avoid them, you're in the clear, right? Not even close. Things can *always* go wrong, even when you've done everything right. Besides avoiding common mistakes, you have to know how to react to bad times. You need a strong damage control plan, and it must be in place before anything actually goes wrong.

Carly Simon had a hit song called "Anticipation." That's exactly what you need here. Damage control is all about anticipation, the ability to see problems coming, determine what problems might occur that you don't see coming, and be ready to deal with them before they hit.

Of course, each business has its own potential problems, and I can't possibly list everything that can go wrong for your business. If you're selling things via retail outlets, you're going to have one set of possible pitfalls. If you're offering a service, rather than a tangible product, the things that can go wrong will be very different. What's important is that *you* know what can go wrong and how to plan for the Murphy's law possibilities.

We can divide the potential pitfalls into two general categories: *technical problems* and *message problems*. The first group is much easier to tackle while you're still designing your website, choosing whether to hire a host service, and making your choice among the available services. The second group of problems is more directly under your personal control; your actions can have considerably more direct impact.

Technical Problems

In this chapter, we've already discussed what can happen if you choose the wrong host service for your website or if you design your website to be slow or confusing. But many technical problems can arise even if you make these choices correctly. Some of them can have just as devastating an effect on your business if you don't anticipate and provide for them.

For example, your system might crash. Remember the problem that ToysRUs.com had when its huge catalog went to 60 million people in one day, and the number of visitors to the website suddenly spiked beyond all expectations? The problem there was twofold: First, the company should have made sure there were enough backup servers to handle *any* possible capacity. Second and more important, the staff should have anticipated the increased demand.

Maybe there's no way to be ready for a huge onslaught of potential visitors to an E-commerce site, but any business should certainly know what its customer base looks like, and have an idea as to how many of its potential customers are likely to be shopping on the Internet. In a business like toy retailing, where such a huge percentage of gross sales happen between November 1 and December 31, there is no excuse for being unprepared when sales activity increases drastically—especially when you have made sure your website is prominently featured in a print catalog that your company is distributing to tens of millions of people in one day.

Estimate your best possible day for traffic on the Web. Triple that. Now double that. Now you're ready for traffic spikes.

Another potential problem in the technical area can come from following the rules of a good website: change and expansion of the site can cause downtime and glitches.

It's important, therefore, to build time into the process. Test everything and test it again before you make any changes to your site live. When something shows up on the visitor's screen, it had better be safely in the realm of the tried and true, even if it's the first day that visitor had access to see it.

To adequately anticipate any bugs in changes to your website, you have to have your site's software available at your business headquarters or be able to spend time at the host service where you have the site kept. Make sure to have your Web master or someone you trust from the host service with you when changes are being proposed, planned, and implemented. Before you spend time and money, find out what is possible and what is not. Make sure that the links work and that the renovation achieves the goals for which it was designed.

The smart guerrilla leaves nothing to chance.

Message Problems

It's much more common that something will go wrong with the way your message is disseminated. These are not techno-glitches that you can blame on your server, your host, or your hardware. These problems occur when you've neglected something or implemented a plan that was flawed from its beginning.

Levine's Lessons for Guerrillas: Lesson #9

There's no use crying over spilt milk. If you've made a mistake, own up to it, analyze it, figure out what you did wrong, then undo it. And most importantly: never make that mistake again. You're allowed to make new errors, but if you repeat one, you are part of the problem yourself.

Some of the pitfalls we find in this area have already been discussed. For example, you already know not to overhype your story, not to lie, and not to be too technical or use too much jargon. But sometimes your message just isn't getting across. Why?

It's possible you didn't communicate your message adequately from the beginning. Sometimes, those who have been working in a particular industry for an extended period of time tend to forget what it's like to be a "civilian" and not know the ins and outs of that industry. You have to remember that many, if not most, of the people who visit your site will be civilians, and they don't have the same background you do. Explain things in simple terms, and use the old formula: tell people what they need to know, tell them what you just told them, and then tell them again. Use words you would understand if you were listening to a lecture on a business other than your own. Use examples. Make sure it's simply impossible to misinterpret what you're trying to say.

At the same time, it's equally possible that someone has misinterpreted your message. That has the potential to be extremely dangerous. Word on the Web travels fast. If one or a few people think your company has done them wrong, or that what you've told them on your website isn't true, they can spread the word quickly, and to every corner of the World Wide Web.

Of course, the easiest way to anticipate this problem is to be crystal clear in your message. But that's not always enough. Some people will misunderstand or misinterpret, no matter how precise your language may be.

So be prepared for damage control. Have your company spokesperson ready to answer any questions that come through E-mail regarding your problem. And don't try to bury your head in the sand. If there's a vicious rumor going around about your company (something we'll explore in detail in Chapter 14), make sure your website addresses it prominently—on the home page, where everyone can see it. Rumors are made to be dispelled.

If you've made a legitimate error and posted something on your website that is incorrect, own up to it *immediately*. Don't deny, don't fudge, don't ignore it. Say, "We made a mistake, and here's the truth." It may not eliminate the possibility of damage to your company, but it will certainly minimize the amount of destruction that's done.

Portrait of a Guerrilla: Connie Connors, President/CEO, Connors Communications

Gathering publicity is a question of networking. You have to know who to call, where to find them, and what to say. You have to develop a network of contacts, which takes time and effort, and use that network to spread the word.

Nobody is better at networking than Connie Connors, whose public relations company specializes in emerging technologies and who worked with Amazon.com before everyone knew exactly what an Amazon was—or, for that matter, what a dot-com was. She's one of the reasons you know what those words mean today.

Connie is a consummate pro who knows her business inside and out. She also understands that sometimes things go wrong, and she has plans in place to deal with those times. Even though her clients generally have generous budgets, she knows guerrilla tactics and how to use them.

Her core philosophy is to build contacts with your unique circumstances in mind. "Almost every business has a core set of influencers in a particular niche of a particular industry," she says. Connie says *influencers* are the people to whom everyone in a particular industry goes for opinions and sage advice, and to convince the influencers in your industry that you are an expert takes you a long way toward getting favorable publicity.

"Your local councilman, any other high-profile business owners, local media—those are the people you want to get to first and say, 'This is what I'm trying to do,'" she explains. "Word of mouth is very important. If you have a restaurant in a certain town, a party for the influencers is a good guerrilla way to attract their attention."

Working with Amazon when it was new, Connie says much of the work was done on a grassroots level. "Our goal was to make them the poster child for E-commerce," she says. "We emphasized that it's impossible to search through thousands and thousands of books in a bookstore, but you could do it at Amazon."

The danger in websites, she notes, comes from not planning well enough and not anticipating changes and problems. "You have to have the foresight to see what's coming next," Connie says. "Business moves very quickly. Using the Web can increase even a local business's business by 500 percent."

Her rules for public relations on the Internet are simple: "Number one, you have to have a website. Number two, you have to have it searchable. Number three, it has to be linked to as many resources as you have in your community."

Advertising on the Web is something Connie says has proved to be less than useful. "Advertising as we know it on the Web is not viable. It isn't working now. There is a next generation [of Web advertising] out there somewhere, but we don't know what it is yet. The Internet will continue to be used more for marketing than advertising in the foreseeable future."

A website, she contends, is a very effective type of self-promotion. "People don't look at the website as a brochure, but it is a brochure, one that you can get lots of traffic from," says Connie. "You have to sell them; you have to tantalize them."

Connie can be found at www.connorscommunications.com.

What People Learned if They Read This Chapter and Didn't Skim

- Things can *always* go wrong. The trick is to anticipate what can go wrong, and do what the Boy Scouts do—be prepared.
- The top 10 mistakes made by guerrilla publicists are:

    1. Not being familiar with the publication or program you're pitching
    2. Creating a dull, unimaginative, hard-to-use website
    3. Choosing a hosting service badly
    4. Sending too much E-mail to an editor

5. Taking no for an answer
6. Not taking no for an answer
7. Lying to the press
8. Making your site too slow to download
9. Thinking the Internet is the only necessary medium
10. Publicizing a nonstory

- Choosing a host for your website should hinge on service. Ask questions about server capacity, technical support, and above all, the ability to anticipate and deal with problems.
- Don't be the boy who E-mailed wolf. Send a message only when you have a message to send.
- Don't take no for an answer, but don't be so stubborn nobody will ever speak to you again. Know when to quit and when not to quit.
- The Internet has a broad and far reach, but it doesn't reach everybody. Don't forget you want to be seen on more traditional media, and the Net can help you achieve that goal.
- Technical glitches may not be your fault, but they're your responsibility. Work with your host service to eliminate as many problems as you can, particularly when you're making widespread changes to your site.
- If your message isn't clear to the general public, you risk being misunderstood. Bad publicity comes from such situations. Be clear, and be honest.
- Make a list of influencers in your area and your business, and do your best to convince them that you're a serious player in your business. Then stand back and let them use their influence.

13

IT'S GOING WELL—NOW WHAT?

*"There are moments when everything goes well;
don't be frightened, it won't last."*

—JULES RENARD

Some people just can't handle success. They strive, sometimes for years, to achieve it, and when they attain the goal they've been seeking, they find they have no idea what to do next. Business history is full of examples of people and companies that worked like a charm, then fell off the face of the earth because nobody knew how to handle success. Bad choices were made. Expansion was too ambitious. Things happened too quickly.

But if you think that means success is something to avoid at all costs, I suggest you go back to page 1 and start over; you've missed the point of this book.

Let's illustrate: you have launched your website. You can now track the number of hits it receives and how many separate pairs of eyeballs that represents. You know there's interest, and there have been inquiries from the press about some press releases you've sent out and information you've E-mailed and posted on the website. Things couldn't be going better.

What to do next? Well, if you're driving down the highway at sixty-five miles an hour, you don't suddenly take your foot off the gas unless something is in front of you, right?

The best thing to do when things are going well is to keep them going well. That means you should continue the things that have gotten you this measure of success—careful planning, hard work, and a guerrilla's daring—but don't lose sight of the obstacles, and don't become complacent.

Levine's Lessons for Guerrillas: Lesson #10

A guerrilla is *never* satisfied. That doesn't mean you should make foolhardy choices and expand your business at a rate the market won't bear. It means you should never sit back and say, "It's going well now, so it will continue to go well." There's always someone right behind you with your company in his gun sights. Grow, continue, and strive for more, but in a well-considered, guerrilla style.

Retail chains are notorious for overexpansion. When they begin, most chains are striving to be different, to carve out a niche of the market by attracting a segment of the population that hasn't been directly catered to before. If the stores show a high level of profit, however, the temptation for a company to add more and more stores is inevitable.

Chains like Office Depot, Boston Market, Crazy Eddie, and many others have been forced to cut back on the number of outlets they own, and in some cases to go out of business altogether, because they tried to become too big too fast. The market will let you know very quickly when you have overstepped your boundaries. It's not always easy to recover, so it's a much better plan to let cooler heads prevail when you're successful and not try to take over the world. Most guerrillas have a goal in mind, and it's rarely so ambitious that it will send the company into a spiral.

When things start to take off, self-knowledge is key. Know who you are and what your company is, and have realistic goals. Take it a little bit at a time—a baby step here, a baby step there. Do not try to go from being a corner hot dog vendor to the next Microsoft in six months. Even if that were to happen, it would probably take so much capital to achieve that you'd never see any profit. That's one of the most common success mistakes made by business owners.

Five Major Success Mistakes

1. Overexpansion in response to unrealistic expectations
2. Failure to deliver what you promised
3. Refusal to acknowledge threats
4. No expansion as a result of timidity
5. Losing sight of the guerrilla credo (small steps, taken quickly)

As the name suggests, a success mistake is a miscalculation made because things are going well. These mistakes are common. They're easy to make, but they can be very difficult to undo. It's a much better strategy to avoid the common success mistakes before they happen to you. The trick is knowing how to recognize and avoid them.

OVEREXPANSION IN RESPONSE TO UNREALISTIC EXPECTATIONS

We've already discussed the risk of overexpansion, but it's important to note the words *in response to unrealistic expectations*. In these cases, the business has grown too quickly or too large because the business owner refused to acknowledge legitimate boundaries made by a reasonable market. A florist shop every square mile may be a reasonable expectation; two on every block is more than likely not.

Make sure you have studied your industry well, and don't let your current success blind you. Success is like a drug; it can get you feeling so euphoric that you forget the reality that brought you this far. Have a well-thought-out business plan, and no matter how well you do, stick to it. You'll grow, but you won't grow yourself out of the market. Guerrillas like to strike while the iron is hot, but not so much that they get burned.

FAILURE TO DELIVER WHAT YOU PROMISED

It's easy to get people interested in your business if you promise them things that seem to be too good to be true. The problem is, they most often are.

Imagine being offered a new car for $100. Loaded: air conditioning, automatic transmission, leather seats, CD player, and power everything. You'd take that offer in a minute, wouldn't you? And how long do you think the company that offered it would stay in business?

Make sure that your claims made in press releases, advertisements, and on your website are absolutely realistic. Be certain you can deliver everything you say you can deliver—and a little bit more. That's the way you keep a business successful. If you try to make a big splash by offering things that you know you simply can't provide, you're not only setting yourself up for a big fall, you may very well be committing fraud. It's best to avoid that.

REFUSAL TO ACKNOWLEDGE THREATS

When things are going well, who wants to think about the possibility that someone is watching, learning from your success, and planning to top it? The smart guerrilla, that's who.

It's a natural response to ignore unpleasant realities when your business is booming and things are rolling along. But it's a dangerous impulse, and one you have to resist at all costs. The enemy is always out there, lurking in the bushes, and if you ignore your enemy, you won't be the guerrilla who laughs last.

Keep vigilant. Remember that business has no natural end point; even if you've achieved the level of success you had initially hoped for, there's no reason not to set the bar a little higher and try to achieve more. But also make sure you're not leaving yourself vulnerable to attack. Keep those press releases coming out; make sure you still stage events and have a story to tell.

You still want press coverage, even if you've already had some. The oldest thing on this planet is yesterday's news, so you have to find a way to continue to be interesting and vital, and to make sure the media know about it. The media are the best avenue through which you can reach your customers. The Internet works to attract attention, and your website will inform that segment of your clientele that has the means and chooses to visit the site, but that's far from your entire potential customer base. You need news coverage, and the way to get it is through vigilance.

NO EXPANSION AS A RESULT OF TIMIDITY

If there's anything worse than a lazy guerrilla, it's a frightened one.

Too much expansion is clearly a problem. But no expansion at all, because you're afraid of doing too much, is just as serious a pitfall. It's easy to get paranoid, especially when you're aware that someone is waiting to ambush you at every turn. But you have to make sure that you don't fold your tent and give up before the competition even has a chance to do you in.

Remember, a guerrilla is always moving. Standing still is not our nature, and worse than that, it's bad for business. The key is to find moderation. Don't expand until you can't support the weight of the structure you've built, but continue to expand.

Small steps are important. With small steps, with the idea that you've achieved one level of success, so now you can implement your plan to achieve the next level, you can continue to thrive and grow your business. If you try to jump three steps, you will find yourself with nothing to grow. At the other extreme, if you don't move on to the next step, sooner or later, someone will come up from behind and pass you on the way to the step you should have taken.

A good guerrilla is disciplined. Now, don't assume that disciplined is the same as cautious or slow. It's not. It means that you need to keep a level head, keep the goal in mind at all times, and be watching in all directions. Keep your discipline, and you can grow at the proper pace for your business.

LOSING SIGHT OF THE GUERRILLA CREDO: SMALL STEPS, TAKEN QUICKLY

All this leads up to the concept of small steps, taken quickly. Trying to jump hurdles is too fast; waiting until something happens around you will immobilize you while others are passing you by.

If you remember those four words—*small steps, taken quickly*—you can capture the essence of this chapter. When success comes (and it will, if you use your guerrilla skills properly), you have to have your plan already in place. It must call for a series of steps, up a ladder, to be taken immediately. Begin the plan right away. But start with a small jump, from a one-store operation to a two-store business, let's say. Do all the same things for the second store you did for the first, but don't neglect the business that got you here. Keep paying attention to everything; that's a guerrilla's job.

When you find that you can handle both stores, it's time to implement the next step of the plan, which might be selling a limited number of franchises in your geographic area, say, two or three. Keep it local, and keep it small. You don't need to be McDonald's by the end of the week.

Every step of the way, keep the press releases coming. Keep planning events. Expand the website to include more information and interactivity for your customer base. Make use of every single guerrilla technique we've discussed. But not just for your expanded business. Do it for all your outlets. Make sure nothing is neglected, even as you hire more people. You don't have to micromanage, but you are responsible for the ultimate success of your business. Don't forget that.

Small steps, taken quickly.

ON THE WEBSITE

How should your website respond to success? In the same way. Make sure to change it periodically. Keep the pages that attract the most traffic, even if you change some of the graphics or update the copy. Discard the ones that are not seeing many visitors, except the essential pages (press room, contact us, basic company information, home page). Add interactive features. Add graphics and text. Add any information about your business as it evolves. Hold nothing back.

As the business grows, you'll probably want to hire on a *Web master*, someone who actually runs the site's technical end. The Web master does not control the creative end of the site but is responsible for implementing the ideas, making sure that software changes are compatible with the rest of the site and that everything works generally. A Web master is the person you would be if you wanted to take the time to learn everything about computers just for the purpose of running your own site. You may have the inclination, but few guerrillas have the time. The Web master, then, handles that end.

A *system operator*, or sysop for short, runs the computer server. Most of the time, the term refers to someone who keeps the peace on a bulletin board or in a discussion group, but it can sometimes mean the person with the responsibility for running a company's website. In contrast to a Web master, a sysop doesn't so much run the technical end. Rather, he or she contributes to the creative end, coming up with new ideas and answering site visitors' questions about the site itself, not the company. For example, if someone is having trouble downloading a certain page or needs a particular plug-in to make your site work and doesn't know how to get it, E-mail to the sysop will get the question answered.

The person who will answer questions about the company is still your company spokesperson. When your site is up and running, however, the spokesperson's duties expand to include answering E-mail about the company from visitors to the site and media members who might find E-mail the best avenue for a quick response. Your spokesperson should be well versed in all things about your company and should check his or her E-mail often. You don't want journalists or customers to have to wait long for a response.

Portrait of a Guerrilla: Alan Weiss, Ph.D.

At Summit Consulting Group, one of the most highly respected organizational development consulting firms in the country, Alan Weiss helps companies improve their nonfinancial, nontechnical skills. Summit specializes in executive coaching, improving innovation, and organizational restructuring or, as Alan puts it, "anything to do with improving people's performance."

These days, of course, a lot of that has to do with the Internet, and companies often come to Summit asking about online issues. So Alan, the company's president, is well versed in Internet considerations. He often consults with top companies on problems and solutions that begin and end online.

He sees the Internet as a helpful tool, but not the revolution some have touted. "People who say the Internet is replacing everything else are the technical people who see everything through that prism," he says. "People think we're in the middle of a digital revolution or an electronic revolution, but we're not. What we're in is the latest iteration of the revolution from Gutenberg called movable type. The hubris, the absolute arrogance that says this is anything far beyond that is crazy."

Given that, Alan still believes the Internet can be an enormously useful forum for companies. He recommends having a website that is user-friendly and easily manageable. "The Internet is more important for what I call passive marketing than aggressive marketing," he says. "It's important, for example, to have a good website and important to have professional-looking E-mail, important to have people find you easily on the Internet, because those are all credibility statements about you."

Using the Net as an advertising device, Alan believes, is worse than useless. "Nobody takes a drive on the highway to look at the billboards," he says. "They don't go on the Internet to do that, either."

The most important thing you can offer your customers via your website and your other Internet activity, Alan says, is value. "Value compels the visitor to return to the site and also to mention the site to others," he says. "If you have a new article free to download every month, or if you have '10 tips to do x' or links that are constantly changing, you are offering value. And you have to offer some kind of value, because even if they visit once, you have to answer why they should return."

Alan knows that speed on the Net is very important, but he believes other factors can be just as valuable to the online guerrilla. Chief among these are quality and targeting. Quality includes the idea of value but also means that the information and presentation on the website must be well developed and worthwhile to the user. Targeting is more specific, meaning that the online guerrilla should clearly aim at the most likely customer and tailor the information on the website and in press releases to that demographic.

"Targeting and quality can be more important than speed," he contends. "It's no good getting there firstest with the mostest if the people you're in front of don't care. Understand exactly who your prospective buyer is and what precisely you bring to them. You constantly have to ask, 'Who's the buyer?'"

The future growth of the Internet and promotion will be inevitable, Alan believes. There is no question that more people will become involved in the years to come. They simply won't have a choice, he says.

"The issue is whether someone will choose not to use the telephone today," he says, drawing an analogy. "In the future, ten or twenty years from now, you'll have to use the Internet, because the utilitarianism of it will be there."

Alan Weiss can be found at www.summitconsulting.com, and you can reach him by E-mail at alan@summitconsulting.com.

What to Do When You've Done Well

- When your business has found success on the Internet, it's not the time to sit back and bask in glory. Put the pedal to the metal, then pull back a little. Keep up a nice, steady speed.
- There's always another guerrilla coming up behind you. You have to keep moving.
- Adopt the guerrilla's credo: small steps, taken quickly.
- Success mistakes can sneak up on you when you least expect them.
- The five most common success mistakes are 1) overexpansion as a result of unrealistic expectations, 2) failure to deliver what you promised, 3) refusal to acknowledge threats, 4) failure to expand as a result of timidity, and 5) losing sight of the guerrilla credo (small steps, taken quickly).
- Your website has to respond to success, too. Expand. Change. Keep what works, and lose what doesn't—on a regular basis.
- You might need to hire a system operator (sysop) and a Web master. They can help with creative and technical website questions as your business expands.
- Your company spokesperson should be well versed in all the progress you make. He or she should answer E-mail regularly and promptly.
- Passive marketing is an Internet strength. People will find out about you from your website, but you shouldn't expect the Internet to do all the work for you. People have to be interested before they get there.
- Advertising on the Net isn't a high-payoff proposition. Nobody gets into a car and drives on the freeway to see the billboards.
- Value is necessary to a website. Offer visitors something they can use.
- Targeting is essential to a Web campaign or any promotion. You absolutely must determine your most likely customer and tailor your message and its medium toward that customer.
- Always ask, "Who's the buyer?"

14

IT'S A SMALL WORLD WIDE WEB, AFTER ALL

*"If you can keep your head when all about you are losing theirs,
it's just possible you haven't grasped the situation."*

—JEAN KERR

The Internet, as we've established, is a huge, complex, interconnected series of communications lines between people (or more
accurately, between computers) that shares information. Its size, if
it could be properly calculated, would be mind-boggling.

It's also a small town. People hang out the back window, they
gossip over the clothesline, they create and destroy reputations while
having lunch. Or, more precisely, the Internet is the largest collection of interconnected small towns ever devised.

Think of each newsgroup, each bulletin board, each posting on
each website as a means of conversing with people whose interests,
in one way or another, coincide with yours. Consider that every
time you send out a message, as long as it's not specifically made
private, it can be seen by friends, neighbors, and strangers literally
worldwide. Keep in mind that anything you read on the Net can be
read by millions of other people. Think of the number of messages,
posts, facts, figures, and opinions you read on your computer screen
every day.

Now assume that someone wants to make your life miserable.

Let's say someone is holding a grudge against you or your company. Someone with access to the Internet (which doesn't leave out many possible suspects). Someone who wants to cause you trouble, sully your reputation, cut into your sales, or just generally make things awful for you.

It could be a consumer who feels your product didn't perform up to expectations. It could be someone who simply feels like playing a prank. It could be a covert competitor, trying to cut into your market share or slow your momentum. After all, it's a guerrilla-eat-guerrilla world out there.

The fact is, it doesn't matter who might want to do you damage. If the desire is strong enough, and the knowledge of the Internet broad enough (it doesn't have to be very complete at all), it's very easy to do. Starting a rumor is about 400 times easier than stopping one once it gets out. Type, point, and click, and the next thing you know, a complete untruth can be zipping its way to computers in every country on every continent in the world.

Or try on another scenario: Maybe your company really has messed up in some way. Your product has a defect you didn't foresee. Your service plan doesn't cover a fundamental need. A member of your staff makes a statement to the press that offends some segment of the population. Sometimes, even companies with the best of intentions make mistakes. But once a story like that gets rolling on the Internet, it's dreadfully difficult to stop in its tracks.

All of a sudden this whole worldwide community doesn't seem so friendly, does it?

Don't panic. Damage control is what public relations was invented for. The Internet just adds a few new wrinkles and a few new advantages, both of which we'll examine in this chapter. But if you take nothing else away from this topic, remember two words—and they're the same ones the Boy Scouts use, so it should be easy: be prepared.

Once again, anticipation is worth pure gold here. Crisis management—and that's what this is—hinges on the ability of the guerrilla to respond in a heartbeat to a threat, be it real or imagined. And that ability, the speed you need, is going to be in direct proportion to the amount of preparation you've done ahead of time.

In other words, the better your plan and the more practice you have, the better your crisis response will be.

Crises come from two areas: from without and from within. Preparation is equally important, no matter which kind of crisis you confront. But the type of preparation will certainly differ.

THE EXTERNAL CRISIS

A crisis that comes from outside your organization is an *external crisis*. It can come from a competitor, a former customer, a disgruntled former employee, or from anyone or anywhere not within your organization. The most difficult thing about external crises is that they are utterly unpredictable; you get no warning signs, and you can't begin damage control until after the problem has become public.

That means your preparation has to be considerably more general than it would be for something that can come from within your company. You have to be ready for more varied circumstances, and you have to be ready to move quickly—remember, the Internet can send millions of messages about your company, either positive or negative, into the world in a split second.

Preparation

When a P.R. problem comes at you from outside, your course of action must be multipronged. First, you have to determine whether any charges made against your company are true. If they are, you'll be obligated to address them and come clean to the public. That'll involve your website, because, as we've said, your website is the one place you can be sure your message is getting out unedited and uninterpreted. The words you choose to use are the ones the public will see. You'll also send press releases to the media, but make sure the website responds immediately.

Why? Because in this technological age, your website is where the public will turn first. If people hear something negative about your company, they will go to your website because they don't want to wait for the story to show up on their local news. They don't want to wait through commercials, weather reports, and sports scores. If they're interested enough, they want their information *now*. So they're going to turn to your website. And that's an advantage, because it's your message, not that of the media, that the interested consumer will see first.

If the charges made against your company are false, if a rumor has been started that has no basis in fact whatsoever, your website will still disseminate the information before any other medium. It's an easier message to write, but a harder one to sell. The fact is, the public tends not to believe company spokespeople when a crisis hits. So press coverage, which the public sees as more credible, will be more crucial in this case.

That doesn't mean you should eschew the website for press releases. For one thing, journalists, like everyone else, will go to your website to see your response, and again, they will be able to see it in exactly the presentation you have chosen. The quicker you can convince reporters that your response is honest and the rumors are untrue, the faster they can bring that information to the public.

Your company spokesperson will be under siege at this point. You may have to have extra people answering phones, and you might even need the services of a public relations firm on a temporary basis, if the crisis is bad enough. But make sure the spokesperson who speaks to the press is from your company, that she or he is totally informed on the subject, and that a lie about this issue is never, ever issued from anyone in your company. Be assured: any untruth you tell *will* be uncovered by a journalist, and your reputation will suffer considerably more damage.

It is always, of course, a bad idea to make any kind of statement when an ongoing legal matter is at the center of your crisis, so that may complicate your strategy. Some other tips for crisis preparation include:

- Designate a spokesperson, and make sure to choose someone who copes well under pressure.
- Make sure there's space on your website, with at least a link from your home page (it's better if the space is actually on the home page) to present your response to the crisis.
- Have a list of journalists with whom you've established a good relationship, and "leak" the news to them before other reporters. But do it anonymously—in other words, make sure the reporter doesn't quote you by name as giving out information other media members don't have.
- Talk to your employees before any press statement is made *anywhere*—even on your website. Make sure they understand the situation, so everyone can be on the same page when media inquiries begin. If your business is too large to talk to all the employees at once, at least be sure to send E-mail to everyone.
- Establish good relationships with some reporters, who might give you a little warning before airing or printing a major story. In crisis management, extra time is gold.

Execution

Preparation is the key, but after a situation develops, execution becomes imperative. You can't sit back and expect everything to work perfectly just because you've established contingency plans. You, as the head of the company, have to make sure you keep your finger on the pulse of the situation. Oversee all you can, and make sure you're available to answer questions from anyone inside your company. If you are the company spokesperson, you also have to be ready to field questions from the press.

The most important thing to remember is that the information you give out must be true. That, of course, means that you have to know the truth about the situation before you make any statements. If you don't already know when the story breaks, find out as quickly as possible via direct contact with the people in your company who might be involved. When the press asks a direct question, don't duck, just answer it.

This does *not* mean you have to shoot yourself in the foot by giving out more information than will help your image or divulging trade secrets that will give your competitors an edge. You're not required to say everything you know. Just answer the question in the most direct, honest way you can, then move on.

An Example of Managing an External Crisis

Suppose the information damaging your reputation comes from a completely external source, a consumer who makes trouble for you on an Internet bulletin board. This person posts messages claiming your product doesn't perform the way it's supposed to, and actually includes ingredients that are harmful to small children and pets.

You know this isn't true. But the word is spreading like wildfire, you've gotten thousands of phone calls in the past two hours, and some of them are from reporters demanding to know whether there's going to be a recall of your product.

This is where your preparation comes into play. Your company spokesperson immediately begins weeding out the press phone calls and E-mail from the messages that come from consumers. After all, the media will reach your customers faster than you can if you're communicating with the public one at a time.

You also draft, or have the spokesperson draft, a statement declaring in no uncertain terms that the rumor being spread on the Internet is absolutely false, that your product does exactly what you say it does, and that it contains nothing that is of any harm to anyone. You make sure the statement is posted on your website as soon as it's finished and approved. Then you call sympathetic reporters back and answer their questions, fax the statement, or direct the reporter to the Internet.

Once your statement has been leaked to a few reporters, it's time to draft and disseminate a general press release. Once again, you include the statement and direct consumers and the press to your website for further clarification. While the press release is being drafted, post on your website information about your product's purity and effectiveness, taken from your own research and any you might have on file from outside sources.

After all that information is in place, it's time to call the rest of the media representatives back and give out a few strong, honest quotes about the vicious rumor. State over and over again that it is absolutely untrue and that you have documentation proving so. Let the first few news stories run, see how the public (and, if your company is publicly traded, the stock market) reacts, and get ready for another round of interviews. If you tell the truth, and if the rumors really are unfounded, you should be able to ride out the crisis.

THE INTERNAL CRISIS

Sometimes, a situation that can damage your business's public relations (that is, damage your reputation) can come from inside your company. This is an internal crisis.

An internal crisis has a few advantages, in terms of crisis management, over an external one. The biggest advantage is that in most cases, you'll know about the situation before the press does. This is an enormous advantage, since it allows you more time to prepare for the oncoming questions, and more time to craft your response.

Internal crises generally come from one of two possible sources. One possibility is that a disgruntled employee leaks an unflattering story to the press anonymously. The other is a situation about your company's product, service, or internal structure that will alter the way the organization runs and may affect your dealings with the public.

The first type of crisis is more difficult to manage. For one thing, a leak to the press takes away the advantage of time on your side, since you won't know the problem is about to become public until very little time is left. Also, because human emotion often takes over in these cases, the desire to smoke out the source of the information may overshadow the problem at hand, which is dealing with the crisis and the way it will appear in the press.

If a press leak comes from inside your organization, fight the impulse to investigate the source. There will be time for that after you've put the best face on the situation. Work instead on crisis management as described for external crises. Get the facts about the situation. If you have indeed done something wrong, make sure you own up to it in a statement, and do everything you can to repair the defect or the misbehavior. Don't lie to the press or the public. Get your website up and running with your statement, in which you apologize for the problem and explain exactly what is being done to rectify it. Denying there is a problem is fruitless; the media will make sure it is publicized. You might as well do the best you can with what you have, and don't make matters worse with a cover-up.

This may be the best possible place to use the Tiffany Theory. Yes, you have to deliver bad news, but no, it doesn't have to sound awful. Wrap your message in Tiffany paper, make sure the message is true, and release it to the public the best way you can. The trick is to make as big a splash with your side of the story as there will be with the sexier, more inflammatory side the press will be leading with.

If your crisis comes from some problem or practice from within your company, not from an anonymous leak to the press, you have more time to prepare. You don't get to hide the problem completely, because if it's important enough to merit crisis management, it will eventually be discovered by some member of the media. But you *can* determine the timing of the revelation and the method by which the problem is revealed.

In this case, make sure your company spokesperson is well briefed in advance, since he or she will be the best person to explain the problem to the press when it becomes necessary. Then draft a statement using your best Tiffany paper, and determine when you should release it. If there's time pressure and you feel the news will become public soon, you can't wait very long. But if possible, time your statement late on a Friday afternoon or early evening, since fewer people read or watch the news on Saturday than any other day.

Of course, if the crisis involves a product defect that can harm people and you have to recall the product, you have to make the information available immediately, explain how the product will be repaired or altered to be safe, and make *that* the story. Remember how ToysRUs.com gave $100 gift certificates to online consumers who weren't going to get their Christmas presents on time? That's a perfect example of a company turning the announcement of a huge problem into a news story about how they were acting to rectify the situation.

The strong guerrilla has to stay in control of his or her emotions during a crisis; it's what guerrillas do best. Letting yourself give in to anger, despair, worry, or depression isn't going to help at all. The adrenaline rush of doing, putting on a push to get the coverage you need done the way you need it, is what keeps a guerrilla going. Crisis management is what a guerrilla was born to do. So go out there and do it.

Portrait of a Guerrilla: Craig Black, President, Blackstone Audio Books

No, Craig Black doesn't have a horrible crisis story to tell; his company, Blackstone Audio Books, is among the most renowned and respected suppliers of unabridged audio books in the world. But he does know how to promote, how to market, and how to use emerging technology.

Craig looks to the future and sees a time when public relations on the Internet will be the most mainstream, vital area of the P.R. process. And he knows the difference between public relations and marketing, a distinction few people can make in as articulate a manner.

"Public relations and marketing are closely aligned," he says. "Marketing is selling your product, and public relations is selling you or your company."

So if P.R. is the art of creating an image that makes your business more attractive, more friendly to the potential customer, Internet P.R. must be the art of making your business more friendly to those who frequent their computer screens for information and entertainment. Craig says that over the next ten years, the use of P.R. on the Internet will not only grow, it will evolve.

"Public relations on the Web is incredibly important. It's also a great opportunity," Craig says. "You have a chance through the Web to make people like you, or at least not dislike you."

Businesses must have a website, he maintains, admitting that his own website, www.blackstoneaudio.com, is not the most high-tech site on the planet. He does not believe in complicated, slow-to-download sites, no matter how sophisticated.

"One of the big no-nos is when you have an unclear home page," Craig states. "People are extremely busy, so when they click on your home page, they want to be able to get to the content quickly and easily. Don't make it take too long to load up. Most people don't have a lot of free time."

As the medium progresses, Craig expects that more and more specialization will occur. Eventually, consumers will be able to find very specific products and information, and companies will be able to tailor their messages and, in some cases, their product lines to consumers who have specific tastes.

"The future is tremendous, unlimited, because the Web allows you to design your message to a very specific group," he says. "We could eventually get to a point where [Blackstone] knows each of our customers who have a taste for, say, historical fiction. The Web is a medium, but it is unique in that it allows you to design very specific messages to very specific groups of people."

Craig has his own suggestion to add to the Guerrilla Commandments: "Thou shalt not confuse." He can be reached at www.blackstoneaudio.com.

What Can You Do in a Crisis?

- A P.R. crisis can be internal or external.
- An external crisis is most likely to come from a disgruntled consumer, an ex-employee, or a competitor, but it can come from anywhere outside your organization.
- External crises are more difficult, because they usually happen with no warning, so you should be well prepared to cover as general a situation as possible.
- First, you have to determine whether the charges made against your company are true. If not, gather information proving so.
- In a P.R. crisis, the public will look to your website first. Make sure your statement is there as soon as possible and states clearly what your company's reaction to the crisis will be.
- Also alert the press. Outside media carry more credibility than statements made from within your company, so press coverage will be crucial.
- Designate a spokesperson.
- Make sure there's enough space on your website.
- Have a list of journalists with whom you've established a good relationship. Leak the information to them before other reporters.
- Talk to your employees before any press statement is made anywhere—even on your website.

- Establish good relationships with some reporters, who might give you a little warning before airing or printing a major story.
- *Never* lie about the situation, to the public or the press.
- Use the Tiffany Theory to tell your story.
- In an internal crisis, the bad publicity is usually generated by a disgruntled current employee or because of a flaw or mistake made in your business.
- Internal crises give you more time to prepare, but you still have to make a statement to your consumers and the press.
- All the same steps apply in internal and external crises. Make sure the website has correct information, and disseminate that information to the press.
- Answer all questions honestly, but don't give away unnecessary information that can damage your business.
- Make it very clear that your company is taking steps to resolve the situation, and make sure the public knows what those steps are.
- The Internet makes it possible to tailor a public relations message to a very specific audience. Use that ability to cater to your consumer.

15

SPREAD THOSE WINGS
AND SURF!

"Eighty percent of success is showing up."

—WOODY ALLEN

There comes a time when the mother bird has to push her babies out of the nest. This may seem cruel to humans, but without that motion, the small birds might never find their way out into the world to live their lives.

That's the way it is with guerrillas, too. Now that you have gotten through the entire process of *Guerrilla P.R. Wired*, you have to leave the nest (that is, the comfort of studying theory with this book) and get out there into the jungle. Keep the dangers of the jungle fresh in your mind, because there are predators and natural disasters out there. But you don't need to be afraid, because you have your guerrilla training behind you, and you know how to handle any situation that may come up.

Still, there are a few things left to learn before you close the cover of the book and begin your own chapters in the Guerrilla Chronicles. There is nothing a promotional campaign needs so much as momentum, and in this chapter, you can learn about how to develop momentum, and how to keep it going. Consider it the last piece of advice before that gentle beak nudges you to spread your wings and surf the Net for publicity.

Levine's Lessons for Guerrillas: Lesson #11

Somewhere along the way, you're going to make a mistake, because everyone on the planet does. Your momentum will evaporate, and you'll be back at a standstill. If that means that you fold your tents and give up, you're not a guerrilla. You're a sheep. The whole point of guerrilla marketing is to keep going, no matter what. There's always a way to continue, to persevere. Some of them have been outlined in this book; others you'll have to make up on the fly. But if you've learned anything by reading this book, you've learned that there are always options, and the practiced guerrilla will know one or invent one when needed.

WHAT IS MOMENTUM?

Everybody thinks they know what momentum is. But very few can clearly define it; they just know it when they see it. Or, more accurately, when they *feel* it.

Webster's defines *momentum* as "a property of a moving body that the body has by virtue of its mass and motion and that is equal to the product of the body's mass and velocity; broadly: a property of a moving body that determines the length of time required to bring it to rest when under the action of a constant force or movement."

Well, that's not terribly helpful, but notice the constant references to a "moving body." In terms of business, that means an organization that's already had some success. You can't have momentum if you're standing still, so you have to have your promotional campaign up and running before you can count on that wind at your back to boost you through.

In a baseball game, when the team that's behind scores a run and draws closer, the announcer will often say, "The momentum in this game has shifted." It doesn't have to be a tangible thing. Momentum is a feeling, the idea that suddenly Nature or Fate is on your side, the planets have aligned in your direction.

Some momentum comes from pure luck. That's not the kind we're talking about here. For purposes of *Guerrilla P.R. Wired*, momentum is the product of hard work and intense preparation. It is manufactured, not caught or bestowed. It is everything you've read about in this book. It comes to you because you know your guerrilla training. What you need to know now is how to keep your momentum once you have started it rolling.

To a certain extent, it's easy. Momentum, by nature, is hard to stop once it gets going. But because this is the type of a roll that comes because you've created it, your momentum in P.R. is more under your control. That's good news and bad news: If you do everything right, you can stay on this good streak. But if you make even one crucial mistake . . .

HOW TO KEEP
THE MOMENTUM GOING

Once your campaign begins to succeed, the steps come easily. Remember that big follows small, and a local newspaper story can lead to one in a larger publication, a guest spot on a radio talk show, or eventually, exposure on a TV program, still the P.R. holy grail, in that it reaches more people with more power than any other public relations placement.

So let's examine a possibility. Let's say that our Baltimore T-shirt store has gotten some exposure, through the clever "Free T-Shirt on Your Birthday" promotion. A local weekly wrote an article about that, which turned into a profile of the business in the feature section of the Baltimore *Sun*.

How does our store keep the momentum going? You can't simply wait for the electronic media to notice the print story. As soon as that article hits the streets (or before, if you can get an advance copy), you've got to be poised to capitalize on the publicity.

The first step is to utilize your website. Immediately on publication, find out if the newspaper is going to include the article about your business on its website (the reporter may know or will know who to ask). If they are, create a link to the URL for your story, and put it on your home page. Make sure as many people see that story as is possible.

If the newspaper is not using your story on its website, scan a paper copy of the article into your computer, and upload it onto your website directly. It is a good idea to seek the newspaper's permission before (or at least while) posting an article online since most newspaper articles are copyrighted. A link to the newspaper's website posting will not require permission. If you don't want to put it on the home page, create a link to the copy right away. That will get as many eyeballs on the story as you can quickly.

But that alone will not manufacture more press coverage for your business. Keeping your momentum going will be a matter of sweat and hard work, and you have to act, in the best guerrilla tradition, very quickly. Use the following steps as a guideline for staying on top of your campaign once you have generated some press.

1. Make tearsheets of the article(s).
2. Create a new promotion that will serve as the centerpiece of a new press release.
3. E-mail the press release to media on your E-mail list.
4. Include in the E-mail a link to the Web address (URL) for your article.
5. Mail a press release, including the Web address for your article.
6. Check E-mail you receive about the article, making note of any press contacts.
7. Follow up on the press release and E-mail by making phone calls.
8. Have another promotion in mind, just in case. Make sure any news stories generated from your company are exploited.

The process is the same as ever, but you'll have it running concurrently with your first promotion. In other words, you're milking the first promotion for all it's worth while beginning to pitch the second and planning the third. It becomes difficult to keep all the balls in the air, but with enough planning, it can be done, and it can work beautifully.

If your first promotion has not generated any press coverage, and your momentum has not begun yet, you still have to have the second and third ideas ready to go. On the Web, this is a subtle process that seems to have cross-purposes: generating buzz while appearing to do nothing.

The idea is to make one promotion, or guerrilla campaign, blend into the next seamlessly. You don't want your loyal website visitors to feel there's been a dramatic switch in direction on the site or in your company, since that might send the wrong signal. (Drastic changes in a company's image—and your website is a large part of your public image—often mean turbulence inside the organization and can make outsiders think something's wrong.)

How does a guerrilla move from one campaign to the next without signaling a problem? It's an art, but one that can be learned. On your website, it's a question of changing things a little at a time, and never starting with your home page.

Because the home page is the first thing your visitors see, and because it's the welcome mat for your company on the Internet, it's important to change it periodically but not drastically or so often it seems you don't know what your image should be. This is where your consumer base finds the personality of your company. If you change your home page from top to bottom every day, you're going to appear to have multiple personalities.

This doesn't mean you can *never* change a thing on your home page. That's absolutely false and would be horrible advice. News updates, for example, should be added as often as possible. However, you should only periodically overhaul the look of the page, its structure, and the way it works. Those changes should occur no more than a couple of times a year.

Luckily, there are other places on your website that can be changed more frequently. The other pages on your site, which provide information in more specific areas, can have overhauls pretty often, so long as their look conforms to the rest of the site. These are places where you can start adding hints and teasers for upcoming promotions and news stories that you don't want to announce immediately.

For example, let's say you're about to begin a T-shirt alliance with a local rock band. You're going to be the exclusive supplier of shirts for their concert dates, their fan club and, yes, their website. That's a good news story, especially if the band has been attracting attention outside your area and may eventually become a national name.

You start by linking to the band's website before you announce the deal. Then you place hints on any pages devoted to music-related shirts. Perhaps you could post a small graphic with the band's logo and the words *Watch this space!* or a listing offering their latest shirt but not mentioning that it's an exclusive product.

Remember that during all this activity, you're still running your first promotional campaign, hopefully getting some press coverage about that. Your announcement about the band contract is still waiting, to come when the publicity from your first promotion dies down.

When you're ready to announce the contract, the first thing to do is issue the standard press release, and be sure it is posted in the press area of your website. At that time, post an announcement on your home page (for maximum visibility) and go through the usual press lists—who likes pitches via E-mail, who prefers fax or snail mail, who responds to telephone calls. Your first campaign will have taught you much of this information, and you might even have some contacts waiting for your next promotion. This is the time to cash in those chips.

In the back of your mind, of course, is the information about your *next* campaign being planned. You're about to put a teaser on your website about that, and you have another idea for something that might attract some interest . . .

It's an ongoing process. And it can't ever end entirely. Guerrillas always have a trick or two up their sleeve, always keep another round of ammunition in their belt. If one thing doesn't work, the next one will. If this campaign didn't raise your level of visibility but kept it at the same height, that's not a defeat; it's a smaller victory.

Your goal should always be to broaden your appeal just a little bit, one step at a time, from tiny weekly newspaper to appearances on all network talk shows in one week. But don't expect anything to happen overnight; smart guerrillas know they won't take over the world in a week. But if you can pass one competitor in market share, if you can get from a placement in that tiny weekly to a local daily, you have made progress, and that's what momentum is all about.

COMMUNITY

There has been a lot of talk in this book about "building a sense of community" and "the Internet community." It's hard to be even casually involved with the Web without running into that idea. Community on the Net is difficult to explain but inescapable once you begin exploring, and before you know it, you're a part of a community—in fact, many communities.

The people who spend time on bulletin boards, in chat rooms, and with newsgroups have chosen to become part of those communities, those groups of people who share a common interest and are devoting their time to discussing it. Personal relationships have begun on the Internet. Business deals have been done. Deaths have been mourned, and births have been celebrated. There have been close friendships forged between and among people who have never met each other face-to-face in their lives.

Much fun has been made of those who spend their time in front of computer screens, communicating with others from other cities, states, or countries. But they aren't all that different from the old ham radio operators, whose consuming passion was for talking to those in other places and making connections.

When you're trying to publicize your business, in one way or another, on the Internet, you are becoming part of a community, and you are joining that of others. You are a guest everywhere but at your own website. Keep that in mind, and behave as a good guest should. Don't insult the locals, since they are your hosts (and your potential customers). Don't condescend to them. Treat them as peers, and invite them to your home (page), where they will be treated like the honored guests they are.

But since you are also trying to create some viral marketing, you are trying to create and build your own community on the web. Give people something around which they can rally. Give them something they'll want to recommend to their friends.

The creators of *The Blair Witch Project* didn't think they were doing something revolutionary by creating a website for their movie; they are children of the Internet age, and it seemed like a natural progression to have a presence there. What *was* revolutionary—the thing that earned them the first seats in the *Guerrilla P.R. Wired* Hall of Fame—was their bravery in promoting a product (their film) by never mentioning that it even *existed*. They understood the concept of viral marketing well enough, and had enough enthusiasm for their movie, that they could do that.

But another concept was at work, one that subsequent attempts to duplicate *Blair Witch*'s success have lacked: The filmmakers had strong respect for the community toward which they were marketing their film and aiming their website. They knew that if they told their story in a way that was intriguing enough, they could trust the community to pass the information along. That's an incredibly bold step for people whose careers were hanging in the balance before they could begin. If it had gone wrong—if, for example, they had tried to hide the fact that their story was a fictional creation and had pushed the "myth" too far—it could have been a disaster.

Since they respected the intelligence of the people who would find something interesting in their story, Dan Myrick and Ed Sanchez made the right choices. They never mentioned the movie, but they never denied that there was one and that it was entirely fictional.

The community paid them back in spades. Viral marketing reached new heights as the website took off with virtually no promotion at all. Eventually, the film's success at the Sundance Festival led to more interest, and the rest is film history. Like it or hate it, *Blair Witch* made tons of money for the studio and began the careers of its creators on a very high note.

Respect your community. Trust your target audience. If you deliver what you promise, they'll take you where you want to go.

Portrait of a Guerrilla: Mark Vega, Information Technology Attorney, Greenberg Traurig

If there are five preeminent law firms in the country that specialize in matters involving the Internet and news media, Greenberg Traurig is one of them. And Mark Vega, the firm's resident expert in information technology (IT), is the man to talk to about high-tech communications, E-mail, Internet matters, and other high-tech legal questions.

In other words, he knows the Internet inside and out. He's seen it grow and has watched the issues swirling around it. And Mark has insight into the present—and the future—of promotion and marketing online.

"The Internet environment is the most volatile environment we have ever experienced in technology or media," he says. "It's so heavily influenced by investment markets and investment sectors, more than any other medium we know of. The landscape changes once a month, once a week, sometimes every other day. I wrote an article yesterday and said, 'The information you read in this article may only be good for as long as it takes you to read the article.' It's almost that fast."

Although he wasn't involved in *The Blair Witch Project* in any way, Mark, like everyone else in the entertainment and online industries, watched the phenomenon closely. He interprets its success as a revolutionary and groundbreaking event.

"In hindsight, everyone involved in the project from the Artisan side [the film's distributor] will tell you [the website] was an incredibly important element that got people into the theaters, and they're going to tell you they did it all themselves," he says. "But the reality was the public relations firm that took on that project, without money, on the come, put a lot of hard work and effort into getting that picture recognized and submitted to the Sundance Festival. Because of the guerrilla style of independent film, it is apropos."

But what made the film's website work, he continues, is the fact that it had an identity of its own, independent of the movie itself. "They made it all the more interesting by making it possible to be intrigued by the Blair Witch story without ever seeing the film at all," he marvels. "What they did was slap up all they could and could not use to make the film interesting, and created all the more mystery by making the website be an entity unto itself."

That site illustrates, Mark says, the basic idea of P.R., online or off. "If you can capture those people [your target audience] and get them interested in you and/or your product in a way that's not offensive to them, and in a way that is not forced upon them, you've taken the first step toward getting new customers."

That phrase—in a way that is not forced upon them—is crucial. It's why Mark is such an adamant opponent of spamming, and why he says companies must take care in compiling and using their E-mail lists, adding names of only those people who have expressed some interest in your product or service.

"Public relations is not unsolicited mailers," he says. "Public relations is targeted mailers and targeted contact with people who might help you and/or your business because they're interested in you and/or your product."

That's why Mark's suggested Guerrilla Commandment is one you've seen a number of times in this book: "Thou shalt not spam." Beyond that, he says, the only rule is, "There are no absolutes."

"Once [people] realize that P.R. online is as important as P.R. offline, I think we'll start to see some standards jumping forward," he says. "I think we'll start to see some rule we can accept as a given. I think we'll start to see some programs that really work that will attract customers."

You can find Mark on the Web at www.gtlaw.com.

Pay Attention! There May Be a Test on This Material!

- Momentum is the feeling of inevitability that occurs once a project or operation starts on the right path.
- To create momentum, a guerrilla can have one promotional campaign running, another beginning, and a third in the planning stages.
- Maintaining momentum involves eight steps:

  1. Make tearsheets of the article generated by your publicity campaign.
  2. Create a new promotion that will serve as the centerpiece of a new press release.
  3. E-mail the press release to media on your E-mail list.
  4. Include in your E-mail a link to the URL for your article.
  5. Mail a press release, including the Web address for your article.
  6. Check E-mail you receive about the article, making note of any press contacts.
  7. Follow up on the press release and E-mail by making phone calls.
  8. Have another promotion in mind, just in case. Make sure any news stories generated from your company are exploited.

- Moving from one promotional campaign to the next on your website should be seamless. Begin your new campaign while the original one is still ongoing, with small teasers and hints on interior pages.
- Wait to announce your new campaign or news story on your home page until after the first promotion has run its course.
- Use links to direct those interested to the websites of publications that have featured your business, or post the article on your own website and add a link to that page.
- On the Internet, a community is a group of people sharing an interest. You can join one via bulletin board or chat room, or help create one via your website.

- Respect the community you're targeting. Give its members something they want on your website.
- Public relations is not about blanketing people with unsolicited E-mail. It is about targeting *interested* individuals and giving them the information that you hope will intrigue them so they look more closely at your business.

16

A GUERRILLA QUIZ

"How much is that guerrilla [sic] in the window?"

—OGEE, *THE MAGILLA GORILLA SHOW*

See? I *told* you there'd be a test on this material!

It's time to go back over the rules, concepts, and techniques we've discussed, to make sure you're ready to go out into the jungle and face the quicksand traps and ferocious cheetahs lurking behind every tree. Consider it your final exam from the University of *Guerrilla P.R. Wired.*

Give yourself five points for each correct answer. We'll tally up at the end. And in case you need to go back and check, the questions are arranged in order of the chapters from which they've been taken. Good luck, guerrilla!

Chapter 1

1. All of the following words belong in the Guerrilla Dictionary *except*: (a) fastest; (b) excuse; (c) always; (d) will.

Answer: (b). There are no excuses.

2. The most important weapon in the guerrilla publicity war is: (a) speed; (b) creativity; (c) technology; (d) all of the above.

Answer: (a). The two speeds for Guerrilla P.R. wired are: fast and dead.

3. Publicity on the Web is about: (a) you; (b) your company; (c) your customers; (d) none of the above.

Answer: (c). It ain't all about you. If you're creating a website and generating publicity to feed your ego, perhaps you're in the wrong line of work. Have you considered acting?

4. Sending out promotional E-mail to thousands of people who haven't requested information about your company is: (a) bold and daring; (b) absolutely horrible and not permitted in the *Guerrilla P.R. Wired* world; (c) called "spamming"; (d) both (b) and (c).

Answer: (d). Even if Spam is your favorite lunch meat, spam is a complete and total no-no in the world of promotion. Potential customers can be completely turned off to your company, which is, I feel compelled to point out, a bad thing.

5. The lifeblood of the guerrilla is: (a) innovation; (b) speed; (c) creativity; (d) all of the above.

Answer: (a), (b), (c), or (d). The chapter reads, "Innovation is the lifeblood of the guerrilla," but each of these qualities is vital. Give yourself five points for any of the answers.

6. Public relations is the art of "offering people reasons to persuade themselves." This means that: (a) it's the same as advertising; (b) P.R. gives people all the facts and lets them decide; (c) P.R. gives the people selected facts and offers a gentle nudge in one direction; (d) all of the above.

Answer: (c). We are not Madison Avenue, but we're not ABC News, either. Our job is to persuade with the truth.

7. The Tiffany Theory states that: (a) something bought at Tiffany's is better than something bought at Kmart; (b) a gift delivered in a box from Tiffany's will have a higher perceived value than one in a box of less value; (c) a publicity campaign should be modeled on the movie *Breakfast at Tiffany's*; (d) none of the above.

Answer: (b). The key is perceived value. If you deliver your message wrapped in a Tiffany design, or in a positive "wrapping" of compliments and optimism, you'll get farther than you will with cold, hard truth.

8. Because a website allows you to wrap your message any way you want, the Tiffany Theory: (a) applies to the Internet in ways it never could with traditional media; (b) is less applicable on the Internet; (c) requires outside media attention to work on the Internet; (d) has to have moving graphics.

Answer: (a). You can include pictures, charts, quizzes, and raffles if you want, but the best thing about the Internet is that you control the information and the Tiffany wrapping that covers it.

9. *The Blair Witch Project* Web campaign worked in large part because: (a) the movie had already generated lots of great buzz; (b) the movie was really scary; (c) no witch was shown on screen; (d) no mention of the movie was made on the website.

Answer: (d). Believe it or not, the ability to create a community of *Blair Witch* fans and have *them* publicize the movie to their friends—an example of viral marketing—was key to the Web success of *Blair Witch*.

10. Public relations is: (a) sending out press releases; (b) getting attention for you or your business; (c) controlling the perception of yourself or your business; (d) all of the above.

Answer: (c). While the other three answers could be part of what P.R. is about, the best working definition of the process is (c). Public relations is giving your side of the story to as many people as you can.

11. The following is *not* one of Levine's ten commandments of Internet P.R. for guerrillas: (a) Thou shalt not overspend; (b) Thou shalt not spam; (c) Thou shalt seek out and provide links; (d) Thou shalt choose none of the above.

Answer: (d). The first three choices are three of the commandments. If you need a refresher course, the other seven are in Chapter 1.

Chapter 2

12. The World Wide Web is: (a) a spider-centric tourist attraction; (b) the same as the Internet; (c) one part of the Internet; (d) an Internet service provider.

Answer: (c). The Web is the "www" in many Internet addresses, and it includes mostly public-access sites. About 45 million people access it every day.

13. Areas of the Net where people can post and read messages about specified topics are called: (a) newsgroups; (b) bulletin boards; (c) both (a) and (b); (d) none of the above.

Answer: (c). Newsgroups and bulletin boards are great places to gain a reputation as an expert on your subject, but you can't try to sell a product or service on them.

14. The only area of the Internet where products and services can be offered for a fee is: (a) the World Wide Web; (b) Amazon.com; (c) any URL ending in ".org;" (d) none of the above.

Answer: (a). The prefix "www" stands for World Wide Web. The suffix ".com" stands for commerce. You can't try to sell people something in newsgroups or on bulletin boards; they'll get mad at you. E-mail is a different matter (although recipients might still get mad at you, particularly if they haven't asked for information about your product or service).

15. Your website should be: (a) flashy and exciting to look at; (b) a living brochure for your company; (c) changed every day; (d) easy to use and quick to download.

Answer: (d). Nobody will see your fabulous graphics and streaming video if they don't sit in front of the computer long enough to download your website. Make it come up fast and be easy to use.

16. A good website should *not* include: (a) company information; (b) links to other sites; (c) a search engine; (d) a press room.

Answer: (e) none of the above! Trick question! All those things should be on a good company website.

Chapter 3

17. Overload of information has created: (a) the Magilla Gorilla Syndrome; (b) the Mr. Magoo Effect; (c) the Tiffany Theory; (d) Bill O'Reilly.

Answer: (b). The Mr. Magoo Effect is characterized by a vague understanding of input, because we can't retain every fact that's thrown at us in the course of a day. A good guerrilla publicist knows how to capitalize on the Mr. Magoo Effect.

18. When trying to attract media attention: (a) small follows big; (b) attack big and small at the same time; (c) big follows small; (d) small is irrelevant.

Answer: (c). Big media outlets often get ideas from small media outlets. If you can place your story with a small newspaper or radio show, it's possible larger markets will be alerted and follow up.

19. You can't sell everything to everybody. In marketing, it's important to identify: (a) a target demographic; (b) the limits of your local reach; (c) your product's limitations; (d) all of the above.

Answer: (a). Give yourself half points for (d). A target demographic includes the type of person most likely to be interested in your product or service. By determining who your target demographic might be, you can make it easier to target your publicity campaign to the people most likely to become your customers.

20. In creating your website, you should *not* give one-third of the budget to: (a) development; (b) maintenance; (c) marketing (promotion); (d) none of the above.

Answer: (d). Each of those three factors should control one-third of the website budget.

21. Data smog is: (a) a type of air pollution over Silicon Valley; (b) a contributing factor to the Mr. Magoo Effect; (c) a mishmash of information collected during the course of an average day; (d) both (b) and (c).

Answer: (d). Because data smog combines all the information a person encounters in the average day and blends it together, it makes understanding and remembering all that information much more difficult. This leads to the Mr. Magoo Effect.

Chapter 4

22. The number of websites now exceeds: (a) 42 million; (b) 68 million; (c) 116 million; (d) 4.2 billion.

Answer: (c). Any way you slice it, that's a lot of opportunity for a guerrilla publicist. (Note: If you answered (d), wait a few years.)

23. A core audience is: (a) a TV news program's viewership during the dinner hour; (b) the demographic most likely to show interest in your product or service; (c) the same as an ancillary customer; (d) none of the above.

Answer: (b). Your core audience is the center of your target's bull's-eye. The outer rings are ancillary customers, who might be interested if your message is presented properly.

24. Make links with related websites by: (a) placing a link to their website on your home page, without asking; (b) paying a fee; (c) E-mailing owners of websites you think are compatible; (d) all of the above.

Answer: (c). The proper request, stressing how your link will help the *other* website, will help you get the link you need.

25. You can be listed on search engines by: (a) submitting your Web address in the proper area on the search engine's website; (b) paying a submission service a fee of less than $100; (c) both (a) and (b); (d) none of the above.

Answer: (c). It's important to be listed on search engines, to attract as many Web surfers to your home page as possible. But either do it yourself, or pay a low fee. Don't spend a huge amount of money on something that can be had for less.

Chapter 5

26. Because big follows small, you should always: (a) aim for the biggest, then work down; (b) buy clothes that are too big for you; (c) start with a small goal and work up; (d) always sweat the details.

Answer: (c). Start with a local news goal and work your way up. Give the outlets with larger audiences as many places to discover you as possible.

27. All the information in a press release: (a) should be included in your website's press room; (b) should discuss only the story you're trying to place; (c) is made up; (d) none of the above.

Answer: (a). The press area of your website will be there a long time. Make sure every press release that is still current (that is, anything in which the information is still true) stays posted.

28. Press releases should be sent: (a) the day they are written; (b) via E-mail; (c) via snail mail; (d) both (b) and (c).

Answer: (d). It doesn't matter whether you send the release out as soon as it's written, unless you're responding to a crisis. But you do have to send it by E-mail to media outlets that prefer E-mail, and by snail mail or fax to those that don't read E-mail pitches.

29. The following is *not* a rule of the buyer/seller relationship: (a) find out what the buyer wants; (b) lower your price; (c) both (b) and (d); (d) get it to them.

Answer: (b). There are a buyer and seller in every business relationship. The fundamentals of the relationship from the seller's point of view are to find out what the buyer wants and get it to him or her. And you're the seller.

30. If an editor says he or she can't use your story, try to: (a) convince the editor of the story's merits; (b) pitch another story; (c) maintain the relationship for the next assault; (d) none of the above.

Answer: (c). You can try to point out the story's news value, but an editor doesn't want to be begged, and your odds of changing the editor's mind are, at best, slim. Live to fight another day.

Chapter 6

31. The following is *not* one of the steps in a successful guerrilla raid: (a) package a news story toward the media outlet you're targeting; (b) create a colorful brochure that explains your story and include a gift for the editor; (c) alert the media outlet to your news story; (d) add fresh information to your website.

Answer: (b). Flashy press materials and small gifts have their place in P.R., but not on a guerrilla raid. Guerrilla P.R. is down and dirty, not cute and frilly.

32. You should always hear the voice of your customer, asking: (a) "How much does it cost?"; (b) "Who are you?"; (c) "What's your Web address?"; (d) "What's in it for me?".

Answer: (d). You're in business to serve your customers. It's not about you, it's about them. And if you're constantly asking yourself how you can help your clientele, you'll end up serving yourself more efficiently.

33. An editorial gatekeeper is: (a) an editor or producer who decides which news is covered and which isn't; (b) the person who opens the gate at the entrance to the newspaper offices or TV studio; (c) the editor who decides which editorials and opinion segments are used; (d) none of the above.

Answer: (a). The person you have to convince first is the gatekeeper. The gatekeeper answers to his or her audience or readership. Figure out what the audience wants, pitch it to the gatekeeper, and you have a very good chance of making a placement.

34. Gatekeepers especially appreciate: (a) publicists who get to the point; (b) publicists who don't call during the deadline crunch; (c) publicists who actually read the publication or watch (listen to) the program; (d) all of the above.

Answer: (d). Editors and producers are people like the rest of us. If you appeal to their needs and preferences, your chances of getting publicity go up.

35. One guerrilla raid should lead to: (a) four news placements; (b) two news placements; (c) another guerrilla raid; (d) none of the above.

Answer: (c). A guerrilla campaign isn't a one-shot deal. Have a second raid planned and ready before the first is executed.

Chapter 7

36. A website must be: (a) easy to use; (b) easy to use; (c) easy to use; (d) all of the above.

Answer: Give yourself five points.

37. Your page will download too slowly if it includes: (a) too many graphics; (b) more than 40K of material; (c) a slow server; (d) all of the above.

Answer: (d). Streamline, but not to the point that your website looks cheap and boring. Make sure you're using your memory economically.

38. To avoid boredom: (a) put nude pictures on your website; (b) change the content periodically; (c) use lots of red; (d) none of the above.

Answer: (b). You don't have to completely overhaul the site every day, but change the content as often as possible to keep regular visitors interested. "Throw in a grenade" and change the site fundamentally once in a while.

39. Links should be limited to: (a) twenty per page; (b) five per page; (c) ten per page; (d) one per page.

Answer: (c). It's not a hard-and-fast rule, but more than ten will start to be confusing to the visitor, and that's certainly not something you want.

Chapter 8

40. You can find addresses and phone numbers for media gate-keepers (or at least their companies): (a) on the company's website; (b) in trade publications; (c) in the phone book; (d) all of the above.

Answer: (d). There are plenty of places to find addresses, phone numbers, fax numbers, and E-mail addresses for the gate-keepers you need to reach. Use all of them, including the public relations reference books you can find at your local library.

41. Some gatekeepers don't read E-mail pitches. You should: (a) send them E-mail after E-mail until they see the light; (b) disguise your E-mail as something else; (c) send them a fax or letter, or call them on the phone; (d) none of the above.

Answer: (c). Being tricky can work for some guerrillas, but not in this situation. Find out how the gatekeeper prefers to receive pitches, and send yours that way. Why add another obstacle to the process?

42. What's most important is: (a) to get the placement on this story; (b) to establish a relationship with the gatekeeper so you can live to pitch another day; (c) to reach the widest number of gate-keepers with one E-mail; (d) none of the above.

Answer: (b). Don't miss the forest for one tree. If you get this story placed but the gatekeeper never returns your phone call again, you have won the battle and lost the war. Step back and remember you will need this gatekeeper again.

Chapter 9

43. The Mr. Magoo Effect can help you create goodwill among site visitors by: (a) delivering *more* than the site promises; (b) contributing to the data smog; (c) blinding the visitor to your site's drawbacks; (d) all of the above.

Answer: (a). If your site is so well designed and packed with information that even muddled Mr. Magoos can find what they want there, you will have gone a long way toward establishing a good reputation on the Web.

44. Free-for-All (FFA) websites that can link any site to any other site: (a) are great for a cash-strapped guerrilla; (b) will tarnish your Tiffany image; (c) will be developed in the future; (d) none of the above.
Answer: (b). It doesn't cost so much to get links that you should link up with any site anywhere that might align you with a business that doesn't fit your image. Be selective in choosing your links, and use the Tiffany Theory.

45. How many hits your site receives: (a) is as important as any factor in website publicity; (b) isn't as important as the demographic of the people who are visiting; (c) can be counted by a person with 10,000 toes; (d) all of the above.
Answer: (b). You're aiming at a target audience. If 35,000 people visit your site every day, and only 35 of them are potential customers, you have not achieved success.

Chapter 10

46. You should be able to raise some capital for your website through: (a) a bake sale; (b) paid links; (c) affiliate programs; (d) none of the above.
Answer: (c). An affiliate program compensates you for a small percentage of any transaction done on another website, if the link from your website sent the other business that customer. If you can make such an agreement with another (preferably larger) company, you can generate some income.

47. If disaster strikes: (a) deny, deny, deny; (b) impose a media embargo; (c) use the Tiffany Theory; (d) don't hide, invoke damage control.
Answer: (d). Even if you haven't done something wrong, hiding will make it seem like you have. Denial is appropriate only if it's honest. Create a message, and use it.

Chapter 11

48. Viral promotion is: (a) a campaign that counts on the public to spread the word; (b) a way to promote medication; (c) an E-mail virus to avoid; (d) none of the above.

Answer: (a). Think *Blair Witch*. The idea of telling a story and letting an interested public spread it is the P.R. wave of the future. Ride the wave.

49. The inverted pyramid is: (a) a seventies game show with Dick Clark; (b) a description of a news story's structure; (c) one of the Eight Wonders of the World; (d) both (b) and (c).

Answer: (b). The inverted pyramid reminds publicists and journalists to put as much information at the beginning of a news story as possible, to avoid the reader stopping before he or she reaches the important facts.

50. Thou shalt not: (a) overspend; (b) send an E-mail with a heading in ALL CAPS; (c) waste a gatekeeper's time; (d) all of the above.

Answer: (d). All good advice.

Chapter 12

51. The following is *not* a valid reason to choose a host for your website: (a) clean, tidy offices; (b) server capacity; (c) technical support; (d) contingency plans.

Answer: (a). If your host can handle your needs, will offer 24/7 tech support, and has plans in place to deal with problems, the neatness of the host's offices is irrelevant. But you might want to check the seat before you sit down.

52. Traditional publicity routes off-line are: (a) unnecessary; (b) ready to be phased out; (c) still viable; (d) none of the above.

Answer: (c). There's no sense in ignoring television, radio, and print. They reach far more people than the Internet, and are still the most used sources of information, although that may change in another generation. If it does, I'll write another book.

53. Influencers are: (a) a high-tech weapon found in James Bond movies; (b) an association of high-tech decision makers; (c) drugs; (d) people in your local area whose opinions sway others.

Answer: (d). Frankly, if you answered anything *but* (d), you worry me. Persuade influencers that you are a serious player in your business, then let them use their influence to help you.

Chapter 13

54. The guerrilla's credo is: (a) praise the Lord and pass the bananas; (b) small steps, taken quickly; (c) big follows small; (d) none of the above.

Answer: (b). Don't try to do too much, and don't waste a lot of time taking steps. Have a strong plan, and put it in motion when you're ready.

55. A sysop is: (a) the guy who makes your glasses; (b) the person who operates your server; (c) the person who provides technical support; (d) none of the above.

Answer: (c). A system operator (sysop) is usually a person who hosts bulletin boards and newsgroups and tends the server. Together with a Web master, a system operator can be a very important website employee.

56. People find out about you via your website. This is called: (a) passive marketing; (b) an incredible stroke of luck; (c) the Mr. Magoo Effect; (d) viral marketing.

Answer: (a). Because the potential customer may not be actively seeking a company like yours but finds it anyway because of your website, the process is called passive marketing. But only those who have some interest are likely to find your site and use it.

Chapter 14

57. An external crisis is likely to come from: (a) an unsatisfied consumer; (b) an ex-employee; (c) a competitor; (d) all of the above.

Answer: (d). External crises can come from anywhere, but your plan already has to be in place in order to deal with one effectively.

58. Before you post a reply to a crisis on your website, you should: (a) have a good, stiff drink; (b) talk to your employees; (c) talk to sympathetic media members; (d) all of the above.

Answer: (b). Your employees need to be briefed before there's any response. A company spokesperson must be designated, and all communication should be through him or her.

Chapter 15

59. Momentum is: (a) a term used in sports; (b) a new Sylvester Stallone movie; (c) the feeling of inevitability that occurs once a project or operation starts on the right path; (d) something that can be created from nothing.

Answer: (c). Half points for (d). It's extremely difficult to *create* momentum, but possible. It's much more common to have it going and maintain it through the proper steps.

60. The following is *not* one of the steps in maintaining momentum: (a) make tearsheets; (b) E-mail the media; (c) send out copies of previous news coverage; (d) none of the above.

Answer: (d). All these steps should be taken to keep momentum flowing.

Scores

0–25: It's very important that you start reading this book again from page 1, right now.

26–50: You were skimming. Now read the whole thing.

51–75: You're not a guerrilla yet. Maybe you're a plebe at the academy.

76–100: Don't start a guerrilla raid. Stock up on supplies and read about Che Guevera.

101–125: You absorbed some of the information in the book. Do more research on websites you go to regularly.

126–150: You're starting to show some promise. Next time, maybe we'll give you a gun with ammo in it.

151–175: You can come along on a guerrilla raid, but you're not the leader. Pay attention.

176–200: You graduated from the Guerrilla Academy! Congratulations!

201–225: You are an official guerrilla. Maybe you could look back on a couple of chapters to upgrade your technique a little.

226–250: Very impressive. You're officer material for sure.

251–275: Wow! A guerrilla raid leader!

276–300: You're an expert! Call me, I might have a job opening.

CONCLUSION

*"Let me tell you the secret that has led me to my goal.
My strength lies solely in my tenacity."*

—LOUIS PASTEUR

We have come a long way. Hopefully, you've learned something about making your splash in the world and doing it your own way. I can only tell you about the rules; it is up to you to bend or break them as your needs dictate.

But if you put down this book with only one thought, let it be this: The only thing you can be sure about is you. Your strengths and your talents will determine how far you can go, and as long as you don't ever give up on yourself, you always have a brighter future.

Keep in mind this old Japanese proverb: Fall seven times; stand up eight.

Good luck, Guerrilla!

Michael Levine
levinepr@earthlink.net
Los Angeles, California

Appendixes

APPENDIX A

THE WOODS ARE FULL OF GUERRILLAS: AN EXCLUSIVE INTERVIEW WITH DANIEL MYRICK, COWRITER/CODIRECTOR, *THE BLAIR WITCH PROJECT*

"When you have a choice between the truth and the myth, print the myth."

—BILLY WILDER

As described in Chapter 1, *The Blair Witch Project* may be the defining moment for Guerrilla P.R. wired. Admittedly, as Daniel Myrick, one of the film's writers and directors, points out, a movie that makes it to the Sundance Film Festival didn't do that strictly on the merits of its website. But there's no denying that the ingenious Web publicity campaign for *Blair Witch* was a touchstone for Guerrilla P.R. practitioners, driving home the scope and influence of the Internet with a power that hadn't even been imagined before.

Because it is such an important event, I think you should read about the anatomy of the *Blair Witch* campaign from the man himself. Here's a talk I had with Dan Myrick, the cowriter and codirector (with Eduardo Sanchez, for their company, Haxan Films). Myrick explains and defines the concepts of Guerrilla P.R. wired through the practice of possibly the most successful campaign ever conducted on the Web.

Michael Levine: There are various and sundry stories about the genesis and development of the original *Blair Witch* website. How did that actually come about?

Daniel Myrick: We came up with the idea to do a website pretty early on, about six months before we went to Sundance. I had met with John Pearson, who had a show called *Split Screen* on the Independent Film Channel, which highlighted film shorts, and he was coming down here to Florida to shoot a segment for that. I got hired as a shooter [cameraman] on that. So at that time, we had an eight-minute trailer for *Blair Witch*, which was a mini version of the movie, a mock documentary, and he bought it hook, line and sinker. He aired it on the show, and that generated a huge response on his "Grainy Pictures" website. Everyone on his website was saying, "How can I get more information? Who is Haxan Films, and who are these guys?" and so on. That prompted us to start a website which basically encompassed all the mythology. Ed Sanchez had some experience in developing and designing websites. We threw all the material onto the website that we had shot for this eight-minute trailer.

ML: So the exposure on one website led you to develop your own website?

DM: That's right. We just kept expanding on the mythology, and that went on for months. The website helped generate all of the pre-Sundance buzz. Artisan picked it up after they saw it, and they took the website as well.

ML: You made the decision not to mention the movie at all on the website. Wasn't that risky?

DM: The website didn't reference the film at all in the early days because it was all about the mythology. Once [the film] got into Sundance, we were faced with that dilemma: do we tell people this is just a movie, or do we play this off as real, or what? The decision we made was that we wouldn't hide the fact that it was just fiction. So all the interviews we did in the trade magazines, we described in detail how we made this film, and we let the website just be ambiguous. People who wanted to find out the truth could pretty easily look around and find out the truth that it was all fiction. Those who wanted to remain immersed in the mythology wouldn't find anything on the website that would point to the fact that it was a fictional feature film.

ML: Did you decide that based on the fact that people had believed in the trailer, or did you factor in the idea that your audience for this movie would be people who spend a lot of time on the Internet and are interested in scary stories, so you'd cater to them? Which came first, the chicken or the egg?

DM: That's a really good question, because the Internet for us wasn't a big step. We're part of that whole generation of people who have the emerging Internet mentality. It was a really cheap way for us to raise awareness about our film. It was motivated by economics, for the most part. It was just $40 a month to have a website. We could do it ourselves. We could throw it up there and be one click away from Universal's website. It was the great equalizer. That was a real cheap way for us to generate a fan base. The interactivity of the Internet ended up being this undiscovered potential. Our fans were able to interact with us, and it became such a huge tool for us, but we didn't anticipate that at the beginning.

ML: You were just looking for an inexpensive way to get the word out.

DM: Yeah. People seemed to be interested based on the response from the John Pearson show. The way it kind of ballooned into this big, deep, interactive mythology didn't happen until later.

ML: Were you surprised by it?

DM: Oh, yeah. Totally. You have to keep in mind, we shot for eight days in the woods in Maryland on a $400 video camera. Really, what do you think your expectations are for something like that? Theatrical release? No, probably not. Maybe we'd get on cable. It would be kind of a cool HBO thing if we were lucky. We had no idea, even up to the release of the movie, that there was such a following for the film.

ML: How did you generate buzz for the website? How did people find the *Blair Witch* website for the first time?

DM: At first, you just throw something up and see if it sticks. The *Split Screen* show was really instrumental in getting the initial awareness going. *Split Screen* airs in New York on the Independent Film Channel, so you get a lot of film people watching it, film geeks like us. They all tuned in, and they were all tuning into the "Grainy Pictures" website, and we steered them to ours, so we had this initial following.

ML: Was there a one-click link from "Grainy Pictures" to the Blair Witch website?

DM: Yeah, there was a link. Then we started having a couple of fan sites pop up. Jeff Johnson, who did our first fan site, called a phone-in show in L.A. and said, "Hey, man, this is a cool, scary website; tune into it," so they tuned in and brought the website up on the air, and our hit count went up by ten thousand hits in one day. From there, it started growing and growing. Once we were finally finished with the film and had a final cut, we distributed that around, and that also had on the end of it our website address, pointing people to the website. But at first, it was just a gradual climb for the first few months, then we had a spike when they did that radio interview, and once it hit Sundance, it just went berserk.

ML: How many hits were you getting at that point?

DM: Oh, we were up to eight million hits or something by then. And then Artisan took our basic website design and stripped it all down and started again. Now we were on a national level, and we've got millions of people looking at it, so let's start at the beginning again and just keep adding to it, as they keep orchestrating this publicity campaign toward the eventual release of the movie. They took the basic idea of the original website, stripped it down, and built it up again, and I think that was really effective.

ML: What changed at that point on the website?

DM: Not much in content. We literally E-mailed them all the things we had on the original website. It was basically design. They had a little slicker design, technically upgraded. It had some music in it. The original site was a bit more raw, which was kind of the way we liked it.

ML: Because it looked more real?

DM: It looked less corporate. It didn't look like anybody trying to promote a movie, or anything. It still was an effective site; I don't want to take anything away from Artisan. They made it a bit more approachable on a broader scale. They used the same material we had before, down to the time line we had typed up for it.

ML: Do you still get people who think it was all real?

DM: Yeah, occasionally. Usually foreign people who may not have had all the exposure to the press that we had here in the States. Occasionally I get an E-mail from somebody overseas who asks if the filmmakers survived, and do we ever hear from them? They're still buying it, it's real, and that's pretty amazing that it's still holding up.

ML: *Blair Witch* was the first time something like this had been done, and it worked like a charm. Do you think it can still be done, now that the Internet is so much more pervasive, and given that *Blair Witch* set the standard? Is it still possible to catch so many people so off guard?

DM: That's the big question. In some sense, people compared what we did with *Blair Witch* to *War of the Worlds*. We just happened to do something more than just the website or just a movie. People were ready for *Blair Witch*. So much of it had to do with timing. I think people are really savvy now, but I don't think that precludes someone coming up with a really clever, creative way to market a mythology or idea they have that just takes people by storm. There really is no rule and no limit. That's the beauty of this business.

ML: It's the beauty of the Internet, as well. That something like this can be done for virtually no money, and anybody can do it.

DM: It's really pretty profound. We've never had this kind of accessibility in the history of mankind. There are no rules right now, and that makes it pretty exciting and scary at the same time. That's what was great about *Blair Witch*, that it came so out of left field, and nobody was expecting it. I don't think there'll be another *Blair Witch*, but there will be something different.

ML: Still, you could have the greatest website in history and a really strong marketing plan, but if the movie wasn't any good, it wouldn't have worked.

DM: I like to try to remind people of that. You have to have some merit to get into Sundance. That was the first step. The fact that people went to the movie. Not everyone liked it; it certainly polarized audiences. But the people that liked it *loved* it. So the film has got to pay off. The hype is only hype until people see the product. If it pays off for people, you've got a real success story on your hands; otherwise, it's just a flop.

Dan Myrick can be found on the Web at www.haxan.com.

APPENDIX B

MAGILLA GUERRILLA:
AN EXCLUSIVE INTERVIEW WITH
CABLE NEUHAUS, EXECUTIVE EDITOR,
ENTERTAINMENT WEEKLY

*"If I were to begin life again, I should want it as it was.
I would only open my eyes a little more."*

—JULES RENARD

"I think, therefore Descartes exists."

—SAUL STEINBERG

When Time Warner Magazines launched *Entertainment Weekly* in the early 1990s, the Internet was a vague, esoteric issue that was supposed to become part of our lives one day in the future. But my good friend Cable Neuhaus, the magazine's general editor and director of its new media coverage, knew better then, and he knows better now.

Cable oversees all coverage of the Internet, including website reviews, coverage of online chats, and features devoted to the technology and content on the Net. Like every good journalist—and Cable is a *very* good journalist—he knows his beat inside and out. And here, he offers some opinions, facts, and insights that very few people on the planet could possibly bring to the table. He also talks freely and candidly about the process of pitching—and in his case, receiving pitches about—news stories. Cable pulls no punches, so hang on.

Michael Levine: You've been a magazine editor for quite some time now. What changes have you noticed over the past few years in the magazine business, as it relates to the Internet and public relations?

Cable Neuhaus: More and more firms are pitching via the Internet, obviously. But fortunately, some of these firms solicit my preference as to whether I want to get pitches via E-mail. And if not E-mail, then what is the best alternative method.

ML: To which you say what?

CN: I say, "Anything urgent, feel free to use my E-mail address to pitch me." If it's not urgent, it may not be the best method for me.

ML: What is the best for you when it's not urgent?

CN: Plain old U.S. mail is just fine. Faxes are fine. The problem with E-mail is that it all looks kind of alike when it shows up on your desktop. If you're getting tons and tons of this material, you have to make a decision as to what to open up and what to read. Some of it, I must tell you in all honesty, I will delete before I open it. A lot of these will say in the subject line that it's a P.R. pitch. They don't try to come in under the radar. But if it's a P.R. firm I've never heard of, or a firm I don't respect, or a firm that in the past has pitched me stories that clearly were way off the mark, I will very frequently just delete those messages without ever opening them.

ML: You're pretty assiduous about responding to people.

CN: If I feel there's a need to. I don't feel any responsibility to respond to P.R. pitches that just come in over the transom.

ML: How much E-mail do you receive in a day?

CN: A busy day is a hundred E-mails for me.

ML: What percentage of those would be from outside your company?

CN: About 55 percent.

ML: So you get a tremendous amount of external E-mail.

CN: Yeah. But the internal E-mail I'm going to read.

ML: Is that coded in such a way that you can tell what's from inside the company?

CN: Yes. I can tell.

ML: What about websites? How have websites changed the process of public relations from your point of view?

CN: Some firms, not that many, have websites, and they encourage you to go to that. But I must say, I haven't seen that much of that, and if I haven't, probably not too many people have. This is my business. Very few P.R. firms have websites. In fact, often I will talk to the head of a company, and they will inquire of me as to whether or not they should bother, make the investment. I think it's a good idea if you have a good website and you maintain it on a daily basis.

ML: What defines a good website?

CN: That depends on what function you have in mind for your website. If you're trying to attract clients, that's one thing. If you're trying to attract my attention, that's another. Those are two different things.

ML: Let's say a P.R. firm or a company is trying to attract your attention. What would be a good website, and what qualities would it have?

CN: You should have a component of your website, and a prominent component, that's marked "news" or "hot list" or something like that. You have to update it *all the time*, because if I see old material, I'm not going to go back. You should remind me about this website, because I'm not going to come in every morning thinking about your website.

ML: So you have to give reasons to continue to visit.

CN: Yeah, perhaps an E-mail, or something like a letter, a press release, reminding me that you have a website, and here's the address, updated daily with information that might be valuable.

ML: What about the ability to navigate quickly? How important is it to you that a website not have too many bells and whistles, and simply give you what you need?

CN: You know, bells and whistles aren't important when you're trying to talk to an editor. What's important is information. Most websites these days, business-to-business websites, are fairly smartly done. Most people have figured out that editors don't want to wade through tons of beautiful pictures to get to the information. They are really more informational.

ML: At this point, minorities and senior citizens are not very well hooked up to the Internet. This may be a little out of your area of expertise, but do you think that will change in the next decade?

CN: Oh, yeah. I think so.

ML: Television and mass communication are the most powerful media to promote a product or service. How would someone attract news coverage through a website, other than the obvious example of the *Blair Witch Project*?

CN: The movie industry is really starting to figure this out. They understand storytelling better than most of us. It's not like A&P, the supermarket, which might have a website. They're storytellers; that's what they do. Unlike novelists, who might focus on the written word or the story, moviemakers are very visual, as well. They think three-dimensionally, so the movie industry has been very aggressive and fairly smart about promoting films online. The smartest are the ones who use what is called viral marketing.

ML: OK, we've already discussed this in the book, but can you give me a good working definition of viral marketing?

CN: Viral marketing is where you plant a sort of seed on the Web, and it becomes something like a game that is very interactive. People pick up your game or your device or contrivance, and they on their own will forward it on to other people. They see something and send it to a friend: "Did you see that thing from this new movie;

it's so cool, you've gotta see it," and then I forward it to you. The movie company hasn't spent another penny on it, and now they've got people who are forwarding their messages basically to others who are going to be customers at the box office.

ML: So viral marketing is going to be a very important concept.

CN: Yes, viral marketing will probably become so commonplace before long that the term may not even apply anymore. Viral marketing has been pretty effective so far, but only a couple of industries have figured it out.

ML: You make the point that Hollywood has done so well with this because they are by nature good storytellers.

CN: Yes, and that they're very technically advanced and technologically adept. They are early adopters of this stuff.

ML: And you, as an editor, tell stories to your readers.

CN: That's part of what we do, but we also impart information.

ML: Yes, but you do use the story form, so for people who are trying to pitch you, it's important to get good at telling a story.

CN: That's always been true. It's no more true on the Internet. Big people can hire people who make a lot of money to do this for them. But small people and entrepreneurs should bear in mind that most people aren't as excited about what they do as they are. If they're selling really cool key chains and they're really amped up about their key chains, they've got to bear in mind that everybody in the neighborhood isn't going to be as amped up about their key chains.

ML: What are some of the mistakes you've seen publicists and entrepreneurs make in their use of the Web for public relations?

CN: Because it's so easy to do, people broadcast their messages to too many people.

ML: Spamming?

CN: Yeah. It's easy to send a message to a hundred people when probably it should be targeted to twenty. Also, I think a lot of these messages are way, way too long. I opened a bunch of them this morning, and I'd say many of them are too long. They're 250 words when they could have been 50. Some of them provide links to a website, which can be helpful.

ML: Can you recommend any websites where this sort of thing is done well?

CN: It's doesn't relate to public relations, but a website like www.salon.com does it well, because it's clean, fairly clear in terms of its navigation, and it's not so media rich that you have to have the top-end computer to get to all that it has to offer. Some people can't access all the bells and whistles because they don't have the horsepower.

ML: Your website is . . . ?

CN: www.ew.com. That's the magazine's website.

APPENDIX C

MEDIA OUTLETS

A well-equipped guerrilla needs information. If you want to contact gatekeepers in the media, you need to know where to look.

The following list identifies major media outlets and how to contact them. Media outlets that have no E-mail listings have E-mail forms on their websites for Internet correspondence. This list is the last piece of the puzzle you need. Now go out there and launch your guerrilla campaign!

GENERAL-INTEREST MAGAZINES

American Legion
www.americanlegion.com
575 N. Pennsylvania Street,
    #325
Indianapolis, IN 46204
317-226-7918
info@americanlegion.com

Cosmopolitan
www.cosmopolitan.com
224 W. 57th Street, Floor 4
New York, NY 10019
212-649-2000

Ladies Home Journal
www.lhj.com
125 Park Avenue
New York, NY 10017
800-374-4545
515-433-1018 (fax)

Newsweek
www.newsweek.com
251 W. 57th Street
New York, NY 10019
212-445-4000
webeditors@newsweek.com

People
www.people.com
1271 Avenue of the Americas
New York, NY 10020
212-350-1212
editor@people.com

Playboy
www.playboy.com
680 N. Lake Shore Drive
Chicago, IL 60611
312-751-8000
dearbp@playboy.com

Prevention
www.prevention.com
1901 Bell Avenue
Des Moines, IA 50315
1-800-813-8070

Redbook
www.redbook.woman.com/rb
224 W. 57th Street, Floor 5
New York, NY 10019
212-649-3330

Southern Living
www.southernliving.com
P.O. Box 62376
Tampa, FL 33662
800-272-4101
southernliving@customersvc
     .com

Sports Illustrated
www.si.com
Time Life Building
New York, NY 10020
212-522-3233
letters@si.timeinc.com

Time
www.time.com
1271 Avenue of the Americas
New York, NY 10020
212-522-1212
daily@timeinc.net

Woman's Day
www.womansday.com
1633 Broadway
New York, NY 10019
212-767-6418
212-767-5785 (fax)
womansday@hfmmag.com

INTERNET-RELATED MAGAZINES

Business 2.0
www.business20.com
5 Thomas Mellon Circle,
   Suite 305
San Francisco, CA 94134
415-656-8699
415-656-8600 (fax)
jdaly@business2.com

Computer World
www.computerworld.com
500 Old Connecticut Path
Framingham, MA 01701
508-879-0700
maryfran_johnson@computer
   world.com

E-Business
www.advisor.com
P.O. Box 429002
San Diego, CA 92142
858-278-5600
858-278-0300 (fax)

Fast Company
77 North Street
Boston, MA 02114
617-973-0300
617-970-0373 (fax)
100P@fastcompany.com

Industry Standard
www.industrystandard.com
398 Fifth Street
San Francisco, CA 94107
info@industrystandard.com

Info World
www.infoworld.com
155 Bovet Road, Suite 800
San Mateo, CA 94402
650-572-7341
mark_jones@infoworld.com

Internet Magazine
www.internet-magazine.com
Angel House
338 Goswell Road
London EC1V7QP England
020-7880-7438
020-7880-7441
subs@ecm.emap.com

Internet World
www.internetworld.com
CMP Media Inc.
600 Community Drive
Manhasset, NY 11030
516-562-5000
lsafina@cmp.com

Linux Magazine
www.linux-mag.com
P.O. Box 55731
Boulder, CO 80323
800-950-1974
editors@linuxmagazine.com

PC Magazine
www.pcmag.com
650 Townsend Street
San Francisco, CA 94103
415-551-4800
415-551-4813 (fax)
zdnetcare@zdcommunity.com

PC World
www.pcworld.com
501 Second Street
San Francisco, CA 94107
415-243-0500
415-442-1891 (fax)
pcwletters@pcworld.com

Smart Computing
www.smartcomputing.com
131 W. Grand Drive
Lincoln, NE 68521
800-544-1264
402-479-2104 (fax)
editor@smartcomputing.com

Wired
www.wired.com
660 3rd Street, 1st Floor
San Francisco, CA 94107
newsfeedback@wired.com

Wireless
www.wbt2.com
135 Chestnut Ridge Road
Montrale, NJ 07645
201-802-3000
info@sys-con.com

Yahoo Internet Life
www.yil.com
28 E. 28th Street
New York, NY 10016-7930
212-503-4782
212-503-4703 (fax)
yilmail@ziffdavis.com

OTHER MAGAZINES

Advertising Age
www.advertisingage.com
711 3rd Avenue
New York, NY 10017
212-210-0100
webinfo@adage.com

Adweek
www.adweek.com
1515 Broadway
New York, NY 10036
212-764-7300

American Baby
www.americanbaby.com
249 W. 17th Street, Floor 3
New York, NY 10011
212-645-0067

Architectural Digest
www.architecturaldigest.com
370 L'Enfant Promenade S.W.
Washington, DC 20004
202-646-7476
letters@archdigest.com

Atlantic
www.theatlantic.com
77 N. Washington Street
Boston, MA 02114
617-854-7700
letters@theatlantic.com

Automotive News/Auto Week
www.automotivenews.com
1400 Woodbridge Avenue
Detroit, MI 48207
313-446-6000
Kcrain@crain.com

Barron's
www.barrons.com
200 Liberty Street
New York, NY 10281
212-416-2000
editors@barrons.com

Billboard
www.billboard.com
1515 Broadway
New York, NY 10036
800-449-1402

Bon Appetit
www.bonappetit.com
6300 Wilshire Boulevard
Los Angeles, CA 90048
323-965-3600

Broadcasting
www.broadcasting.com
1705 DeSales Street, N.W.
Washington, DC 20036
staff@wn.com

Business Marketing
www.businessmarketing.com
740 Rush Street
Chicago, IL 60611
312-649-5401
312-649-5462 (fax)
ebooker@crain.com

Business Week
www.businessweek.com
1221 Avenue of the Americas,
   43rd Floor
New York, NY 10020
212-512-2511

Car and Driver
www.caranddriver.com
2002 Hogback Road
Ann Arbor, MI 48105
734-971-3600
editors@caranddriver.com

Communications News
www.communicationsnews
   .com
2500 Tamiami Trail N.
Nokomis, FL 34275
941-966-9521
941-966-2590 (fax)
lori@comnews.com

Country Living
www.countryliving.com
224 W. 57th Street, Floor 2
New York, NY 10019
212-649-3204
countryliving@hearst.com

Direct Marketing
224 7th Street
Garden City, NY 11530
516-746-6700
516-294-8141 (fax)

Discount Store News
www.dsnretailingtoday.com
425 Park Avenue
New York, NY 10022
212-371-9400

Ebony
www.ebony.com
Johnson Publishing Company
P.O. Box 690
Chicago, IL 60690
312-322-9250

Electronic News
www.electronicnews.com
350 Hudson Street, 4th Floor
New York, NY 10014
212-519-7685
jcassell@cahners.com

Elle
www.elle.com
1633 Broadway
New York, NY 10019
212-767-5800
editors@elle.com

Entertainment Weekly
www.entertainmentweekly
  .com
1271 Avenue of the Americas
New York, NY 10020-1300
212-522-1212
letters@ew.com

Entrepreneur
www.entrepreneur.com
2392 Morse Avenue
Irvine, CA 92714
949-261-2325
editor@entrepreneur.com

Esquire
www.esquire.com
1790 Broadway
New York, NY 10019
212-459-7500

Essence
www.essence.com
1500 Broadway
New York, NY 10036
212-642-0700

Forbes
www.forbes.com
60 5th Avenue
New York, NY 10011
212-620-2200
letters@forbes.com

Fortune
www.fortune.com
Time Life Building
New York, NY 10020-1293
212-522-1212
212-522-6412
letters@fortune.com

Gentleman's Quarterly
www.gq.com
350 Madison Avenue
New York, NY 10017
212-880-7901
gqmag@aol.com

Gourmet
www.gourmet.com
4 Times Square
New York, NY 10036
212-371-1330

Harper's Bazaar
www.harpersbazaar.com
1700 Broadway
New York, NY 10019
212-903-5000

House Beautiful
www.housebeautiful.com
1700 Broadway
New York, NY 10019
212-903-5084

Inc.
www.inc.com
38 Commercial Wharf
Boston, MA 02210
617-248-8000
editor@inc.com

Information Week
www.informationweek.com
600 Community Drive
Manhasset, NY 11030
516-562-5000

Mademoiselle
www.mademoiselle.com
350 Madison Avenue
New York, NY 10017
212-880-8800
mllemag@aol.com

Media Week
www.mediaweek.com
770 Broadway, 7th Floor
New York, NY 10003
646-654-5115
ldadamo@adweek.com

Modern Bride
www.modernbride.com
249 W. 17th Street
New York, NY 10011
212-462-3600

Modern Health Care
www.modernhealthcare.com
740 N. Rush Street
Chicago, IL 60611
312-280-3173
312-280-3183 (fax)
mhcedit@aol.com

Money
www.money.com
1271 Avenue of the Americas
New York, NY 10020
212-522-1212
money-online@money.com

Mother Jones
www.motherjones.com
731 Market Street, 6th Floor
San Francisco, CA 94103
415-665-6637
415-665-6696 (fax)
backtalk@motherjones.com

National Enquirer
www.nationalenquirer.com
5401 N.W. Broken Sound
    Boulevard
Boca Raton, FL 33487
561-997-7733
letters@nationalenquirer.com

New York
www.newyorkmag.com
444 Madison Avenue, Floor 14
New York, NY 10022
717-560-2001
nyletters@primediamags.com

New Yorker
www.newyorker.com
4 Times Square
New York, NY 10036
212-840-3800
212-286-5047 (fax)
themail@newyorker.com

Opportunity
www.opportunitymag.com
73 Spring Street
New York, NY 10012
212-925-3180

O Magazine
www.oprah.com
1700 Broadway
New York, NY 10019
212-649-3843

Outdoor Life
www.outdoorlife.com
2 Park Avenue
New York, NY 10016
katie.donovan@tmm.com

Parade
www.parade.com
711 3rd Avenue
New York, NY 10017
newspaperrelations@parade
.com

Parent's Magazine
www.parentsmagazine.com
PMMcustserv@cdsfulfillment
.com

Popular Mechanics
www.popularmechanics.com
810 Seventh Avenue
New York, NY 10019
212-649-2000
212-586-5562 (fax)
popularmechanics@hearst
.com

Popular Science
www.popularscience.com
2 Park Avenue
New York, NY 10016
212-481-8062
letters@popsci.com

Premiere
www.premiere.com
1633 Broadway
New York, NY 10019
212-767-5400
212-767-5450 (fax)
premiere@hfnm.com

Publishing News
www.bookzonepro.com
P.O. Box 9642
Scottsdale, AZ 85252
aphillips@bookzone.com

Rolling Stone
www.rollingstone.com
1290 Avenue of the Americas
New York, NY 10104
212-484-1616
letters@rollingstone.com

Rosie Magazine
www.rosiemagazine.com
800-451-2020

Saturday Evening Post
www.saturdayeveningpost
.com
1100 Waterway Boulevard
Indianapolis, IN 46202
317-636-8881

Science
www.science.com
1200 New York Avenue, N.W.
Washington, DC 20005
202-326-6400
science-feedback@forsythe
.stanford.edu

Scientific American
www.scientificamerican.com
415 Madison Avenue
New York, NY 10017
212-754-0550
editors@sciam.com

Self
www.self.com
350 Madison Avenue
New York, NY 10017
212-286-2860
comments@self.com

Seventeen
www.seventeen.com
711 3rd Avenue
New York, NY 10017
feedback@seventeen.com

Software Magazine
www.software.com
1900 W. Park Drive
Westborough, MA 01581
508-366-2031

SPIN
www.spin.com
104 E. 25th Street
New York, NY 10010
212-633-8200
goingpostal@spinmag.com

STAR
660 White Plains Road
Tarrytown, NY 10591
914-332-5000

Sunset
www.sunset.com
80 Willow Road
Menlo Park, CA 94025
650-321-3600
editservices@sunset.com

Teen
www.teen.com
8490 Sunset Boulevard
Los Angeles, CA 90069
310-854-2222
editor@teen.com

Telecommunications
www.tr.com
1333 H Street, N.W.
Washington, DC 20005
202-842-3006

Television Digest
www.1-news.com
2115 Ward Court, N.W.
Washington, DC 20037
202-872-9200

Town and Country
1700 Broadway
New York, NY 10019
212-903-5000

Travel and Leisure
www.travelandleisure.com
1120 Avenue of the Americas
New York, NY 10036
212-382-5600
letters@amexpub.com

Travel Weekly
www.twcrossroads.com
500 Plaza Drive
Secaucus, NJ 07094
201-902-1500
twcrossroads@cahners.com

USA Weekend
www.usaweekend.com
1000 Wilson Boulevard
Arlington, VA 22229
800-487-2956

U.S. News and World Report
www.usnews.com
1050 Thomas Jefferson, N.W.
Washington, DC 20007
202-955-2000
202-955-2685
webmaster@usanews.com

US Weekly
www.usmagazine.com
1290 Avenue of the Americas
New York, NY 10104
212-484-1616
usmagazine@palmcoastd.com

Vanity Fair
www.vanityfair.com
4 Times Square
New York, NY 10036
212-286-2860
vfmail@vf.com

Variety
www.variety.com
245 W. 17th Street
New York, NY 10011
212-645-0067
212-337-6977 (fax)

Video Magazine
www.videomagazine.com
460 W. 34th Street
New York, NY 10001
212-947-6500

Vogue
www.vogue.com
4 Times Square
New York, NY 10036
212-286-2860
feedback@style.com

Woman's World
270 Sylvan Avenue
Englewood Cliffs, NJ 07632
201-569-6699

Women's Wear Daily
www.womensweardaily.com
7 W. 34th Street
New York, NY 10001
212-630-4000

Working Mother
www.workingmother.com
230 Park Avenue
New York, NY 10169
212-551-9412
wmeditor@workingmother.com

Working Woman
www.workingwoman.com
230 Park Avenue
New York, NY 10169
212-551-9500
letters@workingwoman.com

WIRE SERVICES AND SYNDICATES

Associated Press
www.ap.org
50 Rockefeller Plaza
New York, NY 10020
212-621-1500
221 S. Figueroa
Los Angeles, CA 90012
213-746-1200
2021 K Street, N.W.
Washington, DC 20006
202-776-9400
10 S. Wacker Drive, Suite 2500
Chicago, IL 60606
312-781-0500
info@ap.org

Canadian Press
1825 K Street, N.W.
Washington, DC 20006
202-736-1100

College Press Service
P.O. Box 2831
Orlando, FL 32802
407-425-4547

NATIONAL TELEVISION NEWS AND TALK SHOWS

ABC World News Tonight
www.abcnews.com
212-456-7777

CBS Early Show
www.cbs.com
524 W. 57th Street, 7th Floor
New York, NY 10019
212-975-2824

CBS Evening News
www.cbs.com
212-975-3691
212-975-2161 (for WCBS)

CNN
www.cnn.com
One CNN Center
100 International Boulevard
Atlanta, GA 30348
404-827-1500

Entertainment Tonight
www.et.com
5555 Melrose Avenue
Los Angeles, CA 90038
213-956-4900

Fox Broadcasting Company
www.foxnews.com
10201 W. Pico Boulevard
Los Angeles, CA 90035
310-203-3442

Good Morning America
www.abcnews.com
1965 Broadway
New York, NY 10023
212-496-4803

Larry King Live
www.cnn.com
820 First Street, N.E.
Washington, DC 20002
202-898-7983

Late Night with David
    Letterman
www.cbs.com/lateshow
30 Rockefeller Plaza
New York, NY 10112
212-664-5908

Live with Regis and Kelly
www.regisandkelly.com
7 Lincoln Square
New York, NY 10023
212-887-3054

The Montel Williams Show
www.montelshow.com

NBC Nightly News
www.nbc.com
212-664-4444

Nightline
www.abc.com
47 W. 66th Street
New York, NY 10023
212-887-4995

The Oprah Winfrey Show
www.oprah.com
110 N. Carpenter
Chicago, IL 60607
312-633-0808

Public Broadcasting Service
www.pbs.org
1320 Braddock Place
Alexandria, VA 22314
310-203-3442

The Rosie O'Donnell Show
www.rosie.com
30 Rockefeller Plaza
New York, NY 10112

Sally Jessy Raphael
510 W. 57th Street
New York, NY 10019
212-582-1722

Today
www.today.msnbc.com
30 Rockefeller Plaza
New York, NY 10112
212-664-4238

The Tonight Show
3000 W. Alameda Avenue
Burbank, CA 91523
818-840-2222

USA Network
www.usanetwork.com
1230 Avenue of the Americas
New York, NY 10020
212-408-9100

ALTERNATIVE PUBLICATIONS

Austin Chronicle
www.austinchronicle.com
P.O. Box 49066
Austin, TX 78765
512-454-5766
512-458-6910
mail@austinchronicle.com

Baltimore City Paper
www.citypaper.com
812 Park Avenue
Baltimore, MD 21201
410-523-2300
410-523-3222 (fax)
editor@citypaper.com

Boston Phoenix
www.bostonphoenix.com
126 Brookline Avenue
Boston, MA 02115
617-536-5390
617-536-1463
letters@phx.com

Chicago Reader
www.chicagoreader.com
11 E. Illinois Street
Chicago, IL 60611
312-828-0350
mail@chireader.com

City Pages
www.citypages.com
P.O. Box 59138
Minneapolis, MN 55459
612-375-1015
letters@citypages.com

Cleveland/Sun Newspapers
5510 Cloverleaf Parkway
Valley View, OH 44125
216-986-2600
sun@sunnews.com

Creative Loafing
www.creativeloafing.com
750 Wiloughby Way
Atlanta, GA 30312
800-950-5623, extension 1060
steven.poyner@creativeloafing
.com

Dallas Observer
www.dallasobserver.com
P.O. Box 190289
Dallas, TX 75219
214-757-9000
letters@dallasobserver.com

East Bay Express
www.eastbayexpress.com
P.O. Box 3198
Berkeley, CA 94703
510-540-7400
510-540-7700 (fax)
infor@eastbayexpress.com

Isthmus
www.isthmus.com
14 W. Mifflin Street
Madison, WI 53703
608-251-5627

L.A. Weekly
www.laweekly.com
P.O. Box 4315
Los Angeles, CA 90078
323-465-9909
letters@laweekly.com

Maine Times
www.mainetimes.com
P.O. Box 2129
Bangor, ME 04402
800-439-8866
mainetimes@mainetimes.com

Metro Times
www.metrotimes.com
733 Antoine
Detroit, MI 48226
313-961-4060
feedback@metrotimes.com

New Times
P.O. Box 2510
Phoenix, AZ 85002
602-271-0040
feedback@phoenixnewstimes
    .com

Philadelphia City Paper
www.citypaper.net
123 Chestnut Street, 3rd Floor
Philadelphia, PA 19147
215-735-8535
adinfo@citypaper.net

Riverfront Times
www.riverfronttimes.com
6358 Delmar Boulevard,
    Suite 200
St. Louis, MO 63130
314-615-6666
314-615-6655 (fax)
feedback@riverfronttimes.com

San Diego Reader
www.sandiegoreader.com
P.O. Box 85803
San Diego, CA 92186
619-235-3000

San Francisco Bay Guardian
www.sfbg.com
520 Hampshire
San Francisco, CA 94110
415-255-3100
415-255-8762 (fax)
bryce_brygnann@sfbg.com

Santa Barbara Independent
www.independent.com
1221 State Street
Santa Barbara, CA 93101
805-965-5205
805-965-5518 (fax)
letters@independent.com

Seattle Weekly
www.seattleweekly.com
1008 Western Avenue,
    Suite 300
Seattle, WA 98104
206-623-0500
206-467-4338 (fax)
webmaster@seattleweekly
    .com

Shepherd Express
413 N. 2nd
Milwaukee, WI 53203
414-276-2222
414-276-3312 (fax)
editor@shepherd-express
    .com

Tucson Weekly
P.O. Box 2429
Tucson, AZ 85702
520-792-3630
520-792-2096 (fax)
jreel@tucsonweekly.com

Westword
www.westword.com
P.O. Box 5970
Denver, CO 80217
303-296-7744

NEWSPAPERS IN MAJOR MARKETS

For an extensive list of newspapers, visit aol.com/directories/news
paper.adp.

Atlanta Journal/Constitution
www.ajc.com
72 Marietta Street N.W.
Atlanta, GA 30302
404-526-5151
listen@ajc.com

Austin American-Statesman
www.statesman.com
166 E. Riverside
Austin, TX 78767
512-455-3500
512-912-5927 (fax)
letters@statesman.com

Baltimore Sun
www.sunspot.net
P.O. Box 1377
Baltimore, MD 21278
410-332-6000
feedback@sunspot.net

Baton Rouge Advocate
www.theadvocate.com
525 Lafayette Street
Baton Rouge, LA 70802
225-383-1111
genglish@theadvocate.com

Birmingham News
www.bhamnews.com
2200 4th Avenue
Birmingham, AL 35202
205-325-2222
205-325-2283 (fax)
epage@bhamnews.com

Boston Globe
www.bostonglobe.com
P.O. Box 2378
Boston, MA 02107
617-929-2000
letters@globe.com

Boston Herald
www.bostonherald.com
One Herald Square
Boston, MA 02106
617-426-3000
feedback@bostonherald.com

Buffalo Evening News
www.buffalo.com
One News Plaza
Buffalo, NY 14240
716-849-4444

Charleston Gazette/Daily Mail
www.wvgazette.com
1001 Virginia Street, S.E.
Charleston, WV 25301
800-982-6397
304-348-1233 (fax)
haught@wvgazette.com

Charlotte Observer
www.charlotte.com
600 Tryon Street
Charlotte, NC 28232
704-358-5000
feedback@charlotteobserver
    .com

Chicago Sun Times
www.suntimes.com
401 N. Wabash Avenue
Chicago, IL 60611
312-321-3000
stbiz@suntimes.com

Chicago Tribune
www.chicagotribune.com
435 N. Michigan Avenue
Chicago, IL 60611
312-222-3232
bestes@tribune.com

Cincinnati Enquirer
312 Elm Street
Cincinnati, OH 45202
513-768-6060

Cincinnati Post
125 E. Court Street
Cincinnati, OH 45202
513-352-2000
postedits@cincypost.com

Cleveland Plain Dealer
www.cleveland.com
1801 Superior Avenue
Cleveland, OH 44114
216-999-4360
letters@plaind.com

Columbia State
www.thestate.com
P.O. Box 1333
Columbia, SC 29202
803-771-8415
stateeditor@thestate.com

Columbus Dispatch
www.dispatch.com
34 S. 3rd Street
Columbus, OH 43215
letters@dispatch.com
614-461-5000

Daily Oklahoma
www.oklahoman.com
Box 25125
Oklahoma City, OK 73125
405-232-3311

Dallas Morning News
www.dallasnews.com
P.O. Box 655237
Dallas, TX 75265
800-925-1500
gerry@dallasnews.com

Dayton Daily News
www.daytondailynews.com
45 S. Ludlow Street
Dayton, OH 45402
937-225-2000
kevin_riley@coxohio.com

Denver Post
www.denverpost.com
1560 Broadway
Denver, CO 80202
303-820-1010
circust@denverpost.com

Des Moines Register
www.desmoinesregister.com
P.O. Box 957
Des Moines, IA 50304
515-284-8000
dryerson@dmreg.com

Detroit Free Press
www.freep.com
600 W. Fort 321
W. Lafayette Boulevard
Detroit, MI 48226
313-225-6500
webmizz@freepress.com

Detroit News
www.detnews.com
615 W. Lafayette Boulevard
Detroit, MI 48226
313-222-2300
msilverman@detnews.com

Florida Times-Union
www.jacksonville.com
One Riverside Avenue
Jacksonville, FL 32202
904-359-4111

Fort Lauderdale Sun Sentinel
www.sunsentinel.com
200 E. Las Olas Boulevard
Ft. Lauderdale, FL 33301
954-356-4000
sfeedback@sun-sentinel.com

Fort Wayne Journal Gazette
www.journalgazette.net
600 W. Main Street
Fort Wayne, IN 46802
219-461-8333

Fort Worth Star Telegram
www.startelegram.com
400 W. 7th Street
Ft. Worth, TX 76102
jwitt@startelegram.com

Fresno Bee
www.fresnobee.com
1626 E. Street
Fresno, CA 93786
559-441-6111
staff@fresnobee.com

Grand Rapids Press
www.mlive.com
155 Michigan St. N.W.
Grand Rapids, MI 49503
616-459-1400
feedback@mlive.com

Harrisburg Patriot-News
www.patriot-news.com
P.O. Box 2265
Harrisburg, PA 17105
717-255-8100

Hartford Courant
www.ctnow.com
285 Broad Street
Hartford, CT 06115
860-525-2525
comments@ctnow.com

Houston Chronicle
www.houstonchronicle.com
801 Texas Avenue
Houston, TX 77002
713-220-7171
hci@chron.com

Indianapolis Star News
www.indystar.com
P.O. Box 145
Indianapolis, IN 46206
317-444-6300
terry.eberle@indystar.com

Jackson Clarion-Ledger
www.clarion-ledger.com
311 E. Pearl Street
Jackson, MS 39205
601-961-7000

Kansas City Star
www.kcstar.com
1729 Grand Avenue
Kansas City, KS 64108
816-234-7900
thestar@kcstar.com

Knoxville News-Sentinel
www.knoxnews.com
208 W. Church Avenue
Knoxville, TN 37950
615-523-3131
webmaster@knoxnews.com
letters@knoxnews.com

Lancaster New Era
8 W. King Street,
    P.O. Box 1328
Lancaster, PA 17603
717-291-8734

Los Angeles Daily News
www.dailynews.com
21221 Oxnard Street
Woodland Hills, CA 91367
818-713-3636
editor@dailynews.com

Louisville Courier Journal
www.courier-journal.com
525 W. Broadway
Louisville, KY 40202
502-582-4011

Memphis Commercial Appeal
www.gomemphis.com
495 Union Avenue
Memphis, TN 38101
901-529-2211

Miami Herald
www.miami.com
One Herald Plaza
Miami, FL 33132
305-350-2111

Milwaukee Journal
www.jsonline.com
333 W. State Street
Milwaukee, WI 53201
414-224-2000

Nashville Tennessean
www.tennessean.com
1100 Broadway
Nashville, TN 37202
615-259-8000

New Haven Register
www.nhregister.com
40 Sargent Drive
New Haven, CT 06511
203-789-5200

The New York Daily News
www.nydailynews.com
415 W. 33rd Street
New York, NY 10001
212-210-2100

New York Post
www.nypostonline.com
1211 Avenue of the Americas
New York, NY 10036
212-930-8000
jt@nypost.com

Norfolk Pilot
www.pilotonline.com
150 W. Brambleton Avenue
Norfolk, VA 23501
757-446-2989
pilot@pilotonline.com

Omaha World Herald
www.omaha.com
1334 Dodge Street
Omaha, NE 68102
402-444-1000
webmaster@omaha.com

Orange County Register
www.ocregister.com
625 N. Grand Avenue
Santa Ana, CA 92711
714-835-1234

Orlando Sentinel
www.orlandosentinel.com
633 N. Orange Avenue
Orlando, FL 32801
407-420-5000

Philadelphia Inquirer/
   Daily News
www.philly.com
400 N. Broad Street
Philadelphia, PA 19101
215-854-2000
inquirer.letters@phillynews
   .com

Pittsburgh Post Gazette
www.post-gazette.com
50 Boulevard of the Allies
Pittsburgh, PA 15230
412-263-1100

Portland Oregonian
www.oregonlive.com
1320 S.W. Broadway
Portland, OR 97201
503-221-8327
otalkback@oregonlive.com

Providence Journal Bulletin
www.projo.com
75 Fountain Street
Providence, RI 02902
401-277-7000

Raleigh News and Observer
   Record
www.newsobserver.com
215 S. McDowell Street
Raleigh, NC 27601
919-829-4500

Richmond NewsLeader/
   Times-Dispatch
www.timesdispatch.com
300 E. Franklin Street
Richmond, VA 23293
804-649-6000

Rocky Mountain News
www.rockymountainnews
    .com
400 W. Colfax Avenue
Denver, CO 80204
303-892-5000
letters@rockymountainnews
    .com

Sacramento Bee
www.sacbee.com
2100 Q. Street
Sacramento, CA 95852
916-321-1000

St. Petersburg Times
www.sptimes.com
490 First Avenue S.
St. Petersburg, FL 33701
727-893-8111

Salt Lake City Tribune
www.sltrib.com
143 S. Main Street
Salt Lake City, UT 84111
801-237-2045

San Diego Union/Tribune
www.signsandiego.com
350 Camino de la Reina
San Diego, CA 92112
619-299-3131

San Francisco Chronicle
www.sfgate.com
901 Mission
San Francisco, CA 94103
415-777-1111

Seattle Post-Intelligencer
www.seattlepi.com
101 Elliot Avenue W.
Seattle, WA 98111
206-448-8000

Seattle Times
www.nwsource.com
1120 John Street
Seattle, WA 98109
206-464-2111

Shreveport Times
www.shreveporttimes.com
222 Lake Street
Shreveport, LA 71130
318-459-3200

Spokane Spokesman Review
www.spokesmanreview.com
W. 999 Riverside Drive
Spokane, WA 99210
509-459-5485

Springfield Union
www.masslive.com
1860 Main Street
Springfield, MA 01102
413-788-1332

Syracuse Herald-Journal
www.syracuse.com
Clinton Square
Syracuse, NY 13221
315-470-2265

Toledo Blade
www.theblade.com
541 Superior Street
Toledo, OH 43660
419-245-6000

Tulsa Daily World
www.tulsaworld.com
318 S. Main Mall
Tulsa, OK 74102
918-581-8300

Wichita Eagle & Eagle Beacon
www.kansas.com
825 E. Douglas
Wichita, KS 67201
316-268-6000

Wisconsin State Journal
www.madison.com
1901 Fish Hatchery Road
Madison, WI 53708
608-252-6200

Worcester Telegram
www.telegram.com
20 Franklin Street
Worcester, MA 01615
508-793-9100

LOCAL TV NETWORK AFFILIATES IN MAJOR MARKETS

Atlanta
WSB (ABC)
www.wsbtv.com
1601 W. Peachtree N.E.
Atlanta, GA 30309
404-944-6000

WGNX (CBS)
www.cbsatlanta.com
425 14th Street N.W.
Atlanta, GA 30318
404-325-4646
404-387-3003 (fax)
wgcitvnews@wgcitv.com

WXIA (NBC)
www.wxiall.com
1611 W. Peachtree N.E.
Atlanta, GA 30309
404-892-1611

Chicago
WBBM (CBS)
www.cbs2chicago.com
630 N. McClurg Court
Chicago, IL 60611
312-944-6000
wfdehaven@cbs.com

WLS (ABC)
190 N. State Street
Chicago, IL 60601
312-899-8019
Does not accept press releases
via E-mail.

WMAQ (NBC)
www.nbc5chi.com
454 N. Columbia Drive
Chicago, IL 60611
312-836-5555

Cleveland
WKYC (NBC)
1333 Lakeside Avenue
Cleveland, OH 44114
(216) 344-3300

WEWS (ABC)
www.newsnet5.com
3001 Euclid Avenue
Cleveland, OH 44115
216-431-3687
giveme5@wews.com

WKYC-TV (CBS)
www.wkyc.com
1403 E. 6th Street
Cleveland, OH 44114
216-344-3333

Dallas/Ft. Worth
KDFW (Fox)
www.kdfwfox4.com
400 N. Griffin Street
Dallas, TX 75202
214-720-4444

KXAS (NBC)
www.nbc5i.com
P.O. Box 1780
Ft. Worth, TX 76103
817-429-5555

WFAA (ABC)
www.wfaa.com
606 Young Street
Dallas, TX 75202
214-748-9631
news8@wfaa.com

Denver
KCNC (NBC)
www.9news.com
500 Speer Boulevard
Denver, CO 80203
303-871-9999
kusa@9news.com

KMGH (ABC)
www.kmgh.com
1089 Bannock
Denver, CO 80204
303-871-9999
7editorials@thedenverchannel
   .com

Houston
KTRK (ABC)
www.abc13.com
3310 Bissonnet Street
Houston, TX 80204
713-666-0713

Los Angeles
www.abc7.com
500 Circle Seven Drive
Glendale, CA 90028
818-863-7777
abc7@abc.com

KTTV (Fox)
www.kttv.com
5746 Sunset Boulevard
Los Angeles, CA 90028
310-856-1000

Miami
WCIX (CBS)
www.cbsnow.com
8900 Northwest 18th Terrace
Miami, FL 33172
212-975-4111

WTVI (NBC)
www.nbc6.nbc.com
316 N. Miami Avenue
Miami, FL 33128

Milwaukee
WTMJ (NBC)
www.touchtmj4.com
720 E. Capitol Drive
Milwaukee, WI 53201
414-963-4444
news@touchtmj4.com

WISN (ABC)
www.wisn.com
759 N. 19th Street
Milwaukee, WI 53233
414-342-8812
programming@wisn.com

Nashville
WKRN (ABC)
www.wkrn.com
441 Murfreesboro Road
Nashville, TX 37210
615-369-7222
general@wkrn.com

New Orleans
WDSU (NBC)
www.wdsu.com
846 Howard Avenue
New Orleans, LA 70113
504-207-WDSU

WVUE (ABC)
www.nbc10.com
2 Canal Street
New Orleans, LA 70130
504-581-2600
abc26news@aol.com

Philadelphia
WCAU (NBC)
www.nbc10.com
City Avenue and Monument
   Road
Philadelphia, PA 19131
610-238-4700

KYW (CBS)
www.kyw.com
301 City Avenue
Philadelphia, PA 19131
212-975-4111

WPVI (ABC)
www.wpvi.com
4100 City Line Avenue
Philadelphia, PA 19131
215-878-9700

Phoenix
KNXV (ABC)
www.knxv.com
515 N. 44th Street
Phoenix, AZ 85008
602-273-1500

Pittsburgh
KDKA (CBS)
www.kdka.com
P.O. Box 1100
Pittsburgh, PA 15230
412-392-2200

WPXI (NBC)
www.wpxi.com
P.O. Box 1100
Pittsburgh, PA 15230

WTAE (ABC)
www.wtaetv.com
400 Ardmore Boulevard
Pittsburgh, PA 15221
412-242-4300

St. Louis
KDNL (ABC)
www.kdnl.com
1215 Cole Street
St. Louis, MO 63106
314-436-3030

KSDK (NBC)
www.ksdk.com
1000 Market Street
St. Louis, MO 63101
314-421-5055
newstips@ksdk.com

San Diego
KGTV (ABC)
www.kgtv.com
P.O. Box 85347
San Diego, CA 92186
619-237-1010
webstaff@thesandiegochannel
   .com

KNSD (NBC)
www.nbc739.com
P.O. Box 719739
San Diego, CA 92171
knsd.feedback@nbc.com

San Francisco/Oakland
KRON (NBC)
www.kron.com
P.O. Box 3412
San Francisco, CA 94119
415-441-4444

KGO (ABC)
www.kgo.com
900 Front Street
San Francisco, CA 94111
415-954-7777

Seattle
KOMO (ABC)
www.komotv.com
100 4th Avenue N.
Seattle, WA 98109
206-443-4000

KING (NBC)
www.king5.com
333 Dexter Avenue N.
Seattle, WA 98109
206-448-5555
news@king5.com

Washington, DC
WJLA (ABC)
www.wjla.com
3007 Tilden Street, N.W.
Washington, DC 20008
202-364-7777

WUSA (CBS)
www.wusatv9.com
4100 Wisconsin Avenue, N.W.
Washington, DC 20016
202-364-3900
9news@wusatv9.com

WRC (NBC)
www.nbc4.com
4001 Nebraska Avenue, N.W.
Washington, DC 20016
202-885-4000
nbc4@nbc4.com

RADIO STATIONS

www.netradiosearch.com

PROFESSIONAL P.R. JOURNALS AND NEWSLETTERS

International Public Relations
  Review
Editor: Raymond Argyle
IPRA
Cardinal House
7 Wolsey Road
Hampton Court, London
  KT89EL England
44-181-481-7634
44-181-481-7648 (fax)
jprasec@compuserve.com

Journal of Business
  Communication
Editor: Robert J. Myers
Baruch College
Department of Speech
17 Lexington Avenue
New York, NY 10010-5526
212-387-1655
212-387-1340 (fax)
myersabc@compuserve.com

Journal of Communication
www.oup.co.uk/jnlcom
Editor: Alan M. Rubin
Oxford University Press
Journal Subscriptions
  Department
2001 Evans Road
Cary, NC 27513
800-852-7323
919-677-1714 (fax)
jnlorders@oup-usa.org

Journal of Employee
  Communications
  Management
www.ragan.com
Editor: Carol Jackson
Ragan Communications
316 N. Michigan Avenue,
  Suite 300
Chicago, IL 60601-3702
312-960-4100
312-960-4105 (fax)
carolj@ragan.com

Public Relations Quarterly
www.newsletter-
  clearinghouse.com
Editor in Chief: Howard Penn
  Hudson
44 W. Market Street
P.O. Box 311
Rhineback, NY 12572-0311
914-876-2081
914-876-2561 (fax)
hphudson@aol.com

Public Relations Review
www.jaipress.com
Editor: Ray E. Hiebert
JAI Press
10606 Mantz Road
Silver Springs, MD 20903-1247
301-445-3231

NEWSLETTERS

Bulldog Reporter
www.infocomgroup.com
Editor: Aimee Grove
5900 Hollis Street, R2
Emeryville, CA 94608
510-596-9300
800-959-1059
510-596-9331 (fax)
bulldog@infocomgroup.com

Communication Briefings
www.combriefings.com
Editor: Jack Gillespie
1101 King Street, Suite 110
Alexandria, VA 22314-2944
703-548-3800
703-684-2136 (fax)
customerservice@briefings
    .com

Community Relations Report
www.jwcom.com
Editor: Joe Williams
300 S.E. 4th Street
P.O. Box 924
Bartlesville, OK 74005
918-336-2767
918-336-2733 (fax)
joewmscomm@aol.com

Contacts Newsletter
Editor: Nora Madonick
Merrcomm Inc.
500 Executive Boulevard
Ossining, NY 10562
914-923-9400
914-923-9484 (fax)
contactpr@aol.com

Corporate Public Issues
Editor: Teresa Yancey Crane
207 Loudoun Street, S.E.
Leesburg, VA 20175
703-777-8450

Entertainment PR Newsletter
www.westcoastpr.com
Editor: Darren Shuster
5928 Lindley Avenue
Encino, CA 91316-1047
888-WCPR-NEWS
818-776-1930 (fax)
darren@westcoastpr.com

Healthcare PR and Marketing
    News
www.phillips.com
Editor: Ann McMikel
Phillips Business Information
1201 Seven Locks Road, #300
Potomac, MD 20854-2931
301-340-1520
301-340-1451 (fax)
amcmikel@phillips.com

High Tech Hot Wire
www.media-mark.com
Editor: Art Garcia
99 Brookwood Road, #7
Orinda, CA 94563-3344
925-253-7862
925-253-7864
art@media-mark.com

IEG Sponsorship Report
www.sponsorship.com
Editor: Lance Helgeson
640 N. LaSalle Street,
    Suite 600
Chicago, IL 60610-3769
312-944-1727
312-944-1897
lhelgeson@sponsorship.com

Inside P.R.
Editor: Paul A. Holmes
310 Madison Avenue,
    Suite 2005
New York, NY 10017-6009
212-818-0288
212-818-0289 (fax)
pholmes@prcentral.com

Interactive Public Relations
www.ragan.com
Editor: Sarah McAdams
Ragan Communications, Inc.
316 N. Michigan Avenue, #300
Chicago, IL 60601-3702
312-960-4100
312-960-4106 (fax)
sarahm@ragan.com

Investor Relations Business
www.sdponline.com
Editor: Matthew Greco
Securities Data Publishing
40 W. 57th Street, 11th Floor
New York, NY 10019-4001
212-765-5311
212-765-6123 (fax)
greco@tfn.com

Investor Relations Newsletter
www.kennedyinfo.com
Editor: Gerald Murray
One Kennedy Place, Route 12
Fitzwilliam, NH 03447-3229
603-585-3101
603-585-6401 (fax)

Investor Relations Update
www.niri.org
Editor: William F. Mahoney
NIRI
716 S. Brandywine Street
West Chester, PA 19382-3511
610-430-7057
610-430-0515 (fax)
wfmahoney@compuserve.com

Media Industry Newsletter
www.phillips.com
Editor: Steven Cohn
305 Madison Avenue,
    Suite 4417
New York, NY 10165-0006
212-983-5170
212-983-5144 (fax)
scohn@phillips.com

Media Matters
www.mediadynamicsinc.com
Editor: Ed Papazian
18 E. 41st Street, #1806
New York, NY 10017-6222
212-683-7895
212-683-7684 (fax)

Media Week
www.mediaweek.com
Editor: William Gloede
1515 Broadway, 12th Floor
New York, NY 10036-8986
212-536-5336
212-536-6594 (fax)
wgloede@mediaweek.com

Multinational PR Report
Editor: John M. Reed
Pigafetta Press
P.O. Box 39244
Washington, DC 20016
202-244-2580
202-244-2581 (fax)
110104.1310@compuserve
   .com

O'Dwyer's Marketplace
O'Dwyer's PR Newsletter
O'Dwyer's Washington Report
www.odwyerpr.com
Editor: Jack O'Dwyer
271 Madison Avenue, #600
New York, NY 10016-1062
212-679-2471
212-683-2750 (fax)
jackodwyer@aol.com

Partyline
www.partylinepublishing.com
Editor: Morton Yannon
1040 First Avenue, Suite 340
New York, NY 10022
byarmon@ix.netcom.com

PR Chicago
Editor: Betty Milton
PRSA, Chicago Chapter
30 N. Michigan Avenue, #508
Chicago, IL 60602
312-372-7744
312-372-8738 (fax)
bmiltonassoc@earthlink.net

PR News Publisher
www.prandmarketing.com
Diane Schwartz, PBI Media,
   LLC
1201 Seven Locks Road
Potomac, MD 20854
301-354-1761
301-340-3169 (fax)
dschwartz@pbimedia.com

PR Reporter
www.prpublishing.com
Editor: Patrick Jackson
14 Front Street
P.O. Box 600
Exeter, NH 03833-0600
603-778-0514
603-778-1741 (fax)
prr@prpublishing.com

PR Watch
users.aol.com/srampton/PRwa
   tch.html
Editor: John C. Stauber
3318 Gregory Street
Madison, WI 53711
608-233-3346
608-238-2236 (fax)
74250.735@compuserve.com

PR Week
www.prweek.us.com
Editor: Adam Leyland
PR Publications Ltd.
250 Fifth Avenue
New York, NY 10001-7708
212-532-9200
212-532-6765 (fax)
adam.leyland@prweek.us.com

Public Relations Tactics, PRSA
www.prsa.org
Editor: John Elsasser
33 Irving Place, 3rd Floor
New York, NY 10003-2376
212-995-2230
212-995-0757 (fax)
j.elsasser@prsa.org

Ragan's Annual Report Review
www.ragan.com
Editor: Bob Sweet
Ragan Communications
316 N. Michigan Avenue, #300
Chicago, IL 60601-3702
312-960-4100
312-960-4106 (fax)
bobs@ragan.com

Ragan's Media Relations
  Report
www.ragan.com
Editor: Candace Dear
Ragan Communications
316 N. Michigan Avenue, #300
Chicago, IL 60601-3702
312-960-4100
312-960-4106 (fax)
candaced@ragan.com

Ragan Report
www.ragan.com
Editor: David Murray
Ragan Communications
316 N. Michigan Avenue, #300
Chicago, IL 60601-3702
312-960-4100
312-960-4106 (fax)
davidm@ragan.com

Speechwriter's Newletter
www.ragan.com
Editor: Kate Vitale
Ragan Communications
316 N. Michigan Avenue, #300
Chicago, IL 60601-3702
312-960-4100
312-960-4106 (fax)
katev@ragan.com

TJFR Business News Reporter
www.tjfr.com
Editor: Dean Rotbart
2020 Arapahoe Street
Denver, CO 80205-2548
303-296-1200
tjfr@tjfr

West Coast PR Newsletter
www.westcoastpr.com
Editor: Darren Shuster
5928 Lindley Avenue
Encino, CA 91316-1047
888-WCPR-NEWS
818-776-1930 (fax)
darren@westcoastpr.com

The Working Communicator
www.ragan.com
Managing Editor:
    Carol Jackson
Ragan Communications
316 N. Michigan Avenue, #300
Chicago, IL 60601-3702
312-960-4100
312-960-4106 (fax)
carolj@ragan.com

WEBSITES MENTIONED IN THIS BOOK

www.amazon.com/toys
www.ariannaonline.com
www.askme.com
www.aspennj.org
www.blackstoneaudio
    .com
www.blairwitch.com
www.callelizabeth.com
www.connorscommunica
    tions.com
www.copernic.com
www.entertainment
    careers.net
www.ew.com
www.gtlaw.com
www.guerrilla-marketing
    .com/authors/jlevinso
    n.html
www.haxan.com

www.inc.com
www.iwon.com
www.kabc.com
www.laradio.com
www.lipservicemag.com
www.macromedia.com
www.microsoft.com
www.overthrowthegov
    .com
www.redherring.com
www.salon.com
www.submit-it.com
www.successmagazine
    .com
www.summitconsulting
    .com
www.thestandard.com
www.toysrus.com
www.variety.com

And, of course, please feel free to check out my website at:
www.levinepr.com.

INDEX